Gender, Criminalization, Imprisonment and Human Rights in Southeast Asia

This exciting new collection reinvigorates prison studies and feminist criminology, by widening the analytical and geographical lens of both. It also offers a critical analysis of the reach and limits of international human rights law. Integrating activist voices with early career and more established scholars, these essays offer a sobering glimpse into the lived reality of prisons in Southeast Asia, while also mapping out possible routes for challenge. In so doing, it reminds us of the salience of gender in understanding incarceration and the urgent need for action.

Mary Bosworth, Centre for Criminology, University of Oxford

As a criminologist and social activist, someone who toils to decolonize both criminal justice and criminology, it is always pleasing to encounter work that privileges the experiences of individuals and communities that are too often silenced within the "wall of noise" that surrounds crime control policy and practice throughout the world. *Gender, Criminalization, Imprisonment and Human Rights in Southeast Asia*, edited by Andrew Jefferson and Samantha Jeffries, is one such book. The collection of essays included in the book cover an impressive range of issues facing cisgender women, transgender persons and sexual minorities, as they encounter criminal justice systems and practice in Southeast Asia. The breadth of issues covered, along with the expressed intent of the editors to give voice to "activist, critical and feminist theorizing and research on gender, intersectionality, criminalization and carceral experiences," makes this contribution an invaluable resource for criminologists, social activists, jurists and policymakers working to enhance the efficacy of criminal justice policy and practice in Southeast Asia and elsewhere.

Juan Marcellus Tauri, The University of Waikato, and the
Centre for Global Indigeniety

In this collection, Jefferson and Jeffries draw together a range of important, expert voices to shed light on gender-based experiences, gendered harms and human rights considerations in the contexts of criminal justice in Southeast Asia. It provides data, analyses, theorizations and experiences of populations that much of the Western world has ignored or overlooked. The chapters aim to juxtapose the personal against the structural in a way that is enlightening for both. In so doing, the book as a whole argues that for transformation to take place, researchers, reformers and activists should consider not just individual need but also the legal, political and cultural constraints and conventions that create structural and gendered inequalities in the first place. The book also reminds us that there are aspects of human experience that are universal, such as the desire for freedom, to be seen as we really are and to be valued for the life that we each breathe into the spaces and societies we occupy. Shifting criminology's gaze toward such issues from a Southeast Asian perspective is a most welcome and much needed adjustment of perspective.

Deborah H. Drake, Senior Lecturer, Criminology, The Open University

EMERALD STUDIES IN ACTIVIST CRIMINOLOGY

Series Editors:
Vicky Canning (University of Bristol), Greg Martin (University of Sydney) and Steve Tombs (The Open University)

Emerald Studies in Activist Criminology is a platform working to identify and address the harms of criminalization and expansive social controls. It draws together academics, activists, progressive policy-makers and practitioners to encourage cutting edge engagement on topics to effect positive social change.

The historical relationships between criminology and activism are contentious. Since criminology in its administrative forms can facilitate increases in state and cultural controls, and was formed within this nexus of social order, the discipline is often complicit in acting on behalf of states and state-corporate collaborators. Critical criminology and zemiology, by contrast, have nurtured conditions under which power and hierarchy can be more fully addressed from radical perspectives, specifically in challenging state-centric focuses on crimes of the powerless. It is from these positions that *Emerald Studies in Activist Criminology* encourages engagement with those working against negative impacts of crime controls on the lives of intersectionally disadvantaged groups in society.

Emerald Studies in Activist Criminology seeks to examine the history of both recent and more established justice campaigns and interventions. It extends across a range of pre-existing sub-fields of criminology that engage in questions of effecting progressive change through activism, such as feminist criminology, juvenile justice, migrant rights, corporate and state crime, green/environmental criminology, sentencing and wrongful conviction, prisons, corrections and abolitionism, and justice for victim/survivors of harm and crime. Campaigns and movements – defensive and progressive – around these issues define what we mean by "activist," while we view "criminology" in its broadest, inter-disciplinary and social science inflected version.

Gender, Criminalization, Imprisonment and Human Rights in Southeast Asia

EDITED BY

ANDREW M. JEFFERSON
Danish Institute Against Torture (DIGNITY), Denmark

SAMANTHA JEFFRIES
Griffith University, Australia

emerald
PUBLISHING

United Kingdom – North America – Japan – India – Malaysia – China

Emerald Publishing Limited
Emerald Publishing, Floor 5, Northspring, 21-23 Wellington Street, Leeds LS1 4DL.

First edition 2022

Reprints and permissions service
Contact: www.copyright.com

British Library Cataloguing in Publication Data
A catalogue record for this book is available from the British Library

ISBN: 978-1-80117-287-5 (Print)
ISBN: 978-1-80117-286-8 (Online)
ISBN: 978-1-80117-288-2 (Epub)
ISBN: 978-1-80117-289-9 (Paperback)

INVESTOR IN PEOPLE

Contents

List of Tables

About the Contributors

Chontit Chuenurah started her career at the Ministry of Justice of Thailand and took part in the Enhancing Life of Females Inmates Project, which was later developed into the drafting of the United Nations Rules on the Treatment of Women Prisoners and Non-custodial Measures for Women Offenders (the Bangkok Rules). Her early career mainly focused on the issues related to crime prevention and criminal justice. Currently, she serves as the Manager for the Office of the Implementation of the Bangkok Rules and Treatment of Offenders Programme at the Thailand Institute of Justice. As part of her work, she supervises and leads several research projects, including Women Prisoners and the Implementation of the Bangkok Rules in the ASEAN Region, National Survey of Female Inmates in Thailand, and Pathways to Imprisonment of Female and Male Prisoners in Thailand. She also played an important role in developing and launching the first comprehensive regional training program on the "Management of Women Prisoners in the ASEAN Region" which was launched by the Thailand Institute of Justice in 2016. She graduated with a Master's of Law from the University of Kent, and a Master's degree, Science in Social Policy and Social Research, from the University of Southampton, the United Kingdom.

Billy Gorter is the Executive Director of This Life Cambodia. He is a passionate activist and advocate for change, bringing more than 20 years of experience tackling conservation, social and human rights and educational issues in Australia and Cambodia to his role as Executive Director of This Life Cambodia. He launched This Life in 2007 based on his founding principles of listening to, engaging with and advocating alongside communities. This development philosophy achieves high-impact outcomes and sets best practice for international development. He is a sought-after speaker and is passionately committed to addressing the rights of children through education, juvenile justice and advocacy.

Philip J. Gover is the Impact Learning & Effectiveness Lead at This Life Cambodia. He has a passion for sustainable development and social economics. Following three years of research and tutoring with Northumbria University Social Science Research Centre, he spent 12 years working as a Senior Public Health Manager with the United Kingdom Government & National Health Service. He has worked in developing countries in East Africa, Southeast Asia and various settings across Europe, supporting a variety of Social Enterprises, Charities and Housing Associations. He is a graduate of Durham University (BA Hons'

Community & Youth Studies), Durham University Business School (MA Enterprise Management) and the University of Northumbria (MPH, Public Health). He is a Fellow of both the Chartered Management Institute and Royal Society for Public Health.

Lucy Harry is a Doctoral candidate in the Faculty of Law, Centre of Criminology at Oxford University undertaking research on gender and the death penalty in Southeast Asia, with a particular focus on Malaysia. Before undertaking the Doctor of Philosophy, she completed the MSc in Criminology and Criminal Justice at Oxford University, graduating with Distinction. She is a Member of Oxford University's Death Penalty Research Unit and is currently providing research assistance on several projects, including a study of foreign nationals at risk of the death penalty in Asia and the Middle East.

Andrew M. Jefferson, PhD, is a Senior Researcher at DIGNITY – Danish Institute against Torture where among other things he is a Principal Investigator on the project Legacies of Detention in Myanmar. He has been with DIGNITY for over two decades occupying academic positions at the cutting edge of theory/ practice within what is a predominantly activist human rights organization. His work focuses on ethnographies of prisons and prison reform processes in the global south and has featured a range of collaborations with activist organizations engaged in torture prevention, human rights work, and prison reform. He co-convenes the Global Prisons Research Network. Aside from issues of prisons and comparative penality, interests include the relation between state and subject in transitional contexts, the hierarchization of human worth, and how to conceptualise human suffering under compromised circumstances. He is the author (with Liv Gaborit) of *Human Rights in Prisons: Comparing Institutional Encounters in Kosovo, Sierra Leone and the Philippines*.

Samantha Jeffries, PhD, is a Senior Lecturer in the School of Criminology and Criminal Justice/Griffith Criminology Institute, Griffith University. Her research focuses on marginalized social statuses, criminalization, victimization, and justice. She has conducted research on LGBTIQA+ domestic violence, the sex industry, problem-solving courts, sentencing, gender, and Indigeneity. In focus more recently, has been the needs and experiences of domestic violence victims in the family law system and restorative justice processes. Since 2015, she has been collaborating with the Thailand Institute of Justice undertaking studies in Southeast Asia and Kenya on gendered pathways to criminalization, women's experiences of imprisonment, as well as re-integration and human rights. She has co-authored a book on domestic violence (*Romantic Terrorism: An Autoethnography of Domestic Violence, Victimization and Survival*, with Sharon Hayes), published articles in high impact journals including *Criminology* and the *British Journal of Criminology*, and conducted training on the United Nations Rules for the Treatment of Women Prisoners and Non-custodial Measures for Women Offenders (the Bangkok Rules) with prison personnel in Thailand, Kenya and Indonesia for the Thailand Institute of Justice and United Nations Office on Drugs and Crime.

Myanmar Research Team

For reasons of safety and security, and given the circumstances in Myanmar following the February 2021 military coup, and with much regret, we are unable to reveal the names, affiliations, or any identifying information for this research team. We are deeply thankful for their contributions to this book, their unwavering dedication to the human rights of Myanmar's people, and stand with them as they continue to fight for democratic freedom.

Barbara Owen, PhD, is an international expert in the areas of women and imprisonment; gender inequality within the criminal justice system; improving operational practice in women's prisons; and women's prison culture, with extensive experience in conducting, ethnographies, large-scale surveys, policy studies; and program evaluation. Internationally, her work involves implementing human rights protections in women's prisons with the Thailand Institute of Justice. A Professor Emerita of Criminology at California State University, Fresno, she received her PhD in Sociology from UC Berkeley in 1984. Before returning to academia, she was a Senior Researcher with the Federal Bureau of Prisons. Her books include *In Search of Safety: Confronting Inequality in Women's Imprisonment* (with James Wells and Joy Pollock), and *In the Mix: Struggle and Survival in a Women's Prison*. Along with Barbara Bloom and Stephanie Covington, she has co-authored a major policy report, Gender-Responsive Strategies: Research, Practice, and Guiding Principles for Women Offenders (2003). More recent works include multiple projects relating to the context of sexual and other forms of safety in women's prisons; an analysis of women's recidivism; research and policy work on Realignment in California and co-authoring the policy report "Unlocking America." Her work has been funded by local, state, and federal agencies. Her consulting experience includes several projects with the California Department of Corrections and Rehabilitation; on-going work with the National Institute of Corrections; extensive work with The Moss Group in providing research and policy review of operational practice in women's facilities; developing architectural design in women's jails; and evaluation efforts within local probation systems. She also serves on the Advisory Council of the Safe Alternatives to Segregation II initiative with the Vera Institute of Justice.

Min Jee Yamada Park joined the International Detention Coalition as the Asia-Pacific Programme Officer in 2019. Prior to that, she worked in the areas of detention monitoring, research, policy advocacy, and capacity building, particularly for government actors in Southeast Asia and Africa. Her previous role as a Policy and Research Coordinator with the Thailand Institute of Justice focused on advocating for the humane treatment of marginalized groups including migrants, stateless persons, and ethnic minorities in criminal detention, and promoting the implementation of the relevant international human rights standards into national laws and policies in Southeast Asia. She has also published and spoken at various international and regional platforms on the experiences and challenges of vulnerable groups deprived of liberty, particularly women and their accompanying children, based on her extensive field research in detention facilities in

Cambodia, Indonesia, Thailand, and Kenya. She received a Master of Arts in Development Studies from the International Institute of Social Studies, Erasmus University Rotterdam in the Netherlands.

Jutathorn Pravattiyagul earned a PhD in Criminology from Utrecht University and Hamburg University in 2018. She has a decade-long experience working as a researcher, ethnographer, university lecturer and consultant for international organizations, the private sector, and universities globally. Since 2016, she has served as an Associate Scholar at Harvard University Asia Center. Her professional specialization is on discrimination and race, gendered migration, and identity politics, reducing gender-based violence, transgenderism, transgender prisoners' rights, policies-making and criminal justice in Thailand and Europe. She has also worked as a Consultant for United Nations Development Programme and United Nations Office on Drugs and Crime on transgender inmates and prisons management policies projects by creating Standard Operation Procedures and technical brief documents for states. Currently, she is lecturing in Anthropology Department at Copenhagen University with a special focus on post-colonial queer, gender stigma and sexuality from non-Western perspectives.

Prarthana Rao graduated with a Masters in Development Studies from The International Institute of Social Studies, Erasmus University Rotterdam, the Netherlands. She currently works as Policy and Research Officer at the Thailand Institute of Justice (TIJ), an organization that aims at strengthening criminal justice reform and enhancing the rule of law through research, capacity building and policy advocacy. In her present role, she works extensively on improving gender sensitivity in the criminal justice system through the use of international human rights standards and norms. As a researcher, she has been involved in multiple projects on understanding women's pathways to prison, their experiences of incarceration and their rehabilitation needs in countries such as Thailand, Cambodia, and Kenya. As a capacity-building specialist, she has trained more than 100 senior correctional staff and prison officers from 11 countries on gender-sensitive prison management. Prior to TIJ, she worked at Leaders' Quest, a social enterprise that helps companies balance profit with purpose, aiming to reduce the structural inequalities in society by focusing on empathetic leadership development.

Tristan Russell is a PhD student in the School of Criminology and Criminal Justice at Griffith University/Griffith Criminology Institute. Her PhD examines the intersection between age and gender, and utilizing prisoners' voices, explores the experiences of older women incarcerated in Thailand. Before this, Tristan was a member of Griffith University's prestigious Honours College, graduated with a Bachelor of Criminology and Criminal Justice with distinction in 2018 and completed her Honours year in 2019. Her Honours dissertation focused on gendered pathways to prison in Thailand. She has a track record of published papers in the areas of gender, imprisonment trajectories, life during and post-incarceration, gender-based violence and restorative justice. She is also engaged in research projects on domestic violence and family law.

Diana Therese M. Veloso is an Associate Professor and the Graduate Studies Program Coordinator of the Behavioral Science Department at De La Salle University. She completed her PhD in Sociology at Loyola University Chicago. She has conducted original research on the life histories and issues of women formerly on death row in the Philippines and the re-entry experiences and challenges of formerly incarcerated women in Chicago, Illinois. She served as the lead researcher in two studies on serious and organized crime threats in the Philippines, as commissioned by the National Law Enforcement Coordinating Committee-Subcommittee on Organized Crime. She was a consultant in a nationwide evaluation of the interventions and rehabilitation programs for children in conflict with the law in the Philippines. She has also conducted research on gender-based violence among internally displaced people in Zamboanga City and Marawi City, two conflict zones in the Southern Philippines. She was also involved in participatory action research projects with First Nations communities in Chicago, Illinois.

Acknowledgments

We owe a debt of gratitude to a range of institutions and people and would like to take this opportunity to register our appreciation. Together we thank the Series editors, Steve Tombs and Vicky Canning for their belief in the project and Katy Mathers and colleagues at Emerald for smooth processing. The project out of which this book grew (*Legacies of Detention in Myanmar*) is funded by a grant from the Consultative Research Committee of the Danish Ministry of Foreign Affairs and we are grateful to the Danida Fellowship Centre who administer the grant and particularly to Pernille Friis. We thank Sriprapha Petcharamesree of Mahidol University and the Southeast Asian Human Rights Network who planned the conference at which we would have presented these ideas were it not for the pandemic. We thank the contributors for putting your ideas and energies at our disposal and for your receptiveness to our input. And, of course, the book would not exist without the people who chose to engage with us (and the book's contributors) during field research sharing experiences of injustice and suffering, oppression and resistance. You take us places we could never go alone, and we are deeply grateful.

Samantha would like to thank Griffith Criminology Institute, Griffith School of Criminology and Criminal Justice, and the Thailand Institute of Justice, in particular the Office for the Bangkok Rules and Treatment of Offenders (OBR) for enabling my research in Southeast Asia with travel funds, an institutional platform, and collaborative relationships through which to undertake joint projects. In particular, from the OBR team, I would like to extend my heartfelt gratitude to Chontit Chuenurah, Yodsawadi Thipphayamongkoludom, Salila Narataruksa, Ploypitcha Uerfue, Wasoontara Sapsaman, Prarthana Rao and Min Jee Yamada Park. Additionally, I would like to thank Barbara Owen and Kathleen Daly for their mentorship and William Wood for his steadfast support throughout my research journey in Southeast Asia.

Andrew would like to thank DIGNITY – Danish Institute Against Torture (my research base for 20 years) and colleagues there for support, encouragement and tolerance. I single out Janne Tornsberg (for helping control the funds in such a friendly and professional fashion), Angelina Tarik Fattah (who is always able to find the literature I need) and members of the LoDiM team who sustained the project from its earliest days. Here I think of Irlin Osaland, Sarah Auener, Eva Zahia Nassar, Hannah Russell, Ergun Cakal, Liv Gaborit, and Tomas Max Martin. We gratefully acknowledge Hannah Russell and Tomas Martin's editorial contribution to Chapter 5. On matters pertaining to feminism, patriarchy, entitlement and mutuality I thank Victoria Canning Brigitte Dragsted, Luisa Schneider, and Bethany Schmidt from whom I am learning much.

Our gratitude is deep and genuine. Our expression of it signals in no way responsibility for the content or tone of this book. For that, we take joint responsibility.

Chapter 1

Introduction to Gender, Criminalization, Imprisonment and Human Rights in Southeast Asia

Samantha Jeffries and Andrew M. Jefferson

Abstract

In this introductory chapter, we discuss the impetus for this edited book. We introduce activist, critical and feminist criminological theorizing and research on gender, intersectionality, criminalization, and carceral experiences. The scene is set for the chapters to follow by providing a general overview of gender, criminalization, imprisonment, and human rights in Southeast Asia with particular attention being paid to Indonesia, Malaysia, Cambodia, Thailand, Myanmar, and the Philippines. We consider trends and drivers of women's imprisonment in the region, against the backdrop of the United Nations Rules for the Treatment of Women Prisoners and Non-Custodial Measures for Women Offenders, also known as the Bangkok Rules, which were adopted by the United Nations General Assembly just over a decade ago. We reflect on the dominance of western centric feminist (and malestream) criminological works on gender, criminalization and imprisonment, the positioning of Southeast Asian knowledge on the peripheries of Asian criminology and the importance of bringing to light, as this book does, gendered activist scholarship in this region of the world.

Keywords: Gender; criminalization; imprisonment; human rights; Southeast Asia; feminism; activism; critical criminology

---

Gender, Criminalization, Imprisonment and Human Rights in Southeast Asia, 1–11
doi:10.1108/978-1-80117-286-820221001

Setting the Scene

Throughout history, women in conflict with the law and those behind prison walls, have been afterthoughts, often ignored because of their small numbers, making them a relatively invisible or forgotten population (Chesney-Lind, 1998; Jeffries, 2014; Owen, Wells, & Pollock, 2017). As a result, criminal law, justice systems, and prisons across the world have shown little evidence of gender sensitivity in policy or practice, leading to discrimination, social exclusion, and violations of human rights. The absence of gender-sensitive perspectives results in systems that are structurally blind to gender-specific challenges and harms within the field of criminal justice in general, and particularly in prisons. It is critical that gendered needs, including how these intersect with other forms of inequality, are paid more attention, better understood, and adequately reflected in law, policy and practice.

Over the last several decades, the number of detained women worldwide has surged (Walmsley, 2017). Women are no longer as invisible as they once were and concurrently, there has been increasing recognition of their human rights when they come into conflict with the law, and especially behind prison walls (Penal Reform International & Thailand Institute of Justice, 2021; United Nations General Assembly, 2010). Just over a decade ago, the United Nations Rules for the Treatment of Women Prisoners and Non-Custodial Measures for Women Offenders, also known as the Bangkok Rules, were adopted by the 193 countries at the United Nations General Assembly (2010).

The adoption of the Bangkok Rules has not interrupted increases in women's imprisonment, even though the Rules contain important commitments concerning non-custodial alternatives that should have reduced population numbers (Fernandéz & Nougier, 2021, p. 4). In Southeast Asia, as is the case globally, there have been substantial upward trends in women's detention (Jeffries, 2014; Jeffries & Chuenurah, 2016; Walmsley, 2017; World Prison Brief, 2021). This expansion in the region is being driven by heightened punitiveness, including government "crackdowns" on the illicit drug trade, human trafficking, and immigration (Jeffries, 2014).

Most notably, the war on drugs (global and local) has resulted in large numbers of women being imprisoned throughout Southeast Asia (Chuenurah & Sornprohm, 2020; Fernandéz & Nougier, 2021; Jeffries, 2014; Jeffries & Chuenurah, 2016). Sentences for drug offending are harsh, incorporating long-term incarceration, mandatory life, and the death penalty in all but two Southeast Asian countries (Cambodia and the Philippines). Furthermore, the number of people being incarcerated pre-trial, and thus presumed innocent, is skyrocketing. In the Philippines, for example, drug laws establish mandatory pre-trial detention (Chuenurah & Sornprohm, 2020, p. 132; Fernandéz & Nougier, 2021, p. 7; Penal Reform International & Thailand Institute of Justice, 2021). While figures by gender are not publicly accessible, data provided by the World Prison Brief (2021) show that in some Southeast Asian countries, around 7 out of 10 people in prison are pre-trial detainees. The overall result is prison overpopulation. Aside from Singapore, all prisons in the region are at over 100% capacity, with some sitting above 400% (Table 1). Custodial overcrowding and concomitant under-resourcing pose obstacles to protecting the human rights of those deprived of liberty, including with regard to healthcare, education, and humane treatment (Chuenurah & Sornprohm, 2020, p. 132; Fernandéz & Nougier, 2021, p. 19; Penal Reform International & Thailand Institute of Justice, 2021). It is important to stress, that representing overcrowding in numerical terms fails to do justice to the experience of living under these conditions. As argued by Schmidt and Jefferson (2021, p. 82),

> overcrowding, we believe, cannot be understood only as a quantitative category. It is not about percentages or about exceeding capacity but bodies in close proximity, living, breathing, infectious, aching, sick, damaged, and sensorially extreme.

Table 1.   Pre-Trial Detention and Prison Overcrowding in Southeast Asia.

Country	Year	Pre-Trial (%)	Occupancy Level (%) Based on Official Capacity
Thailand	2021	19	339
Cambodia	2019	71	355
Indonesia	2021	20	196
Myanmar	2017	15	139
Malaysia	2019	27	132
Vietnam	2019	12	Unknown
Singapore	2020	11	79
Laos	2016	67	Unknown
Philippines	2018	75	464
Brunei	2019	7	144

Source: World Prison Brief (2021).

In 2017, the World Prison Brief listed the top 10 countries with the highest female prisoner numbers, in which 5 were in Southeast Asia: Thailand, the Philippines, Indonesia, Vietnam, and Myanmar (Walmsley, 2017). On average, globally, women constitute around 7% of the total global prison population, and are incarcerated at a rate of 9.9 per 100,000. As demonstrated in Table 2, both figures are higher in nearly every Southeast Asian country. The overuse of imprisonment for women in Thailand is particularly stark, with more women in prison here than elsewhere in the region. Furthermore, after the United States, Thailand has the second highest rate of female incarceration in the world (Chuenurah & Sornprohm, 2020, p. 135; Walmsley, 2017; World Prison Brief, 2021).

Table 2.   Females Imprisoned in Southeast Asia.

Country	Year	Number	Percentage of Total Prison Population	Rate per 100,000 Population
Thailand	2021	37,365	12%	54
Cambodia	2019	3,000	8%	18
Indonesia	2021	13,167	5%	5
Myanmar	2017	9,807	12%	18
Malaysia	2019	3,247	5%	10
Vietnam	2019	13,202	11%	14
Singapore	2020	1,246	11%	21
Laos	2016	1,503	18%	22
Philippines	2018	21,349	11%	20
Brunei	2019	162	12%	36

Source: World Prison Brief (2021).

The Impetus for this Book

In proposing this book on Gender, Criminalization, Imprisonment and Human Rights in Southeast Asia in the Emerald Activist Criminology series, our objective was to capture and collate the emerging work of activist scholars and grassroots advocates grappling to understand the lived experiences of cisgender women, transgender persons, other gender, and sexual minorities, as they encounter criminal justice systems in Southeast Asia. Exploring the complex interplay between conditions, needs, experiences, identities, and trajectories, our goal in the text that follows is to add significantly to our knowledge of the practices of gendered violation, victimization, and vulnerability facing people in conflict with the law and behind prison walls. Covering a range of country contexts – Indonesia, Malaysia, Cambodia, Thailand, Myanmar, the Philippines – and attentive to the variegated gendered experiences of different people on their way into, through, and/or beyond prison, this book contributes toward the development of theoretical and policy-oriented perspectives that are empirically grounded, rather than based on a presumed uniformity of experience.

For the most part, criminological scholarship undertaken within Asian societal contexts has been dominated by academics researching in a limited number of countries, employing masculinist theoretical paradigms (Lee & Laidler, 2013; Moosavi, 2019a). While we have witnessed advancement in criminological knowledge production from East Asia, including Japan, Hong Kong, China, South Korea, and Taiwan, some countries remain on the periphery within the Asian ambit (Lee & Laidler, 2013, p. 144). These tangential sites comprise Southeast Asian countries such as Malaysia, Cambodia, Thailand, Indonesia, Myanmar, and the Philippines (Belknap, 2016, p. 253; Lee & Laidler, 2013, p. 144). Furthermore, even among the relatively active centers of criminological knowledge production in East Asia, most work focuses on testing and reproducing western criminological scholarship, frameworks, and knowledges (Belknap, 2016, p. 256; Lee & Laidler, 2013, p. 150). This work generally coalesces within the domain of new right realist criminology, being "administrative, positivist, quantitative and geared toward reducing crime from a state perspective" (Moosavi, 2019, p. 266). Issues of power, including gender, class, race/ethnicity, and sexuality have not been central to the research agendas of criminologists researching in East Asian countries (Belknap, 2016; Moosavi, 2019, p. 266).

Yet, for the editors of this book, what has become increasingly obvious after years of undertaking collaborative research in Southeast Asia, is the emergence of a burgeoning collection of critical criminological scholarship in the region, including gendered activist work. These endeavors are not limited to academe; they include collaborations with those working at the "frontline" in human rights organizations, NGOs, and government, all of whom seek to effectuate positive change in criminal justice policy, practice, and more broadly. The primary aim of this book is to make this more critical body of work visible.

In contrast to administrative or right realist criminology that has dominated criminological work undertaken in Asia to date, critical criminology is concerned with issues of social structural power. Those working within this activist frame-work make evident the injustice of criminal justice, and unpack how systems of power mark experiences of criminalization and imprisonment. Ultimately, the aim is the creation of a more socially just society across numerous domains, including, and especially within (and sometimes also against) the criminal justice system (Arrigo, 2016; Belknap, 2016; DeKeseredy & Dragiewicz, 2018; White, Haines, & Asquith, 2017, pp. 209–230).

Feminist Criminology, Human Rights and the Chapters that Follow

Feminist criminology sits within the critical criminological paradigm. The collective goal is to speak truth to patriarchal power by centering and valuing the voices of criminalized women and raising awareness of gender oppression (Barberet, 2014, p. 16; Belknap, 2016, p. 14). Ultimately, feminist criminologists have tasked themselves with calling out gendered injustice and advocating for change in the conditions of criminal justice and society more broadly, that is harmful or oppressive to women in conflict with the law (Barberet, 2014, p. 16; Belknap, 2001; Britton, 2000; 2004; Carlen, 1985; Chesney-Lind, 1997; Daly & Chesney-Lind, 1988; Miller & Mullins, 2008; Renzetti, 2018, p. 75). Explicitly or implic-itly, feminist activism presents as the prevailing theme throughout this book. More specifically, the authors of the chapters that follow build on two bodies of feminist criminological work that has, until recently, been dominated by western scholarship – pathways and feminist explorations of women's imprisonment.

Beginning with Daly's (1994) seminal work in the United States, feminist pathways researchers have mapped the life experiences leading women into the criminal justice system, exploring how gender shapes criminalization. These studies revealed a particular and shared gendered backstory in the lives of women who come into conflict with the law, which is qualitatively different from that of men (Evans, 2018, pp. 41–43; Miller & Mullins, 2008, pp. 229–232; Wattanaporn & Holtfreter, 2014). Women's pathways are generally characterized by histories of gender-based violence (e.g., sexual and domestic abuse), associated trauma, substance abuse, economic marginalization, caregiving, problematic familial relationships, and intimate entanglements with men (see Daly, 1994; Owen et al., 2017; Wattanaporn & Holtfreter, 2014 and for studies in Asia, see Cherukuri, Britton, & Subramaniam, 2009; Khalid & Khan, 2013; Kim, Gerber, & Kim, 2007; Jeffries & Chuenurah, 2018; Jeffries & Chuenurah, 2019; Jeffries, Chuenurah, Rao, & Park, 2019; Jeffries, Chuenurah, & Russell, 2020; Jeffries, Rao, Chuenurah, & Fitz-Gerald, 2021; Russell, Jeffries, Hayes, Thipphayamongkoludom, & Chuenurah, 2020; Shen, 2015; Veloso, 2016).

At its core, feminist pathways scholarship highlights how patriarchal social structures play out in the lives of criminalized women, oppressing them through interpersonal, family, and state-sanctioned abuses (e.g., political and economic marginalization). Rather than pathologizing women and seeing their offending as something inherent at the level of the individual, feminist pathways scholars have sought to locate women's criminalization within social structural forces intimately related to gendered power relationships and associated access to resources. Women, it is argued, are frequently criminalized for exacting behaviors of survival within contexts of patriarchal subjugation (Willison & O'Brien, 2017).

In this book, Veloso (Chapter 9), and Russell and co-authors (Chapter 7) have specifically applied a feminist pathways approach to explore the imprisonment trajectories of women formerly on death row in the Philippines, and older women incarcerated in Thailand. The research findings presented in both chapters mirror the themes of previous feminist pathways studies. For the women in Veloso's (Chapter 9) study, economic precarity, victimization, and addiction were dominant themes in their lives, alongside deception, betrayal, and corrupted patriarchal systems of justice. Russell, Jeffries, and Chuenurah (Chapter 7) conclude that the older women in their research had either come into conflict with the law because they were providing for their families against the backdrop of poverty, took "the fall" for loved ones, or had self-medicated with illicit drugs in response to adversity and victimization.

The centrality of pre-existing conditions of gendered social structural vulnerability, putting women at risk of criminal justice system involvement, is highlighted in other chapters. Jefferson and co-authors (Chapter 2) discuss how the criminalization of certain behaviors, normative expectations of womanhood, poverty, relationships, gender discrimination in law, access to justice, and treatment in the criminal justice system, alongside the patriarchy of the Tatmadaw (armed forces), especially in the aftermath of the 2021 military coup, underpin women's imprisonment in Myanmar. Harry (Chapter 3) highlights the gendered vulnerabilities of women sentenced to death in Indonesia and Malaysia. Gorter and Gover (Chapter 4) note that women behind prison walls in Cambodia often come from poor, disadvantaged backgrounds, and lack legal literacy. Rao and co-authors (Chapter 6) highlight similar themes in the life histories of ethnic minority women imprisoned in Thailand.

Around the same time that Daly (1994) was writing, other scholars were attempting to understand the backgrounds and experiences of incarcerated women, alongside the collateral damages of carcerality through a feminist lens (e.g., Bosworth & Carrabine, 2001; Carlen, 1985; 1998; Chesney-Lind, 1991; Owen, 1998; Pollock-Byrne, 1990). In terms of the former, findings align with feminist pathways scholarship. Regarding the latter, women's time in prison was characterized by multiple interlocking gendered harms and abuses. Women experience and adapt to incarceration differently than men due to their distinct incarceration pathways and because prisons are patriarchal institutions built by men for men. Gender exacerbates the pains of imprisonment, with resultant long-term negative implications to women's well-being post-release, including deepening poverty, loss of children and familial connection, stigma, increased socio-economic isolation, trauma, and mental health problems (including substance abuse) (Owen et al., 2017). Feminist criminologists have called attention to the plight of imprisoned women, leveling criticism at prisons for being gender oppressive institutions unresponsive to women's needs (Barberet, 2014, p. 51).

There have been subsequent feminist calls for the development of a women-wise penology that recognizes the impact of patriarchal oppression on women through the development of gender-responsive prisons and increased use of non-custodial sentencing measures (Bloom, Owen, & Covington, 2003, 2004; Evans, 2018, p. 45; Owen et al., 2017). For many, negating the characteristics of women's criminalization trajectories (e.g., poverty, victimization, trauma), their experiences, needs, and concomitant gendered harms behind prison walls and post-release, constitutes a violation of human rights (Gainsborough, 2008; Gundy & Baumann-Grau, 2013; Willison & O'Brien, 2017, pp. 39–40). As argued by Gundy and Baumann-Grau (2013, pp. 106–107) ignoring the effects of patriarchy on women before, during, and after incarceration, the gender-specific factors underpinning their criminalization, and the gendered harms and abuses experienced, constitutes discrimination against women and violates multiple international conventions regulating the preservation of human dignity and equality. These conventions include, but are not limited to, the United Nations Conventions against Torture and other Cruel, Inhumane or Degrading Treatment or Punishment (United Nations General Assembly, 1984) and Elimination of All Forms of Discrimination against Women (United Nations General Assembly, 1981); the United Nations Standard Minimum Rules for the Treatment of Prisoners (the Nelson Mandela Rules) (United Nations General Assembly, 2016), and the United Nations Rules for the Treatment of Women Prisoners and Non-Custodial Measures for Women Offenders (the Bangkok Rules) (United Nations General Assembly, 2010).

As noted previously, the Bangkok Rules were adopted by the United Nations in 2010 and are described as being a "landmark step in adapting the 1955 Standard Minimum Rules for the Treatment of Prisons [currently the Nelson Mandela Rules] to women offenders and prisoners" (Barberet & Jackson, 2017, p. 214). Until their adoption, international human rights standards had not properly reflected the specific gendered needs of women, both as prisoners and regarding alternatives to imprisonment (Penal Reform International, 2013). The Bangkok

Rules reflect the research evidence gleaned from feminist pathways and penal scholarship. They provide a starting point for addressing the appropriate treatment of criminalized women and their children. Spearheaded in Southeast Asia by Princess Bajrakitiyabha Mahidol of Thailand (a prosecutor, jurist, and leading women's rights advocate), the rules were drafted in close consultation with feminist researchers and prison activists from around the world, and taken by a Thai delegation to the United Nations (Barberet & Jackson, 2017, p. 221).

The 70 Bangkok Rules provide a practical and aspirational set of human rights principles via a set of gendered directives to policymakers, legislators, sentencing authorities, and correctional institutions (Gainsborough, 2008). There is recognition that criminalized women and their children are especially vulnerable, that women in conflict with the law have different needs from men, are generally non-violent, subsequently pose minimal risk to society, and that existing systems of corrections are masculinist. The rules consider, amongst other things, high levels of victimization, trauma, substance abuse, mental ill-health, poverty, women's primary childcare responsibilities, and reproductive health care needs. They advocate for non-custodial measures alongside the need for gender-specific prison programs, policies, and practices, that support women's well-being, rehabilitation, and reintegration (Barberet & Jackson, 2017; Carlen, 2012; Gundy & Baumann-Grau, 2013, pp. 11–12; Penal Reform International, 2013). The rules also specifically address the needs of the children who are negatively impacted when their main caregiver (mother) comes into confrontation with the criminal justice system; there is an expectation that the best interests of children are considered (Penal Reform International, 2013, pp. 3–5).

The gendered challenges faced by imprisoned women, and by extension, the need for a more gender-informed approach, are highlighted in several chapters in this book. Gorter and Gover (Chapter 4) discuss the human rights challenges faced by imprisoned mothers and their children in Cambodia. As grass-roots advocates working "on the ground" for an Non-Government Organization, the authors overview a program developed by their organization that aims to support women and their children at risk of separation through imprisonment, recognizing the importance of familial relationships to women's rehabilitation and reintegration. In Chapter 5, a research team from Myanmar[1] explore and critically reflect on the rehabilitative and re-integrative potential of work tasks assigned to female prisoners in Myanmar. Jefferson and researchers from Myanmar[2] (Chapter 2) deliberate on the challenges faced by women imprisoned in Myanmar regarding their basic human right to health care. More broadly, the authors of this chapter summarize findings from an interview-based case-study, examining the gendered experience of imprisonment, the character of prisons, practices of repression and resistance, and reflect on what the future may hold in the wake of the 2021

---

[1]Given the current circumstances in Myanmar and for reasons of safety and security, it is with much regret that we feel unable to reveal the names of the authors of this chapter.
[2]Given the current circumstances in Myanmar and for reasons of safety and security, it is with much regret that we feel unable to reveal the names of the co-producers of this chapter.

Tatmadaw coup. In Chapter 10, Chuenurah, Owen, and Rao consider the progress made, and challenges faced, in implementing and promoting the Bangkok Rules throughout Southeast Asia.

It is important to note that gender-responsive criminal justice and the feminist criminological scholarship underpinning it, has been critiqued for sidelining other crucial aspects of discrimination and oppression, such as race, ethnicity, indigeneity, sexuality, and gender diversity (Barberet & Jackson, 2017; Hannah-Moffat, 2010). While the Bangkok Rules do make a fleeting reference to the vulnerabilities of women from Indigenous, ethnic, and racial minority groups, there is a relative lack of depth around considerations of intersectional oppressions or kyriarchy (Barberet & Jackson, 2017, pp. 225–226). Since the 1990s, feminist criminologists have been calling for and undertaking research exploring the juncture of gender, race, and ethnicity (Burgess-Proctor, 2006; Chesney-Lind, 2006; Collins, 2000; Miller & Mullins, 2008; Potter, 2006; 2013; Richie, 1996). While intersectional criminological feminism is described as profoundly activist, being embedded in effecting structural changes to promote social justice and equity, these endeavors have been dominated by scholarship in western countries (Barberet, 2014, p. 1; Gueta, 2020; Potter, 2013, p. 314).

Utilizing the Bangkok Rules as an assessment framework, Rao, Park, and Jeffries (Chapter 6) employ a feminist intersectional approach to explore axes of gender and ethnicity in the lived experiences of women imprisoned in Thailand. Focusing on Indonesia and Malaysia, Harry (Chapter 3) critically reflects on the implications of calls by activist groups in Southeast Asia for women criminalized and sentenced to death for drug trafficking to be reconceptualized as human trafficking victims. She argues that while this reconfiguration may present as an obvious feminist activist platform to seek reform and remove women from death row, in practice, it may play out in racialized and gendered ways, impeding women's mobility, agency, and livelihood. Intersectionality, this time between gender and age, is also evident in Russell, Jeffries, and Chuenurah's (Chapter 7) exploration of older women's pathways to prison in Thailand. In Chapter 10, Chuenurah, Owen, and Rao reflect on what they describe as the complexity of layers of harm, noting that in implementing the Bangkok Rules in Southeast Asian prisons, we must ensure that women from all racial, ethnic, and cultural groups are accorded full human rights protections, and equal access to programs, services, and opportunities.

There is a tendency within feminist criminology to conceptualize gender in binary terms by focusing on cisgender heterosexual identified women to the detriment of transgender and non-heteronormative sexual identities. Perhaps unsurprisingly, therefore, and as highlighted by Chuenurah and colleagues in Chapter 10, gender and sexual diversity is invisible in the United Nations Bangkok Rules (also see Barberet & Jackson, 2017, p. 225). In academe, this shortcoming has recently been highlighted through the emergence of Queer criminology, a new arm of critical criminological activism seeking to "address a variety of injustices – whether in the form of discrimination, heteronormativity, gender binarism, or invisibility – experienced by queer communities in the realm of criminal justice, criminology, and beyond" (Ball, 2014, 2016, p. 473, Buist & Lenning, 2015; Buist, Lenning, & Ball, 2018; Buist & Stone, 2014; Woods, 2014).

In Chapter 8, Pravattiyagul's exploration of transgender experiences of imprisonment in Thailand examines identity formation and reproduction behind prison walls, how transgender prisoners use gender to strategically negotiate power and offers a corrective to the western scholarly literature on transgender carceral experiences. Jefferson and co-authors (Chapter 2) also illuminate LGBTIQA+ carceral experiences in Myanmar, including encounters with the police and judiciary on the way into prison. They consider how what is coined "shadow law" is implemented in ways that result in sexual and gender minorities being targeted, harassed, and criminalized. Once again, they contemplate what this now means under Tatmadaw rule post-coup.

It is important to note that within feminist criminology, there is some discontent being voiced about the motility toward gender-responsive prisons (Carlton, 2018; Evans, 2018; Hannah-Moffat, 2010; O'Brien, Kim, Beck, & Bhuyan, 2020; Russell & Carlton, 2013; Terwiel, 2020; Whalley & Hackett, 2017; Willison & O'Brien, 2017). Some argue that gender-sensitive prison reform, as per the Bangkok Rules, could be co-opted by the patriarchal state and used to widen the net of confinement (Carlen, 2012, p. 156; O'Brien et al., 2020,p. 7; Russell & Carlton, 2013). Gender-responsive prisons theoretically, by extension, are more rehabilitative, and in place of other options, could become de facto social service agencies where women are imprisoned for "their own good" (Whalley & Hackett, 2017, p. 464).

In Chapter 10, Chuenurah and colleagues argue that in the spirit of the Bangkok Rules, and to achieve gendered human rights, we need to re-imagine punishment by moving away from imprisonment toward community-based sentencing. Yet, this could also result in net-widening, and some feminist scholars have questioned this position. After all, community corrections are rooted in the same structures of gendered oppression as prisons (Whalley & Hackett, 2017, p. 465). Neither gender-responsive prisons nor alternative non-custodial options address the reality that systems of law and justice are patriarchal, and therefore intrinsically and inescapably harmful to cisgender women, transpersons, and sexual minorities (Lawston & Meiners, 2014; Terwiel, 2020; Whalley & Hackett, 2017). The drug wars, for example, have become a war on women waged by patriarchy. Rather than engaging with the masculinist state and tinkering around the edges of the system through non-custodial measures and gender-responsive prisons, maybe feminist activism should be seeking to "dismantle the structural injustices that shape practices of criminalisation and imprisonment" (Carlton, 2018, p. 288; Davis & Rodriguez, 2000; Lawston & Meiners, 2014; O'Brien et al., 2020; Terwiel, 2020, pp. 431–433; Willison & O'Brien, 2017). This theme is evident in the arguments of Chuenurah and co-authors (Chapter 10), who posit that the Bangkok Rules and the feminist principles enshrined therein, should be used as a basis from which to dismantle punitive drug laws alongside the gendered discrimination and oppression that has emerged from them.

Arguably, feminist criminological activists should be investing in the long-term goal of transforming patriarchal social systems, including law and justice. However, in the short-term, and as noted by the authors of numerous chapters in this book, we still need to be investing in change that addresses criminalized cisgender

women, transgender persons, other gender, and sexual minorities immediate concerns and needs, reduces their suffering, and sense of powerlessness (Terwiel,
2020). In the long-term, we should be envisioning a world free of kyriarchy, a
place where social institutions extend substantive equality and conditions of
flourishing to all (Barberet & Jackson, 2017; Carlton, 2018; Davis & Rodriguez,
2000; O'Brien et al., 2020; Terwiel, 2020, pp. 431–433; Willison & O'Brien, 2017).
In other words, as activist scholars concerned with subjugation, we should strive
toward a more egalitarian society where "cage-based" punishment becomes an
impossibility (Davis & Rodriguez, 2000; Terwiel, 2020).

Chapter 2

Gender and Imprisonment in Contemporary Myanmar

Andrew M. Jefferson and Myanmar Research Team[1]

Abstract

In this chapter, we examine historical and contemporary debates about the position and situation of women in Myanmar (and to a lesser extent gender and sexual minorities). Specific reference is made to the patriarchal character of the military coup of February 1, 2021, and the emergent forms of feminist resistance that turned social norms inside out in protest against lethal repression. The way women, as well as sexual and gender minorities, are unequally positioned and face structural and social discrimination in society serves to contextualize our presentation of the findings of a collaborative case-study conducted in 2018 on issues pertaining to gender and imprisonment in Myanmar, based mainly on interviews with former prisoners in three research sites. The aim was to generate field-based knowledge about the carceral experiences of women and LGBTQIA+ persons in Myanmar – focusing on their needs and vulnerabilities, their capacities and rights, their relationships and identities, and their modes of survival as they encounter penal regimes. Findings are summarized focusing on former prisoners' experiences of legal bias; perspectives on encounters with the criminal justice system; the inadequacy of health provision (posed as lethal neglect); and the way certain behaviors and identities are criminalized. The chapter concludes with some reflections on the degree to which there might still be space for critical scholarship in the post-coup world and poses some questions for future research.

Keywords: Myanmar; women; gender and sexual minorities; prison; feminist resistance; military coup

---

[1]For reasons of safety and security and given current circumstances and with much regret, we are unable to reveal the names of the co-producers of this chapter.

Gender, Criminalization, Imprisonment and Human Rights in Southeast Asia, 13–29
Copyright © 2022 by Andrew M. Jefferson and Myanmar Research Team
Published under exclusive licence by Emerald Publishing Limited
doi:10.1108/978-1-80117-286-820221002

Times Changing Hands

The military coup of February 1st, 2021 radically changed the political landscape in Myanmar, almost overnight. In one fell swoop expectations of a new generation, raised during five years of hybrid government (where elected officials shared power with the military), and over 10 years of gradual liberalization, were dashed and the traumas of older generations who grew up, witnessed, and suffered under previous military regimes were reawakened. The coup has disrupted people's lives and interrupted what many believed was a trajectory that would move the country beyond the authoritarian times of the past into a different, more democratic, future. But times have changed hands again[2] and as we write (in July 2021) long-term trajectories of hope are blocked, though the growth of a resistance movement bears witness to the fact that hope is not yet extinguished.

In this chapter, we examine historical and contemporary debates about the position of women (and, to a lesser degree, members of sexual and gender minorities) in Myanmar in light of the military coup and responses to it.[3] Attention is drawn to the patriarchal character of the coup and the forms of women's resistance to it that turned social norms inside out in the face of lethal repression. This examination forms the backdrop for a presentation of the results of a collaborative case-study based on interviews with former prisoners about the gendered experience of imprisonment.

The coup has not made the results of our interview-based case-study irrelevant. In fact, our findings may even illuminate certain aspects of the coup. Parallels can certainly be drawn between punitive and exclusionary policing and penal practices applied to women and sexual minorities in Myanmar's not too distant past and the brutal application of patriarchal power by the military in the face of protest and dissent in the wake of the coup. In the months since February 1st arrests, detention, torture and killing are once more vividly in the public eye and people from all walks of life are at risk. Harassment, detention, and persecution is not a practice limited to minorities, journalists or farmers caught up in conflicts over land. Anyone taking a stand against the military – and they are many – are at risk. According to the Assistance Association for Political Prisoners (AAPP, 2021) over 500 people were killed during the first 2 months since the coup. Over 2,500 were detained at some point. During the first 2 months, around 25% of detainees were women (AAPP 29th March – 668/2570). Whether this proportion (25% women/75% men) is normal under such circumstances would be the subject of mere speculation as, to our knowledge, there exists no baseline. What

---

[2]See Jefferson (2020) for empirical illustration of this notion in the Myanmar context.
[3]We are of course aware that gender is not only about women. However, in this case study, we have not considered the issue of masculinities and imprisonment, though we do touch on the inherently masculinized prison and the patriarchal Tatmadaw (the Myanmar military). We are also aware of the overlapping nature of the experiences related to differently gendered, racialized, classed and sexualized identities but focus mostly on gendered identity and to only a minor degree the experiences of sexual minorities.

we do know is that Myanmar's prison population historically and in recent times features a relatively high proportion of women (around 12%, World Prison Brief, 2021 and Chapter 1) compared to countries in the rest of the world. This was one of the central puzzles that galvanized us to consider the issue of gender and imprisonment in Myanmar (see also Chapter 5, this volume).

We begin by considering the positions, perceptions, and possibilities available to women, and sexual and gender minorities in Myanmar historically and today.

Constructions of Domination

Women in Myanmar do not generally occupy prominent leadership positions or positions of authority. (The now detained State Counsellor Aung San Suu Kyi is exceptional in this respect). In the parliament that preceded the coup women comprise less than 10% of parliamentarians and Aung San Suu Kyi was the only female member of the cabinet (Khin Mra & Livingstone, 2020, p. 247). In the labor market, opportunities for women are limited with many women employed in low paid jobs under exploitative conditions. "Gender inequalities," as Khin Mra and Livingstone (2020, p. 243) put it "persist in many forms." Gender discrimination is deeply structured, even inscribed in the Constitution of 2008 which designates certain positions as suitable for men only. Laws passed in 2015 about population control, religious conversion, marriage, and monogamy are seen by critics as legislating discrimination.

Yet, for a considerable time, scholarship and popular perceptions of women in Myanmar implied that compared to their regional neighbors (and colonial powers) women had, in fact, a relatively high status (Ikeya, 2011; Khaing, 1984). At the start of the twentieth century, the "most compelling and certainly the most enduring popular representation of Burmese society" was that it was "free of customs oppressive to women" (Ikeya, 2011, p. 60). This "traditional" view argues Ikeya (2011, p. 76) in a historical "examination of the construction of gendered discourses" was a result of accounts written by British and Burmese commentators inflected by colonization, modernization, and nationalism. For example, the apparent high opinion of Burmese women held by representatives of Victorian Britain must be understood against their contempt for Burmese men. Furthermore, Khin Mra (2018, p. 383) cites Fielding, writing in 1906 that the future of the nation depended on Burmese men learning to be proper men. The ascription to women of relative influence during this period was thus skewed by the values of the ascriber, and their views on Burmese men and the failed nature of the Burmese state. In turn, post-independence nationalist views, writes Khin Mra (2018, p. 384) "stressed the legitimacy of masculine dominance" contributing to women's marginalization in politics and in some cases to their demonization. Particularly women who married foreigners or non-Buddhists were considered traitors to the nation.

More recently, the history that ascribed high status to women in Myanmar has been debunked as feminist analysis has revealed the lived reality of women's experience of sexism, discrimination, and violence (Thiri Kyaw & Miedema, 2020, pp. 268–269) as well as the structural inequalities including social and religious norms and practices, that position women as subordinate to men and hold them in that position. Contrary to the traditional view, discussed above, conformity to powerful norms about what a "decent" woman is meant to be is expected, and such norms are instantiated through family life and marriage as well as religion and law.

According to Mi Mi Khaing, the author of *The World of Burmese Women*, the idea that "spiritually, a man is higher than a woman… is just not an abstract idea belonging to religious philosophy. Conviction of it enter(s) our very bones" (cited by Ikeya, 2011, p. 56). The key notion at work to sustain women's subordinate position vis-à-vis men and perpetuate gender discriminatory practices is the notion of hpon or "glory" which situates men as superior and women as a potential threat to that masculine "glory." Only men possess hpon (Gender Equality Network, 2015; Thiri Kyaw, 2021a). Women's bodies are understood to be inherently impure (associated with menstruation and childbirth but ultimately rooted in their inferior spirituality) and therefore a threat to men's hpon. The close proximity of a woman to a man threatens to sap the man's inherent, natural power.

Women are expected to be pure – understood as virginal before marriage – and this expectation is used to control mobility and public participation which might put their purity at risk.[4] Women's subordinate position is illustrated by the practice of wives serving their husbands/sons first at mealtimes and walking behind their husbands in public. In another sign of women's riskiness, their garments are washed and hung separately from their husbands/sons/brothers.

Women are supposed to embody yin kyae hmu meaning "politeness or gentleness" (Khin Mra & Livingstone, 2020, pp. 252, 276). Assertiveness is undesirable and women are not expected to aspire to leadership positions. Women's role in reproduction is about protecting and maintaining the culture; failure to fulfill this role appropriately (for example by marrying a foreigner) can be understood as a betrayal of culture and invites censure. Women's sexuality is controlled while femininity is expected. Daughters must be obedient to their parents and are typically "sheltered" more than male siblings during childhood and obligated to a greater extent than sons to their parents' care. The expectation is for men to be leaders and women to be "wives and mothers in need of protection" (Khin Mra & Livingstone, 2020, p. 247). A woman's duty to a husband, as well as being deferential, is to "preserve and enhance" his glory (Fennessy, 2016, p. 64).

In short,

> women are expected to be submissive, polite and marriageable, to have children and maintain modesty without sacrificing femininity. Any deviation from this… is seen as both shameful for the woman and her family, but also deeply threatening to the established order and cultural stability. (Russell & Martin, 2021)

---

[4]In instances where women are raped or otherwise violated they, rather than the perpetrators, are perceived as blameworthy.

Despite these powerful norms, Aye Thiri Kyaw and Stephanie Miedema (2020) trace how today's younger generations are beginning to question such norms and speak out. They document the rise of a nascent women's rights movement and heightened levels of activism around violence and harassment in the light of the global #metoo trend that accelerated during 2020.[5] Perhaps, they speculate optimistically, gender and sexuality norms in Myanmar are changing. Certainly, embedded social norms about gender and sexuality have been subverted in the aftermath of the coup seen at the most basic level in the public and visible presence of women and members of sexual minorities leading demonstrations (see below). And yet the military threatens to undermine any gains with a radical reassertion of masculinized military power. As Phyu Phyu Oo (2021) puts it, "returning to the military regime will impose additional challenges for ongoing development for the gender equality and women's empowerment in Myanmar." Similarly, Jennifer Harriden (2012, p.307, cited by Khin Mra) analyzes of the way that military rule in the past "reinforced the authoritarian, hierarchical and chauvinistic values that underpinned male-dominated power structures." Khin Khin Mra (2021) addresses the more recent situation before the coup:

> Even during the transition to democracy, with the adoption of a new constitution, Myanmar remains a masculine state with its male-dominated institutions where there is no belief in women's equality with men, or support for women to become leaders and politicians. Women remain notably under-represented in all aspects of public and political life in Myanmar's democratising state.

And yet as we shall show below responses to the coup illustrate the grounds for optimism that Thiri Kyaw and Miedema (2020) imply, even against a profoundly troubling backdrop. How gender norms were transgressed in response to the coup suggests that nascent changes may have been accelerated in response to the overt application of patriarchal power.

Khin Khin Mra and Deborah Livingstone (2020, p. 245) document how masculinized and patriarchal practices and norms limited any gains for women during the period of the National League for Democracy (NLD) led government (2015–2020). They argue that "legacies of military rule informed how formal and informal institutions evolved during the democratisation period" and effectively hindered the implementation of gender equality policies. Based on their own experience evaluating a policy initiative (the National Strategic Plan for the Advancement of Women), they describe the normalized patriarchal power structures that are a result of decades of military rule and the consequent limits on space for "feminist action." The 2008 Constitution is seen as propagating

---

[5]See also Hedström's analysis of the rise of a multi-ethnic women's movement with a "gendered political consciousness" (p. 61) forged in response to the secondary position reserved for them within ethnic armed groups (published already in 2015).

male-dominated gender norms and the "primacy of the old order" (Khin Mra & Livingstone, 2020, p. 248). They also describe the idea of women as bearers of culture that needs protecting from internal and external forces. Women are honored as bearers of culture but still seen as subordinate – bearers rather than creators of culture.

Women's Resistance to the Coup

Women's creative response to the coup has been widely documented. It exemplifies both gender norms and the possibilities of transgressing them. Phyu Phyu Oo (2021) situates the pots and pans protests, that emerged very early in response to the coup, within a broader tradition of women's protest going back to Chile in the 1970s. Of particular interest is the merging of meanings attached to this form of protest that combines local cosmologies (beating pans as a form of expelling evil) and global forms [International Women's Day (IWD)]. In addition to this method, as we will consider further below, women have used the culturally embedded beliefs described above about their position, status and potentially polluting nature to push back against the coup. The recent protests took the form of women hanging undergarments (htamein) and sarongs (longyis) on strings across roads blocking armored vehicles from passing under, shaming and embarrassing male security forces whose hpon is believed to be diminished by passing under such impure items.[6] Similarly, htamein have been hung on poles like flags, proudly displayed by men and women during demonstrations and marches (See Beech, 2021; Russell & Martin, 2021).

Other post-coup actions of resistance included putting pictures of the General (patriarchy personified) inside their clothing and under the soles of their feet. One striking image circulating on social media featured a picture of the military chief and usurping head of state with a bloody menstrual pad on his head. The htamein flag protest was deliberately adopted as a campaign tactic on IWD. Khin Khin Mra (2021), writing just a few days after IWD, registers the apolitical, often domestic role of women in society and points with some surprise to the active and activist role women played in the protests. While this mode of protest pre-existed IWD (by a few days), the concurrence of IWD (March 8th) with the growing protest movement created an opportunity to tap into a global discourse and movement indicating the globalized outlook of protesters. "This is a revolution in the making" claims Khin Khin Mra (2021b) optimistically, "opposing the misogynistic dictatorship as well as its underlying patriarchal ideology."

On Twitter, Aye Thiri Kyaw (2021a, 2021b), initially expressed some discomfort about the way women used their imagined polluting nature as a form of resistance, acknowledging perhaps the ambivalence of exploiting a trope of

---

[6]See Khaing (1984, pp. 156–157) for accounts of women at the forefront of strike action in the 1930s.

systemic oppression in an explicit fight against the patriarchal military. But this reversal is not a new tactic in Myanmar. As Khaing pointedly observes,

> the degree of a woman's belief in the concept of hpon can be gauged when, in conflict, a wife "desecrates" her husband's hpon by reversing the usual manners respecting it. (Khaing, 1984, p. 16)

Women's presence at protests modeling creative forms of resistance is a clear sign of an occupation by women of the public sphere. By doing so, women declare their independence from men and send a clear signal that they do not need or wish for the military's "protection" (Khin Mra, 2021). By exploiting their perceived polluting capacity, women expose and undermine patriarchy.

On Sexuality and Gender Identity

Women are not the only subordinated identity group to be differentially treated in Myanmar society. Huge social pressures exist to conform to the sex-gender binary (i.e., biological sex should equate to the presentation of self as masculine or feminine) and heterosexuality. Those who fall outside these heteronormative gender binaries experience marginalization and violence. Around the world, categories related to gender and sexual identity are increasingly understood as not fixed. Cisgender heterosexuality is not universal. The short-hand term LGBT used so often by western agencies promoting liberalizing agendas (but also contested and developing such that the currently accepted term is LGBTQIA+) does not in fact translate as well as might be imagined given the degree to which it is applied globally. We might even argue that the increasing fluidity of gender and sexual identities that current times and specific places bear witness to have quite distinct histories and quite distinct forms, for example in northern Europe and in Southeast Asia. For certain, sexualities situated outside of normative heterosexuality and non-binary gender identity in Myanmar is not the same as being LGBTQIA+ in Denmark.[7]

Same-sex intimacy is illegal in Myanmar and both sexual minorities and people identifying as gender non-binary are subject to discrimination articulated in law[8]

---

[7]Neither our Denmark-based team, nor our Myanmar-based team would claim to be experts in local or global expressions of gender or sexuality so our brief incursion into this field has been a steep learning curve. We have an aversion to the term "LGBTQI people" that is often used in both policy and advocacy circles though we recognize its utility. For us it seems unnecessarily reductionist as if people are only their sexuality or gender identity. It also serves to conflate sexual and gender identities in non-specified ways.

[8]By defining carnal intercourse "against the order of nature" in terms of penetration Section 377 of the (colonial era) Penal Code would seem to imply that it is same sex intimacy between men that is illegal but both men and women who engage in same sex intimacy are discriminated against and harshly treated in Myanmar today.

and driven by social, cultural, and religious norms. We have learned much from secondary sources and would direct the reader to important papers by Chua and Gilbert (2015) and Gilbert (2013) for illuminating discussion of the complexity of subject positions, identities and the "problem of articulation and ascription" (2013, p. 245) in language (in Myanmar), as well as the excellent advocacy work of Colors Rainbow. As well as reminding how poorly western categories translate locally, Gilbert shows how the subject positions related to gender and sexuality involve both external and internal dimensions understood as having to do with image and resemblance on the one hand and mind/heart on the other (as well as past karma). His insightful ethnographically informed analysis clearly illustrates the slipperiness of categories as articulated, ascribed, languaged and, not least, lived.

Color Rainbow's report Facing 377 helpfully discusses issues related to terminology in cultural context and the way section 377 of the Myanmar Penal Code (and the 1899 Yangon Police Act 30 and 1945 Police Act 35) are applied in a manner that discriminates and facilitates harassment, and violence toward sexual and gender minorities. This is the concern of one of the papers resulting from our case-study. As we describe further below the so-called shadow laws impact heavily on two stigmatized groups: sex workers and "apwints." "Apwint" is a term usually translated into English as "open." One local activist organization uses this category to refer to somebody "biologically male who acts as and appears feminine with a preference for male sexual partners" (Gilbert, 2013, p. 242). Apwints, as our interviews reveal first-hand, and Colors Rainbow (2013, pp. 36–46) also document are subject to abuse because of their sexual/gender identity in a range of settings from the home to the street to the police station and prison.

Gendered Prisons

Scholars have taught us that prisons are gendered in quite specific ways. They are masculinized, heteronormative institutions that serve women, gender and sexual minorities exceptionally poorly. This is partially because of their history. Prisons were designed by men, for men with particular versions of masculinity and men's propensity for violence in mind (see Chapter 1 in this volume and Britton, 2003). In fact, in the western world, prisons are some of the only institutions where men and women are still kept separately. Today, schools are increasingly co-ed and even golf clubs and business clubs historically reserved for men are now open to women. But prisons remain almost universally single-sex spaces.[9] Lorna Rhodes (2018), writing about the rather unique therapeutic community prison in UK, HMP Grendon, has noted the irony contained in the practice of trying to help people deal with the problems of sociality in peculiarly anti-social environments. Men (mostly) who are unable to respect the boundaries established by law and often have problems that we might term relational are taken out of

---

[9]Here we are not talking about staff but only prisoners. There are female staff in men's prisons, and, though less often, male staff in women's prisons.

"normal" relations and thrust into a hyper-masculinized abnormal universe and somehow expected to come out better for it. The separation of men from women in prisons (often in the name of protecting women) is one aspect of this slightly absurd paradox.[10]

In Myanmar, there are other men-only institutions, the most important perhaps being the Sangha, that is the Buddhist religious order. There are no women-only prisons in Myanmar (though there are two labor camps for women as well as "education" centers for women charged with minor offenses). Women are mainly held in separate sections of men's prisons. Our case-study confirmed quite clearly the gendered nature of imprisonment and the way hegemonic gender norms are themselves reproduced by the practice of imprisonment and the transactions and dependencies that prison life entails.

Women's (and Sexual and Gender Minorities') Experience of Prison

We come now to a discussion of some primary data. Our overall research project aims to generate new knowledge about the changing character of imprisonment based primarily on first-person accounts gathered through face-to-face interviews. In this case-study on gender, we interviewed 85 former prisoners, including 60 women. We sought to gain insight into their unique experiences of imprisonment and to learn about the dynamics of prison life (and encounters with the police and judiciary) from their point of view.

To our knowledge, there exists no social scientific work on women's experience of imprisonment in Myanmar but there is some literature about women's pathways into and out of prison in other Southeast Asian countries (e.g., Thailand, Cambodia, Vietnam, see Chapters 1, 6, 7, and 9 in this volume). This feminist, criminological literature offers insights into the way women are criminalized in specific ways, the way particular cultural norms affect their journeys into, through and out of prison, as well as the sufferings of ethnic minority and foreign national prisoners. The literature suggests that an overwhelming proportion of women prisoners are poor and are imprisoned for survival-related offenses (Jeffries, 2014; Jeffries & Chuenurah, 2018; Jeffries, Chuenurah, Rao, & Park, 2019, and numerous chapters in this volume). We turn now to a consideration of the gendered effects of criminal justice practices and imprisonment in Myanmar. While not specifically adopting a feminist pathways focus our approach shares with the pathways approach the privileging of the standpoints of the interviewees.

---

[10]Perhaps the segregation of the sexes into prisons for men and prisons for women or separate facilities within the same establishment that seems to be a foundation stone of modern imprisonment should give pause for thought. While institutions around the world are desegregating there is very little evidence of a turn toward co-ed prisons despite some innovations in some places (Denmark, for example, with mixed results). If the thought of men and women serving their sentences together seems unduly provocative an alternative might be to abolish imprisonment all together.

We know that prisons, penal identities and penal relations are gendered. The question for our research team was how that looks exactly in Myanmar. We began our study with a host of important questions and areas of possible interest that were gradually honed down through the experience of fieldwork and subsequent analysis of the material. Our initial research questions, which we share in the hope that they might inspire future studies, were

- Why are so many women imprisoned in Myanmar compared to other places and what are the consequences of this?
- To what extent are women, sexual and gender minority groups more or less vulnerable in Myanmar prisons? How do penal environments impact on their lives in particular and gender-specific ways?
- How is the imprisonment of women, sexual and gender minority groups managed in Myanmar and how has it changed over time?
- Is the legal and policy framework, the service provision, the disciplinary system, the infrastructure and the management culture of Myanmar prisons gender-biased? If so in what way and with what consequence for prisoners, relatives, and staff?
- What does the analysis of the imprisonment of women tell us about perceptions of punishment, penal reform, and state-citizen relations in Myanmar today?

We were especially curious about whether there was something about Myanmar, about the history of the country, about the nature and use of law during the decades of military rule or during the recent transition toward democracy (revealed by the military coup to be a premature prognosis) that marked women's imprisonment in particular ways. Many of these questions remain to be answered and many of these themes could be fruitful topics of future research should conditions in the country ever again become conducive to on the ground empirical work on these sensitive themes. We ended up focusing on four topics each of which have some pedigree in prison literature. We introduce and elaborate briefly on each below.

Women's Harsh Treatment in Prison

One of the papers dives into the heart of women's general experience of incarceration in Myanmar documenting, with the help of six examples, the hardships that women face. The paper draws attention to the way women are poorly treated in the criminal justice system because of the kind of crimes committed or alleged, their social status, and poverty. Women who come into contact with the law face particular challenges. Moral judgments based on social expectations mean that if a woman commits or is suspected of committing a crime, she faces the sanction of the law and the wider society. She may be considered both criminal and "immoral" for failing to live up to norms of womanhood. This may affect sentencing and even legislative practices where what is sanctioned is based on the perceived "immorality" of the behavior rather than the illegality of the activity.

What becomes quite clear is that the trials and tribulations of prison reflect pre-existing hardships and discriminations faced by women in Myanmar society. The experience of prison essentially worsens the circumstances of women so that on release they have little chance of breaking cycles of poverty, or dependencies on criminalized means of maintaining a livelihood or simply surviving. Two quite striking examples are given where a woman is arrested and imprisoned instead of a male relative. In one case a wife and mother plead guilty to a drugs offense because if her husband is found guilty he will serve a longer sentence and his absence as the key income generator, would be keenly felt by their children. In another case, a woman was arrested by police who planted drugs in her house because of a crime committed by her brother. During two or three days at the police station, the police told her that if her brother would come and meet her, they would release her. She ended up serving 4 years of a 15-year sentence. She pointed out that she could not believe the criminal justice system could treat her in this way. If she were a man, she said, they would not have arrested her. She felt this was a case of gender-based discrimination and as a result, she had lost trust in the justice system.

Three key lessons are worthy of iteration. One is about the way pre-existing conditions of vulnerability put women at risk when they encounter the criminal justice system. Poverty for example can contribute to situations where women's livelihood opportunities are reduced and they feel driven to sex work or other criminalized occupations such as drug couriering leaving them exposed and caught up in a vicious and intimidating cycle of behavior and consequences. Another relates to opportunities available to women outside and inside the prisons. Inside prisons in Myanmar women are put to work but the data from our studies suggest this is more to keep them occupied than to contribute to their vocational opportunities on release (see Chapter 5, this volume). Imprisonment for women in Myanmar does not live up to any rehabilitative or reintegrative ideal. A third lesson suggested by our data is that lack of education, illiteracy, and legal knowledge exacerbate the hardships of women coming into contact with the criminal justice system. Lack of awareness of their rights, lack of legal literacy or knowledge of where to seek help or how to acquire the services of a lawyer leave women at a severe disadvantage.

Women's Health

Another of the papers explores what is innovatively termed the "lethal neglect" faced by women prisoners in Myanmar when it comes to their quite specific health needs. This is a topic quite widely researched internationally and our findings resonate strongly with this literature about the challenges women face concerning their health needs in prison.

Six areas of perceived neglect are identified. These are: inadequacy of health-care professionals; inadequacy of reproductive healthcare; inadequacy of HIV/ AIDs healthcare; inadequacy of emergency healthcare service; lack of responsiveness to self-reported medical conditions; and lack of equality of opportunities in healthcare. The scanty provision of care across these areas led women prisoners to believe that prison staff and health professionals in the prison were apathetic, uncaring, and irresponsible. The non-availability, action, and inaction of prison and health staff were found to impact negatively on women prisoners' chances of living meaningful lives in prison and indeed of survival as illustrated by this poignant quote:

> The medical staff rarely came to prison, so prisoners found it difficult to receive medical treatment on a regular basis. They did not care about patients. One of my cell-mates, for instance, suffered from cancer and could not see the medical staff regularly. She became weaker day by day. Eventually, she died. When she died, her dead body covered by a mat was carried to the outside of the prison. I saw this circumstance. It was the most horrible thing I witnessed during my prison life. (Interview, speaking about events in 2014)

Another former prisoner spoke also of the inaccessibility of necessary medical attention during the night. She said:

> One of my cellmates was freezing and trembling at night. She was not able to go to the prison hospital because it was closed at night. With my shocked voice, I yelled for help from some prison staff in fear to get a help in my cell. Yet, nobody showed up there. I needed water to relieve her illness. Eventually, I made for the water in the toilet and fetched the water for her. I made her drink that water because it was the only water to alleviate the pain she was going through. And then, she drank toilet water and I brushed her body with that water. She became relieved. (Interview speaking about events in 2014)

In this situation, the fact that the hospital was closed and no emergency provision was provided meant the cellmate was forced to act quickly with the few resources at her disposal. What we see in both these examples is how the lack of medical care thrusts a burden of responsibility onto prisoners leaving them to deal with health problems and deal with the anxiety and pressure associated with that. The state authorities were failing in their duty of care. One final example drives the point home, this time referring to the experience of a former political prisoner imprisoned in 1990. She describes the inhumanity of conditions. She spoke grudgingly:

> We were human, not animals. When we were sick, we needed to be treated humanely and indiscriminately despite our gender… When patients saw the doctor at the prison hospital, he (the doctor) sat on a chair with crossed legs. Patients had to line up kneeling on the ground. We were not allowed to see the doctor and so we had to keep our head down. That was a prison rule. He did not give

us medicines by hand. Instead, he threw medicines away on the ground. Then, the patient kneeling before him rushed to pick up these medicines on the ground. He did not consider sick patients as human. Moreover, prison staff often bullied sick prisoners with their restrictive rules. For this reason, I did not want to go there whatever I felt. These circumstances forced us to die or they (the prison and authorities) let us go die.

"They let us go die," she says. The stakes are incredibly high here. The data provide a troubling glimpse of the challenges faced by women in Myanmar prisons about health provision.

Women's and Sexual Minorities' Vulnerability and Discriminatory Treatment by Law and the Criminal Justice System

Two further papers address the general topic of vulnerability in the face of the law and discriminatory treatment. The first is about another topic that has received some attention in the literature, namely the issue of legal bias against women resulting in vulnerability and often violation when women encounter the criminal justice system. Looking mostly at the processes leading up to prison – encounters with the police, lack of access to legal aid or a lawyer, and encounters with the judiciary – powerful examples are identified of the obstacles faced by women and the injustices meted out by the so-called justice system. The paper examines how the law works in practice when applied to women and proposes that the reason there are high numbers of women in prison in Myanmar, relative to the rest of the world, is due to a discriminatory system of laws and a consistent legal bias that characterizes the judicial process.

Examples are presented of women's harsh treatment by the police, their lack of access to legal representation and the prejudicial behavior of the courts. Many decades of military rule, abuse of power, corruption and lack of legal knowledge have led to legal bias and lack of faith in the justice system. Women prisoners described how on arrival at the prison they sometimes experienced relief because of the harshness, and unfairness of police detention and judicial practice. Some former prisoners believed that judges and law officers, as well as the police, were involved in bribery and corruption.

Several women interviewed for the study were poor farmers arrested en masse in their villages in cases related to contested land claims. In these cases, the women felt their military opponents held undue power over judges and that the judicial process was fundamentally weighted against them. Generally, judges and clerks in court are likely to be sympathetic to the voices of high-ranking military officials or police or government servants because governmental organizations are so closely knit. Under such circumstance's intimidation and victimization, abuse of power and position is common. Women shared that they did not believe the courts could give justice and the law did not protect them. The military had undue influence even before the coup. Judges claim impartiality but the tales of former prisoners tell a different story. Law officers and judges were influenced by military officers during the period of NLD-led government even as they were under the time of military rule. This implies that institutional practices change very slowly and vested interests play powerful roles in maintaining the status quo even when military regimes seem to relax their grip on power.

Another over-represented group of women facing judicial proceedings are sex workers. Rather than expecting the judicial system to treat them fairly or justly sex workers spoken with during the research believed the courts to be places of danger and the police to be their enemy. Ultimately, the analysis calls out the police, the courts and even the law itself for endemic sexism.

The final paper, emerging from our case-study, broadens the focus to cover important issues about women (specifically sex workers) and also those facing gender and sexually diverse minorities. Mostly staying outside the prison, the paper looks at the way the so-called "shadow laws" mentioned earlier are implemented in such a way that sexual and gender-identity minorities are targeted, harassed, and criminalized because of their apparent sexual or gender identities. The "shadow laws" offer the possibility to police to arrest who they like on the flimsiest of pretexts. The experiences of apwints and sex-workers bring to our attention the attitudes and behaviors of law enforcement and prison actors toward these vulnerable minorities. Myanmar remains a conservative nation with discriminatory attitudes toward apwints and stigmatization of sex-workers. Sex-work is considered an "immoral" profession, given the purity expected of women, and living as an apwint is seen by many as the result of a sin committed in a previous life. Apwints (and sex workers) reported how on arrest and in prison they were subject to abuse that explicitly indexed their gender or sexuality (or their sex-related occupation). For example, an army officer reported about his mistreatment after being arrested at a festival while wearing women's clothing:

> Police came to me saying, "come with us." And I went along with them but they just locked me up in their station. You know right? As a person belonging to the LGBT community, they asked me to undress and they cut my hair as well. That time I have long hair but I always hide it. To speak frankly, I was treated very badly. I was completely naked. They also told me, "you are Akyout mah, we are men. You are not like us." Even when we ate, they treated me discriminatorily. You know sometimes, they asked me to undress and asked me to stand upside down like scorpion.

Sex workers too were taunted by police with requests for sexual favors in exchange for release. Some were entrapped by police via requests for sex and then arrested and harassed.

In prison apwints – incarcerated in men's prisons – were forced to do laborious tasks such as carrying bricks to turn them into "proper men." At the same time, they were obliged to offer sexual favors to other prisoners in exchange for protection. So, their gender identity vulnerabilized them in a double fashion. The victimization of apwints in the prison ranges from inappropriate touching, verbal abuse to sexual harassment and rape. Besides sexual assaults, physical violence, and threats of harsher punishment, apwints are also, in some cases, denied contact with the outside world and medical attention with attendant risks to health and well-being. Prejudice combined with ignorance and embedded habits makes these populations particularly vulnerable to abuse.

Together the four papers that emerged from our case-study shed light on the predicaments that women and also gender and sexual minorities face in contemporary Myanmar when they are thrown into contact with the criminal justice system. As already mentioned, data collection, analysis, and write up took place between 2018 and 2020, that is before the military coup of February 1, 2021. Since then, activists have been quick to note the misogynistic, patriarchal character of the military revealed in their naked power grab and their claim to be protecting the country but also in the aggressive tactics associated with the crackdown on initially non-violent protesters. In line with the troubling history of authoritarian rule in Myanmar, it is almost as though the military are provoked to aggression by the simple presence of opposition staring defiantly back at them. One can almost sense an echo of the classic (perhaps a caricature?) perpetrator line: "what do you think you are looking at?," functioning as a prelude to an act of sometimes lethal violence.

Conclusion

Our core original puzzle was why does Myanmar imprison so many women compared to other countries. It is not easy to answer this, on the surface at least, relatively straightforward question. Statistics are hard to come by in Myanmar. The authorities are notoriously reluctant to share even the most basic information with either the public or interested stakeholders. So solid facts that could reveal patterns related to arrest and charges have not been forthcoming. But it is generally believed that many women are imprisoned on drug charges, or in relation to sex work and illegal gambling.[11] Our sample featured a relatively high proportion of women imprisoned because of conflicts over land and hardly any charged with violence. The proportionally high number of women in Myanmar is likely a product of three interlinked practices namely the criminalization of certain behaviors and identities; the reproduction of gendered social norms resulting in women's ongoing subordination to men and judicial bias; and the history of patriarchy embodied in the Tatmadaw – revealed perhaps most clearly in their claims to be engaged in the protection of the nation through practices of lethal injustice, lethal violence and lethal neglect.

Our project began at an auspicious moment in Myanmar's history with the election of the NLD to a dominant parliamentary position albeit fundamentally compromised by the 2008 Constitution and obliged to partner with the military. As we write these lines (in July 2021), the times have changed significantly and

---

[11]Drug use is extremely high in Myanmar especially in areas that are dependent on opium production as a livelihood source.

dramatically. Economic crisis looms and signs of increasing militancy from the civil disobedience movement, the Committee Representing the Pyidaungsu Hluttaw (CRPH) and the National Unity Government as well as the emergence of autonomous People's Defense Forces are likely to be met with even more lethal force. Escalation of conflict seems inevitable. And the consequences do not bear thinking about.

There have been popular uprisings and brutal crackdowns previously in Myanmar – the most well-known in 1988 and 2007. Two questions present themselves (one way more important than the other). The first relates to how the current crisis will play out, the second to the potential for a new brand of critical social scientific scholarship (that we strive to embody) to thrive in a post-coup universe.

It is very uncertain how the current crisis will play out. Recently, we have witnessed the rise of a digitalized and globalized younger generation (of men and women) with new and different tools at their disposal and perhaps even a new form of political consciousness. They have grown up in a world quite different to that of protesters in 1988 and 2007. The Civil Disobedience Movement emerged and acquired broad support quickly. The CRPH similarly announced themselves as a parallel legitimate government against all the odds while the stakes were high and the shock of the military takeover could not even have sunk in. There is an agility about the resistance and a creativity about the expression of dissent that is arguably novel in contrast to the military tactics which seem to resemble their tried and tested tactics of yesteryear,[12] namely to brutalize, dominate, instill fear, use outsiders to disrupt communities, terrorize, torture and kill and detain people arbitrarily. There are some grounds for hope but also grounds for grief and mourning.

We posed some questions at the start of our study and some new ones present themselves in the light of the coup and its aftermath so far. They illustrate the value of examining the state–society relationship through the lens of the prison. We repose these questions in elaborated form here by way of conclusion as pointers toward research questions worth elaborating on should conditions become conducive.

We asked to what extent are women and LGBTQIA+ persons more or less vulnerable in Myanmar prisons. Today we might also ask whether the whole of Myanmar is now once again a semi-porous prison, a carceral state that will exacerbate pre-existing vulnerabilities. We asked how penal environments impact on everyday lives in gender-specific ways. Today, we might also ask how women and LGBTQIA+ persons in Myanmar might be affected differently to men by the coup. Are they empowered or disempowered? We asked whether the legal and policy framework, the service provision, the disciplinary system, the infrastructure,

---

[12]This resembles responses to COVID-19 around the world where security forces have seen it as an opportunity to utilize their well-rehearsed aggressive tactics in the service of repression and domination whereas civil society groups have operated with considerable agility (see Jefferson et al., 2021). Innovation and novelty are not the handmaidens of authoritarianism.

and the management culture of Myanmar prisons is gender-biased. Today, we might ask the same of the tactics of repression applied by the military. To this latter question, our research and collective experience would posit a resounding yes.

Will there be space for the kind of renewed critical scholarship that Cheesman (drawing on Wittekind & Rhoades, 2018) hoped for in 2019, a scholarship that resists the common ways of thinking of Myanmar in terms of well-worn binaries (center-periphery; Bamar-minorities; democratic or military form of rule) and instead operates from below and is attentive to agency, interaction and everyday life (see Jefferson, 2020, p. 74)? Are the roots of this kind of scholarship firm and strong enough to withstand the new circumstances? It has not had long to take root so this is an open question.[13]

Our research collaboration aimed to contribute to embedding a way of critically analyzing practices and meanings pertaining to the everyday life of prisons and prisoners based on fieldwork and drawing on theory and existing scholarship. The ultimate test of our success is not whether the seeds planted can survive and thrive under the new more blatantly authoritarian conditions for this was not the future we had in mind. But we hope that the research approach modeled and developed through our collaboration and the knowledge generated might thrive and speak meaningfully despite current circumstances and ultimately and authoritatively enable the speaking of truth to power.

---

[13]We might also ask whether this new form of Myanmar scholarship is sufficiently embedded in country or whether it is a field dominated by privileged outsiders protected from current risks and dangers. The current crisis is likely to deepen the physical distance between outsiders and insiders though virtual skills developed during the COVID-19 pandemic may offset this if online digital networks remain open.

Chapter 3

Perpetrators and/or Victims? The Case of Women Facing the Death Penalty in Malaysia

Lucy Harry

Abstract

To reduce the number of women being sentenced to death, this chapter explores and critically reflects on the calls being made by women's rights activists in Southeast Asia for cross-border drug trafficking to be reconstituted as human trafficking. Drawing on interviews with a range of stakeholders, alongside information on 146 cases of women sentenced to death for drug trafficking in Malaysia, this chapter shows that the gendered dynamics of drug trafficking can indeed be understood as a form of human trafficking. However, there are concerns from a feminist activist perspective in representing it in these terms because the discourse of human trafficking, has been used by the patriarchal state to legitimize racialized and gendered oppression of women at borders. This has ramifications in terms of human rights, particularly with regards to women's right to freedom of movement as well as the right to livelihood.

Keywords: Gender; drug trafficking; human trafficking; death penalty; capital punishment; death row

Introduction

The relationship between cross-border human and drug trafficking[1] is most clearly exemplified by the case of Mary Jane Veloso, a Filipina woman on death

---

[1]In this chapter, cross-border refers to the movement of people or drugs across international borders not within national borders.

Gender, Criminalization, Imprisonment and Human Rights in Southeast Asia, 31–44
Copyright © 2022 by Lucy Harry
Published under exclusive licence by Emerald Publishing Limited
doi:10.1108/978-1-80117-286-820221003

row for drug trafficking in Indonesia. Veloso, a single mother of two, was once a migrant domestic worker in Dubai but had fled after an attempted rape. Back in the Philippines, Veloso was recruited for a job as a domestic worker in Malaysia. On the day that she left the Philippines, Veloso was given a bag of clothes to carry with her by the people who had recruited her for the job. Whilst transiting in Yogyakarta, Indonesia, she was stopped at customs and 2.6 kg of heroin was found in her luggage. Despite professing her innocence, Veloso was sentenced to death in 2010 and narrowly avoided execution in 2015[2] (Holmes, 2016). Since then, cases have been brought in the Philippines against the people who recruited her for overseas work, and, indeed, in early 2020, these individuals were found guilty of illegally recruiting three further women for work abroad, and sentenced to life imprisonment (Buan, 2020). It is argued by key actors involved in this case, such as Veloso's lawyers, international legal experts, migrant workers' groups in the region (such as *Migrante International*), and the Indonesian National Commission on Violence Against Women (*Komnas Perempuan*), that Veloso is a victim of human trafficking as she was sent across a border to carry out an illegal activity against her will, and this involved an abuse of her vulnerability (her economic desperation) (Damazo-Santos, 2015; Gerry, Harré, Naibaho, & Muraszkiewicz, 2018; Perempuan, 2018). Additionally, these actors argue that many other women on death row for drug trafficking in the region may also be victims of human trafficking, as the circumstances of Veloso's case are unfortunately all too common.

Concurrently, the plight of women on death row worldwide has begun to receive greater attention amongst death penalty abolitionist groups and international bodies, particularly following the publication of Cornell Law School's report, Judged for More Than Her Crime, which relayed that of the approximately 500 women facing capital punishment worldwide, many are victims of gender-based violence and discrimination, and, in Asia and the Middle East, women are sentenced to death for drug trafficking at a disproportionate rate (Cornell Center on the Death Penalty Worldwide, 2018). Likewise, viewing the death penalty through a gendered lens became a United Nations priority, and indeed, the United Nations Commissioner for Human Rights declared that "[s]tates should also consider protective – rather than punitive – measures towards women who are coerced into the illicit drug trade and other drug crimes" (Bachelet, 2020; Callamard, 2018).

In this chapter, I consider feminist criminological and activist literature on both women's involvement in cross-border drug trafficking – which finds that, like Veloso, female drug couriers oftentimes claimed to have been deceived into smuggling drugs (Office of the United Kingdom Sentencing Council, 2011) – as well as literature that critically reviews international anti-human trafficking measures, and finds that these measures can lead to the increased surveillance and criminalization of women at the border, particularly women of color from the global south (Pickering & Ham, 2014). This ultimately leads to restrictions on

---

[2]More information on this case can be retrieved from Holmes (2016): https://www.thegua rdian.com/world/2016/apr/28/mary-jane-veloso-indon esia-execution-reprieve.

women's right to mobility and right to livelihood (Global Alliance Against Traffic in Women, 2007).

There is tension on the one hand, between lawyers and activists arguing that women on death row are victims of human trafficking to seek reprieve in capital cases, and on the other hand, wider human rights concerns associated with potential restrictions on women's mobility. This chapter draws upon research on women sentenced to death for drug trafficking in Malaysia and seeks to examine whether the human trafficking argument made in neighboring Indonesia regarding the Veloso case applies to other women's cases in this jurisdiction. Alongside this, I consider the potential "collateral damage" that could occur from more protectionist approaches toward women's migration in Southeast Asia.

Perpetrator or Victim?

To begin with, it is necessary to define cross-border drug and human trafficking. In Malaysia, the offense of drug trafficking does not always necessitate movement across an international border. Furthermore, whilst human trafficking offenses often involve cross-border transportation of the victim, the Malaysian Anti-Trafficking in Persons and Anti-Smuggling of Migrants Act 2007 stipulates that the "movement or conveyance of [the] trafficked person is irrelevant" to the prosecution, but instead what is central to this offense is the "exploitation" of the victim. This chapter, however, focuses on cases, similar to Veloso's, that *did* involve drug trafficking across international borders, as – not only are these the most common scenarios – but it is these women's cases that legal experts and civil society groups have argued involve human trafficking, due to the methods of recruitment and transportation involved.[3] The United Nation's Palermo Protocols define "human trafficking" as follows,

> [T]he recruitment, transportation, transfer, harbouring or receipt of persons, by means of the threat or use of force or other forms of coercion, of abduction, of fraud, of deception, of the abuse of power or of a position of vulnerability or of the giving or receiving of payments or benefits to achieve the consent of a person having control over another person, for the purpose of exploitation. (United Nations Office on Drugs & Crime, 2000)[4]

It is therefore argued by lawyers and academics involved in the Veloso case that: "[a] drug mule who is tricked or coerced into trafficking drugs fits the definition of human trafficking victim perfectly" due to the "recruitment" involving "threat,"

---

[3]As opposed to the minority of cases in Malaysia where women were arrested, not having traveled internationally, but with drugs in their possession, which may have been for personal use, but the amount surpassed the threshold of what is considered "trafficking" under the law.

[4]This, again, does not necessitate movement across a border.

"use of force," "coercion" or "deception" with the person being "exploited" for criminal activities (Gerry et al., 2018, p. 180).

Under Malaysian law, a distinction is made between drug "possession" and "trafficking" with the latter subject to a mandatory death sentence. Under the Dangerous Drugs Act 1952, whether you are deemed a trafficker is largely determined by the weight of drugs in your possession. Some limited reforms that occurred in 2017 have given judges the discretion to not impose a death sentence on "couriers" – whose role in the operation "is restricted to transporting, carrying, sending or delivering a dangerous drug" – when certification is provided by the Public Prosecutor attesting the accused person had assisted in disrupting wider drug trafficking activity (Hood, 2013, p. 3). This requirement is nevertheless almost impossible to satisfy because drug couriers, by definition, have little knowledge of the wider drug trafficking operations.[5] An accused person may also put forward an "innocent carrier" defense. Here, it is proffered that the accused person accepts that they were carrying – for example – a suitcase, however, they deny knowledge of the drugs within it; however, this defense – which is frequently invoked by female accused persons – is rarely accepted by the court (Antolak-Saper, Kowal, Lindsey, Ngeow, & Kananatu, 2020, p. 32). Thus, in practice, the death penalty for drug trafficking still operates on a largely mandatory basis.

Importantly, the advantage of arguing that women sentenced to death for cross-border drug trafficking are victims of human trafficking, is that under the Association of Southeast Asian Nations Convention Against Trafficking in Persons, Especially Women and Children (2015), victims cannot be held criminally liable, and the same is true of Malaysia's domestic anti-human trafficking law (Gerry et al., 2018, pp. 174–175).

Gender, Drugs, and Human Trafficking in Southeast Asia: What Do We Know?

The majority of existing literature on women's involvement in cross-border drug trafficking focuses on women from Latin America, the Caribbean and West Africa, usually smuggled to the United States or United Kingdom (Bailey, 2013; del Olmo, 1986; Fleetwood, 2014; Green, 1996; Huling, 1995; Office of the United Kingdom Sentencing Council, 2011; Sudbury, 2005) with the notable exception of two studies of Thai women incarcerated for drug trafficking (Jeffries & Chuenurah, 2019; Jeffries, Rao, Chuenurah, & Fitz-Gerald, 2021). These studies assess the "pathways to crime" or motivations behind women's involvement in cross-border drug trafficking. These pathways can be grouped as follows: poverty or economic factors often related to women's roles as primary familial caregivers or breadwinners; specific vulnerabilities (including histories of abuse and victimization); romance often plays a role with many women recruited by

---

[5]When presenting the findings later on in the chapter, the author will refer to the women on death row as "couriers," in acknowledgment of their limited role in the drug trafficking operation.

their male intimate partners; and, some are drawn to the excitement of travel and potential earnings. Of greatest relevance to the chapter at hand, these studies routinely find examples of women who had been forced, coerced or threatened to carry drugs, oftentimes by a male intimate partner. Indeed, a study conducted with female drug couriers imprisoned in the United Kingdom found that nine of the twelve women interviewed claimed not to know about the drugs they were carrying (Office of the United Kingdom Sentencing Council, 2011, p. 4).

Regarding the existing literature on the possible overlap between cross-border drug trafficking and human trafficking, several studies have compared the two, but with a focus on the organizational structures of syndicates, rather than examining the micro-level recruitment and operations, and particularly the gendered aspects (Cornell, 2009; Shelley, 2012).

Moreover, existing academic studies of human trafficking in the Malaysian context do not currently encompass the consideration of cross-border drug trafficking. Thus far, several studies focus on the policy challenges and governmental responses (Kaur, 2008). Others consider the plight of migrant workers, particularly from Indonesia and the Philippines (Saat, 2009; Sulaksono, 2018). Elsewhere, the focal point is the trafficking and smuggling of Rohingya refugees (Routray, 2019). And, when it comes to the trafficking of women in Malaysia, sex trafficking has been the primary consideration (Hamid, 2019).

Legal and Activist Scholarship

The possible connection between cross-border international drug and human trafficking has been highlighted by legal scholars and activists in the Southeast Asian region. One of the first to link these two phenomena was Irianto, Meij, Purwanti, and Widiastuti (2005) who conducted interviews with six women under sentence of death for drug trafficking in Tangerang Prison, Indonesia. They argue that many of these women were victims of human trafficking "at the hands" of usually male intimate partners from the African continent (Irianto et al., 2005). These women were deemed susceptible to recruitment into the drug trade because of poverty and familial economic need, and due to lacking the courage or power to demand explanations from those asking them to courier items, and being too trusting of those who enlisted them especially when these recruiters were their intimate partners (Irianto et al., 2005).

Civil society groups in Indonesia have also picked up on the relationship between the two, arguing that human trafficking for the purposes of transporting illicit drugs across international borders disproportionately affects female migrant workers. By way of example, Komnas Perempuan (2018, p. 2) – the Indonesian National Commission on Violence Against Women – reported that, at the time of writing, there were 45 Indonesian women migrant workers facing the death penalty in Malaysia and a further 32 on death row in other jurisdictions in Asia and the Middle East. All these women had been sentenced to death for cross-border drug trafficking. The Commission stated that female migrant workers, such as domestic workers, are "easy recruits" for drug trafficking syndicates, as they already possess a passport and are use to international travel, and, given their lowly pay, can be enticed by the promise of extra money (Komnas Perempuan, 2018, pp. 49–53).

The civil society activism in the Veloso case brought the relationship between cross-border drug and human trafficking to the attention of legal academics. In particular, Felicity Gerry QC, has become a vocal advocate for this cause. It is argued by Gerry et al. (2018, p. 167) that Indonesian law needs to recognize the difference between a drug trafficker and "those whom they coerce, deceive, or force to commit crime." The latter need to be protected by international obligations toward human trafficking victims, including non-prosecution. The cases of Mary Jane Veloso and Lindsay Sandiford who were convicted for drug trafficking in Indonesia, and sentenced to death, are cited as examples of human trafficking victims who acted under the control of others, lacked knowledge of the drugs they were couriering and where there was an abuse of their positions of vulnerability (including economic desperation and threats against family members) (Gerry et al., 2018, pp. 168–171).

Relatedly, in death penalty scholarship and activism more generally, there is an acknowledgement that foreign nationals and especially migrant workers are at a greater risk of capital punishment in foreign jurisdictions (Hoyle, 2019). Concerning the cross-border human/drug trafficking relationship, this is touched upon by some abolitionist groups, such as *Reprieve*, but not fully elaborated,

> There are indicators to suggest that a number of migrant workers facing the death penalty for drug offences may have been victims of human trafficking, who were vulnerable people who were forced to act as "drug mules" to transport drugs across the border. (McCulloch, 2018, pp. 1–2)

The argument pertaining to the relationship between human and drug trafficking could be instrumentalized to seek reprieve for women on death row. However, there are several possible unintended consequences of this, which are explored below.

Feminist Critiques

Within the feminist criminological and activist literature, several critiques have been raised that act as a warning against utilizing the drug-human trafficking juncture as a platform from which to challenge the use of capital punishment. These concerns sit at the intersections of patriarchal and racialized subjugation with resultant constraints on women's mobility and in turn, "collateral damage" on human rights which prevent women from exercising the right to freedom of movement, and right to secure a livelihood (Global Alliance Against Traffic in Women, 2007, p. 2).

First, sex work is often conflated with human trafficking even though cross-border labor abuse is more common (Global Network of Sex Work Project, 2011). Here, undue focus on women's cross-border movements operates to deflect from the dangerous working conditions engendered by the criminalization of sex work (Agustin, 2003; Lepp, 2002). International borders become a site of gendered and racialized oppression where women from certain ethnic groups are over-policed (Pickering & Ham, 2014). For example, Pickering and Ham (2014) found that East Asian women are being targeted at the Australian border; here, officials will stop East Asian women and search their luggage for "sexy clothing" (Pickering & Ham, 2014, p. 9). These women become "Third World victim subjects," "Third world prostitutes," devoid of agency and framed within discourses of entrapment, sexual slavery, and submission (Kapur, 2002; Kempadoo, 1998, p. 12). Such narratives are then used to justify infantilizing imperialist interventions to protect women "for their own good." This strips women of their agency over migration, and "reinforces a dichotomy that presents First World women as free and Third World women as forced" (Jeffrey, 2005, p. 34).

Second, gendered and racialized profiling at international borders is used to legitimize the over-policing of women in other ways. For example, research has shown that before 9/11, South Asian women at the US–Canada border were treated in a paternalistic manner by the border force who saw it as their duty to "save" Muslim women who, they thought, were traveling to "escape patriarchal culture" (Ameeriar, 2012, p. 181). However, as a result of the War on Terror, the perception of South Asian women changed and they became "suspects" who are over-policed at the border (Ameeriar, 2012, p. 181). Moreover, in another example, African American women are disproportionately stopped and searched for drugs at the US border, which, it is argued, constrains women's spatial mobility and acts as a wider mechanism of social control (Newsome, 2003, p. 53). Finally, concerning the plight of migrant domestic workers, multiple studies have shown that these women are already subject to scrutiny, surveillance, and criminalization at the border and their places of employment (Constable, 1997; Lee, Johnson, & McCahill, 2018).

The Example of Malaysia

I will now move on to the case of women who have been sentenced to death for drug trafficking in Malaysia. To provide an overview of the Malaysian death penalty: the latest statistics show that there are far more men than women on death row (1,140 men compared to 141 women) (Amnesty International, 2019, p. 19). However, there is a higher proportion of women (95%) than men (70%) on death row for drug trafficking (Amnesty International, 2019, pp. 18–20). Additionally, a higher percentage of women on death row are foreign nationals (86%) compared to the proportion of foreign nationals on the male death row (39%) (Amnesty International, 2019, p. 19). Regarding executions: 469 have occurred since independence in 1957 (229 of which for drug trafficking) and the last known execution occurred in 2017 (4 persons were executed during this year) but since then there has been a moratorium on executions (Amnesty International, 2019, p. 5; Cornell Center on the Death Penalty Worldwide, 2013). The available statistics on executions are not disaggregated by gender. Whilst awaiting execution, the time spent on death row is indeterminate and research has shown that the total length of the criminal proceedings (from pre-trial detention to clemency petition) in capital cases can be up to 27 years in Malaysia (Berrih & Ying 2020, p. 63).

Below I draw on 47 interviews with a range of stakeholders involved in cases of women on death row for drug trafficking in Malaysia, ranging from lawyers, judges, Non-Government Organization (NGO) activists, narcotics officers, religious counselors, NGO activists, journalists, and consular officials.[6] These interviews took place in early 2020. To corroborate and supplement the interview data, I also conducted legal and media database searches and compiled a database with information on 146 women's cases from 1985 to 2019.[7] The key findings of relevance regarding the relationship between cross-border drug and human trafficking are detailed below.

"Drugs Are Different"

Most of the interviews (17) were conducted with lawyers representing women on death row, and when asked about the possible link between cross-border drug and human trafficking, the majority stated that they had never considered this overlap before. There was a sense that, in Malaysia, cross-border human trafficking referred to other forms of exploitation, as one lawyer explained,

> I think human trafficking here is solely for the purpose of using women for other things like prostitutes; slaves; forced labor; domestic workers. I think that is much more of a concern than using them for drug trafficking.

Whilst it was acknowledged that the cross-border routes might be the same, it was argued that the two phenomena are differentiated by the fact that upon arrival in Malaysia, drug couriers are theoretically "free," whereas this is not the case for those subjected to forced labor and other forms of exploitation at the destination. Another difference was identified by a police officer who was interviewed: "for drugs, the drug mule actually makes money, and that's why it is different from human trafficking where they basically become slaves." A review of court testimonies revealed that many of the women (11) were not paid for their couriering services, particularly in cases where they were recruited by a male intimate partner.

As the lawyers interviewed pointed out, whether there is a relationship between cross-border drug and human trafficking is in many ways an academic question, because there is little room in the Malaysian Dangerous Drugs Act 1952 to consider factors such as duress, coercion and exploitation of vulnerability, and the "innocent carrier" defense is very rarely accepted by judges as credible. It was thought that the government would never incorporate drug couriering under duress into existing definitions of cross-border human trafficking because "drugs

---

[6]Owing to ethical and access issues, I did not interview any of the women on death row.

[7]For ethical reasons, I have anonymized all accounts of women's cases from my sample, and I have not directly referenced particular court cases nor media articles due to concerns about re-identification.

are different," and, as one NGO activist speculated, "authorities would think that everybody would use that as an excuse to bring drugs in." Thus, it can be surmised that the injustice of the "means" (human trafficking) does not outweigh the egregiousness of the "ends" (drug trafficking).

Similar Modus Operandi

Although drug trafficking against a person's will is not currently encompassed within Malaysian human trafficking laws, there were plenty of examples that demonstrate the human-drug trafficking nexus in terms of deception, duress and exploitation of vulnerability. If we return to the case of Mary Jane Veloso, which largely prompted this enquiry, we find almost identical factual scenarios in the cases of women on death row in Malaysia, with 14 claiming they were duped into drug trafficking after being recruited for a job overseas, 3 of whom were recruited for domestic work and 7 stated they had previously worked as a domestic worker. Furthermore, the review of death penalty cases from 1985 to 2019 revealed that, of those whose nationalities were listed in court documents, over 90% of the women were foreign nationals from other countries in the Southeast region, such as Thailand (18%), China (11%), Indonesia (11%), and the Philippines (9%), as well as other countries in the global south, including Iran (11%). The trend of the high number of female foreign nationals on death row in Malaysia likely relates to the "feminization of migration" in Southeast Asia, where, from the 1980s onwards, women have increasingly migrated abroad to work within feminized labor sectors, such as domestic work and the entertainment sector (Constable, 2007; Piper, 2008). These women tend to be the primary familial breadwinners and send remittances back home to financially support their families (Sassen, 2000). Indeed, as one lawyer interviewed recounted,

> [My client] she worked in a factory, and she was divorced with two children [to support]. She was given a work opportunity to come to Malaysia to work as a masseuse…The person who offered her a job as the masseuse gave her a bag to take with her to Malaysia, and once she arrived in Malaysia she was supposed to drop that bag off at a particular place to a particular person… She accepted the bag, put her clothes into it, and travelled to Malaysia. When she arrived, the x-ray showed something suspicious in the bag, and drugs were found in the lining.

But the judiciary appeared ignorant of the plight of female drug couriers who may have been human trafficked. A recent Amnesty International (2019, p. 21) report on the Malaysian death penalty found a lack of judicial understanding of "coercion" and "duress" and quoted a judge dismissing a foreign national woman's defense, saying,

> if indeed she was under duress, she had ample time while at the Sao Paolo airport to inform the relevant authorities of her condition. However, she chose not to do so.

Furthermore, a review of cases (1985–2019) found that judges placed the onus on women to realize that they were in an unsafe situation,

> The keeping of her passport by her bosses, the "overprotective-ness" and restriction of her movement upon arrival at each designated destination, the immediate deliverance of the bag of "cloth samples" and all these other things she mentioned in her evidence should have caused alarm and triggered her curiosity.

The judge describes a "modus operandi" that sounds akin to human trafficking, and indeed there were many features like this in the cases reviewed. There were examples of women (or their children) being threatened if they did not comply, as well as women being locked up in hotel rooms or drugged and forced to swallow drugs or insert them into their vaginas. In court testimonies, women would describe the "series of steps" taken at each stage of the journey, and this usually included purchasing SIM cards at various locations on which to contact their recruiter, who withheld information about where they were going, where they would stay, and who they were meeting until the last possible moment. Often flight details were changed at the last minute and they were sent on elaborate routes with up to seven different layovers. Pre-travel it was commonplace for women to give their passports over to their recruiter, who would organize visas and travel tickets on their behalf.

In several cases, women alleged to have been tricked and recruited into drug couriering online. Indeed, the leading academic expert on online scams has published on the topic of online scam victims being unknowingly used as drug mules (Whitty, 2021). The review of cases from 1985 to 2019 found that online recruitment occurred through social media applications such as WeChat, Yahoo Messenger, or specific dating sites such as "date.asia.com." Relatedly, research has shown that technology – including social media – is increasingly used to facilitate cross-border human trafficking in Asia (Mekong Club, 2019).

The Question of Women's Agency

When problematizing the drug-human trafficking relationship, a key question is that of the women's agency and how this relates to her potential victimization at "the hands" of traffickers. It is first important to note that although most popular portrayals of human trafficking victims over-emphasize women's "victimhood" to legitimatize the paternalistic and protectionist state response (Buckland, 2008), in fact, research with women identified as sex trafficking victims in the United Kingdom, sheds light on the fact that sometimes the women "consented" as it was a "rational choice" given their limited circumstances (Hoyle, Bosworth, & Dempsey, 2011, p. 322). However, the "consent" of a trafficked person is considered irrelevant under the United Nations' Palermo Protocols, as well as under Malaysia's Anti-Trafficking in Persons and Anti-Smuggling of Migrants Act 2007 (United Nations, 2000; United Nations Office on Drugs & Crime, 2000).

Nevertheless, according to those who contend that women on death row for cross-border drug trafficking are victims of human trafficking, this argument is underpinned by the acknowledgement that the women lack "autonomy" in the legalistic sense of the term,

> The impacts on autonomy [...] extend to a woman deciding to commit a crime because of a situation of vulnerability relating to external economic of family or abusive factors. She may well be "deliberate" and she may "consent" to commit the crime but criminal responsibility lies firmly with the traffickers if she is not free, informed and deliberate. (Gerry, 2020, p. 17)

From a more sociological perspective, Fleetwood's (2014, pp. 75, 159) research into women involved in the cocaine trade in Ecuador found that most of the participants were "willing" drug mules who agreed to the work, but, once they had committed, there was almost no opportunity to "back out" and at this stage, their agency was more constrained. Furthermore, other research from the region, concerning Thai women imprisoned for cross-border drug trafficking in Cambodia, found that not all of the women were driven by desperation, with one participant being "motivated by self-indulgence or more specifically, money and a desire to travel" (Jeffries & Chuenurah, 2019, p. 50).

As women on death row were not interviewed, this research can only make inferences about the women's agency or lack thereof. But, significantly, the research interviews and review of legal cases (1985–2019) revealed that whilst most of the women claimed in their court testimonies that they were duped into couriering drugs, 51 stated they had agreed – and indeed been paid – to courier items ranging from clothing to electronics across borders in their personal luggage at the behest of a "boss" for them to avoid import duties. This practice is referred to elsewhere as "suitcase trading" or "parallel trading," and research has shown that many women in the global south engage in this economic activity as an agentic response to exclusion from the globalized economy (Laidler & Lee, 2014; Ulysse, 2007). Therefore, we may deduce that the plight of women on death row in Southeast Asia does not fit within the neat victim–agent binary.

Profiling at the Border for Drug & Human Trafficking Based on Gender, Race & Citizenship

The policing and public responses to cross-border drug and human trafficking in Malaysia were also discussed during the interviews. It became clear that there exists gendered and racialized profiling at the Malaysian border. First, from the research interviews, it became apparent that certain groups of women who have been caught at the airport with drugs are more likely to be constructed within a discourse of victimhood than others, as one lawyer explained regarding media coverage of these cases,

> It depends on who the victims are. If it's a Malay girl and the community say, "look at how she was tricked," they can connect,

because it could be one of your sisters, or could be one of your family members... It's very different if it is a Nigerian girl and you portray her, and then they don't relate.

Second, there was a perception that women of certain nationalities – connected to racist and classist assumptions – simply do not engage in this kind of behavior, and thus are less likely to be stopped at the airport and screened for drug trafficking. So, one interviewee explained, that as a white British woman, "I would have relatively few issues carrying drugs through an airport." And, in another case, involving the arrest and conviction of a woman from an affluent East Asian nation, the media extensively reported on the fact that she was caught up in a "drag-net" operation as security at Malaysian airports do not usually profile travelers from her country for criminal activities.

Third, the research interviews revealed a perception that women of certain nationalities were under constant suspicion at the airport but did not engender sympathy nor were viewed through the frame of "victimhood." According to the lawyers interviewed, the "suspicious" countries and nationalities include women from mainland China, Iran, Indonesia, the Philippines, Nigeria, India, Ukraine, and Uzbekistan. In particular, the following stereotype of a "risky" female traveler prevailed,

> There is a profile of a travel-savvy Chinese woman, of perhaps no known sources of income, who then is a professional drug mule, and she gets away with it because she is good looking; she is attractive; she dresses well; she looks professional... [Border control] are also looking out for high-class prostitutes, and tall, lanky, good-looking Mainland Chinese women could also be high-class prostitutes.

As well as for drug trafficking, this stereotype is used to single out women who are deemed at risk of being human trafficked for sex work, yet due to their "savviness," they do not fit the "passive" and sympathetic female "victim" frame and thus are represented as a "vamp" through "linking women's trafficking to her sexuality, her body, or her improper womanhood in ways that shore up neo-colonial heterosexualities and state power" (Schemenauer, 2012, p. 95).

Potential Limitations on Women's Mobility

The argument that women sentenced to death for cross-border drug trafficking are victims of human trafficking could lead to the introduction of restrictions on women's mobility, both in and out of Malaysia. By way of example, back in 2008, as a result of reports that 119 Malaysians were imprisoned abroad for drug couriering – 90% of whom were women and many of whom were thought to have been tricked – a proposal was put forward by the Foreign and Home Ministries which advised that it should be mandatory for women, who plan to travel abroad alone, to first obtain a letter from either their parents or their employers to leave the country; this proposal was strongly condemned by women's groups and was consequently unsuccessful (Asia One News, 2008).

Elsewhere, we have witnessed warnings against women traveling abroad for fear of being caught up in a drug couriering scam. The Malaysian Chinese Association warned women from China of a Nigerian "trafficking ring" targeting women from Guangdong and tricking them into working as unsuspecting drug couriers, which, the Association claimed, has led to more than 20 women being arrested for smuggling drugs to Malaysia between 2013 and 2015 (Moon, 2018). I also found media articles from the Philippines, Singapore, India, Uganda, and Iran, all warning local women about traveling to Malaysia and being tricked into drug couriering (Daily, 2013; Lopez, 2008; Malaysia General News, 2010; Soh & Yuen, 2011; The Monitor, 2011). Placing curbs on women's mobility or warning women not to travel overseas for fear of exploitation represents an affront to their human right to mobility and right to livelihood, particularly for would-be female migrant workers.

Conclusion and Implications

By way of conclusion, this chapter has sought to explore the link between cross-border drug and human trafficking in Malaysia. This exploration was inspired by activism efforts from neighboring Indonesia, where death penalty abolitionists, migrant workers' rights groups and women's groups have argued that many women on death row for drug trafficking are in fact victims of human trafficking. There are overlaps between the official definitions of human trafficking – premised upon the use of coercion, deception and abuse of vulnerability – and the factual scenarios of cases involving female drug couriers in the region; many of whom have been deceived into carrying drugs against their will. However, the Malaysian legislation on human trafficking does not currently encompass people who have been coerced into drug smuggling, and the research participants believed that this is unlikely to change, as the government believes that "drugs are different" and drug trafficking is especially egregious.

However, while conflating cross-border drug trafficking and human trafficking may present as an obvious feminist activist platform to seek reform and remove women from death row, in practice, it may play out in racialized and gendered ways, impeding women's mobility, agency, and livelihood. It could also result in other forms of cross-border exploitation being ignored, the further stigmatization and control of sex work and certain populations of women being racially profiled and over-policed at international borders.

Therefore, to prevent these forms of oppression, I provide the following recommendations. First, the removal of mandatory sentences in drug trafficking cases, and consideration of gendered mitigating circumstances per the United Nation's Bangkok Rules (United Nations General Assembly, 2010). Second, in terms of anti-human trafficking measures, it is necessary to address the disproportionate focus on sex trafficking and to give attention to other forms of exploitation, and instead of "the border" being the focal point of prevention campaigns, there should be a focus on labor laws and decriminalizing sex work to reduce exploitation once in the host country. Furthermore, anti-human trafficking measures should not focus on restricting women's mobility and thus access to livelihood, but, in fact, recognize that by having less restrictive migration policies, women are less likely to resort to unsafe means of travel. Third, concerning the death penalty, I call for the end of the mandatory death sentence and the retroactive review of any cases where an accused person was sentenced to death under a mandatory regime. Additionally, the Malaysian example has highlighted the arbitrary and incommensurate nature of the death penalty for drug trafficking – a punishment that must be abolished globally.

Chapter 4

Supporting Female Prisoners and Their Families: The Case of Cambodia

Billy Gorter and Philip J. Gover

Abstract

Whilst small, the number of women in Cambodian prisons has been growing rapidly. These women are often first-time offenders, detained on drug or poverty-related offenses. Most women are detained pre-trial, then sentenced harshly. Children in Cambodia can accompany their mother in prison, but there is no standardized process for this to occur. Conditions within the prisons have been described as substandard and extremely challenging, with a lack of appropriate nutrition, health care, and environmental stimulation. There is also a lack of humanitarian programs addressing the specific needs and challenges faced by women prisoners, and their children. This chapter provides an overview of the work of This Life Cambodia, a Non-Government Organization (NGO), which delivers targeted programs to both women and their children, during and after imprisonment. It discusses the role of the This Life in Family (TLIF) program, which provides valued support to vulnerable families at risk of separation. The program primarily targets mothers in prison from poor, disadvantaged and multiple deprived communities, who are accompanied by, or separated from, their children.

Keywords: Cambodia; prison; women; children; overcrowding; diversion; public health; prevention; inequality

Introduction

A former French colonial state, Cambodia is a Southeast Asian country bordering Thailand with an estimated population of 16.7 million people (Royal

Gender, Criminalization, Imprisonment and Human Rights in Southeast Asia, 45–57
Copyright © 2022 by Billy Gorter and Philip J. Gover
Published under exclusive licence by Emerald Publishing Limited
doi:10.1108/978-1-80117-286-820221004

Government of Cambodia, 2016). Vietnam sits to Cambodia's east, and to the north, is landlocked Laos. Although rich in culture, history and tradition, Cambodia is beset with social inequalities and laden with poverty (Bylander, 2017). The current Cambodian government has been in power since 1984, and Prime Minister Hun Sen, the fifth longest-serving leader in the world, is now approaching his 37th year as leader.

To fully understand Cambodia is to appreciate the nature of its shared cultural norms, and how these are routinely influenced by the evolving social systems that both surround them and attempt to support them. Equally, it is worth noting how significant historical events have also systematically shaped the Cambodian context, the legacy of which still carries influence today (Time, 2019).

Central to Cambodian culture are core family values that are underpinned by principles of reciprocity and filial piety. Parental respect, conservative behavior and dignity are important representations that drive the common mindset of Khmer society. However, between 1975 and 1979, the nature of this family and community focused lifestyle was severely altered, by the driving presence of the Khmer Rouge. During this short but brutal period, the Angkar Padevat (Stalinist-Maoist Communist Command), fashioned the population into a totalitarian state, rolling back the emerging patterns and perceived threats of western culture and capitalism, with a return to an otherwise pre-industrial model of agrarian social economics. This pitiless period in Cambodia's history fundamentally undermined the foundation of the family unit and forcibly replaced it with a new centralized model of rituals, beliefs, and social control (Delano & Knottnerus, 2018). Estimates suggest that between 1.5 and 3 million people were killed at the hands of this regime. Much has been written about this period of unrest (Becker, 1998), and the long-term legacy that it left, and continues to leave (Sen, 2008). With the end of the Khmer Rouge era, family dynamics slowly reverted to a more traditional, mutual socio-economic system, with families returning to their homes and communities, relying on each other both interdependently and intergenerationally. Many family homes still support multiple generations, who live under one roof. This is particularly evident within communities in rural and remote provincial areas (Ledgerwood & Vijghen, 2002).

A Short Legal History

The Cambodian legal system carries a complex history. Before the Khmer Rouge era, Cambodia's system of both government and law was typified and influenced by the colonial French, who introduced and developed a European styled system of Civil Law (McCarthy & Un, 2017). However, under the Khmer Rouge, the Communist Party of Kampuchea (CPK) abolished all the existing institutions and laws and replaced them with a dictatorial system, which, in keeping with its ideology, exercised absolute power. Beyond this period, and following the four years of Khmer Rouge activity, Cambodia was largely occupied, annexed, managed, and governed by Vietnam, up until September 1989.

After 14 years of calamitous interruptions, Cambodia sought to re-establish itself as a sovereign state, betrothed with new governmental structures, modern civic institutions and embellished with a legal system that was fit for the turn of a century. Yet in the immediate years that followed, this ambition was undermined by a simple lack of capacity. That pool of otherwise existing talent, that would have ordinarily taken up the task in hand (the intellectuals, the government officials and legal professionals), had all been identified and systematically killed by the Khmer Rouge a decade earlier (Hinton, 2005). The long-term effects of this can still be perceived today (Barma, 2012).

This professional vacuum was eventually reconciled under the Comprehensive Cambodian Peace Agreement (Ratner, 1993). In this arrangement, national supervision and control were vested in the United Nations Transitional Authority of Cambodia (UNTAC). During this time (1992–1993), UNTAC supervised the end of foreign military assistance and the withdrawal of foreign forces, as well as the disarmament of all armed forces that were aligned with Cambodian political parties. This demobilization helped pave the way toward the development and adoption of a new constitutional monarchy in 1993 (Kingdom of Cambodia, 2010). In this process, UNTAC helped promote the concept of political pluralism, embed human rights within the rule of law, and coordinate the delivery of fair and free elections (Marks, 1994).

Amidst the fragility of Cambodia, UNTAC controlled and supervised the formation of additional administrative structures, including the police. In totality, it paved the foundations for a fragile state to return to peace and direct its future. However, as we will explore, the subsequent evolution and development of this foundation, including its structures, still leaves much to be desired. No more so perhaps than within the rule of law where significant room for improvement still exists.

The Contemporary Legal Landscape – Legislation and Sentencing

Central to all legal systems is the capability of the state to pursue, prosecute, and secure convictions against those individuals or groups, who are in conflict with or have indeed breached the law. Underpinning this arrangement, and for the most part, domestically at least, are the general rules on sentencing. In this context, the Cambodian Criminal Code (Kingdom of Cambodia, 2011, 2021) is a key source of information that sets out the statutes and guidance for those appointed to enforce, uphold and administer the law. Within Cambodia's Criminal Code Article 96 provides a clear set of directions and guidance that relate to adults, young people and the use of detention within police custody. Article 203, Article 212, and Article 209 set out the administrative and legal terms and obligations, in which young people and adults, in dispute with the legal system, are to be engaged (Kingdom of Cambodia, 2021).

However, Cambodia's judicial process has been seen to consistently fail to operate in line with its legislative guidance. No more so is this the case than within the context of land law (Trzcinski & Upham, 2014), but criminal law too (McCarthy & Un, 2017). The ill-informed use of the guidance, with particular reference to pre-trial detention, occurs systematically, across all age groups in Cambodia, including those that involve children. In a case study example, Rodriguez (2018) highlights "at thirteen years old, Chanlina was detained at a prison in Cambodia where she resided with eighty-seven other prisoners in a one-room cell."

In a report by the Cambodian League for the Promotion and Defense of Human Rights (2015), who were monitoring 61 women, who were either pregnant or living with their children in the prisons, more than 50% were pre-trial detainees, being held on charges associated with minor offenses. All but 2 of the 18 pregnant women were being held in pre-trial detention. In a case study cited by LICADHO (Cambodian League for the Promotion & Defense of Human Rights, 2015), Chanty, a mother of three, was accused of stealing less than a dollar. She spent three months in pre-trial detention, and a further three months behind bars, after she was sentenced. She was not able to see, speak, or maintain her maternal relationship with her children at any point throughout the administrative process. In this case study and a significant number of others like it, it would appear, on the balance of probability at least, that provisional pre-trial detention has been adopted as the de facto rule, and not the exception to it.

Notwithstanding the limits of Cambodian law (West, 2019), if we are to recognize the law and the judiciary that underpins it, as something of an evolving landscape, then we may also consider the legislative process as either incomplete, incomprehensive, or ineffective, in serving the contemporary domestic and democratic needs of its population. Whilst we recognize that the Juvenile Justice Law is relatively new, coming into force as late as 2017, we must also recognize that the widespread discrepancies, underpinned at least via the vagaries of custom and practice, represent in themselves, a breach of both national and international human rights law.

Mothers and Children in Prison: Prison Law, Procedures & International Human Rights

In Cambodia, mothers and children are given explicit consideration in the Prison Procedures Guidance (CPPG) (Kingdom of Cambodia, 2003) and the Cambodian Law on Prisons (Kingdom of Cambodia, 2011), hereafter LOP. Article 40 of LOP (Kingdom of Cambodia, 2011, p. 8) outlines minimum human rights standards (i.e., both Bangkok and Nelson Mandela Rules) (United Nations General Assembly, 2010, 2016) concerning the special accommodations that should be provided to ensure women's pre- and post-natal care and directs that, if possible, arrangements should be made for children to be born in a hospital outside the prison. To protect children from unnecessary stigma, this article also notes if a birth does occur in prison, the place of birth must not be recorded on the birth certificate. CPPG (Kingdom of Cambodia, 2003) Article 34.4.1-14 allows for children to live with their mother in prison until they are six years old when this is in the child's best interests (as per the United Nations Convention on the Rights of the Child, the Bangkok and Nelson Mandela Rules). Directives are also provided around the provision of opportunities to mothers "to exercise and develop their parental responsibilities, duties and skills, to maximise the potential for the child's proper development, and reduce the likelihood of the mother re-offending."

However, LOP (Kingdom of Cambodia, 2011), Article 41 presents a contradiction to the CPPG (Kingdom of Cambodia, 2003) stating that "children accompanying their mother shall be authorized to stay with their mother in prison until the age of three years" after which if there is no custodian outside the prison to take care of them, the children shall become "the burden of the Ministry of Social Affairs, Veterans and Youth Rehabilitation." Prison authorities may also decide to remove a child from their mother if this is deemed necessary by a health care provider. The CPPG (Kingdom of Cambodia, 2003: No3 4.7) directs that

> if the Health Provider believes that the mother is unable to care for the child, the Prison Chief will facilitate alternative arrangements for placement of the child with relatives in the first instance or a suitable foster mother within the prison.

The wording in the LOP (Kingdom of Cambodia, 2011) Article 41, suggests that the responsibility for the provision of food, clothing, and health care of children in prison rests with prison authorities, however, routine neglect in the provision of these goods and services is not uncommon. As such, the nature of this neglect can and has been misinterpreted as a dereliction of duty on behalf of the mother. This in itself, is a direct violation of human rights directives, including the Bangkok and Nelson Mandela Rules. These directives clearly state that prison authorities are responsible for ensuring that the nutritional and wider health care (including developmental) needs of dependent children in prison are adequately met (see Bangkok and Nelson Mandela Rules). Given these issues, a range of pathways exist for a child, either accompanying a mother placed in detention, or born during the mothers' detention, to be separated and relocated to a variety of settings, at the discretion of the prison authorities.

It is perhaps reasonable to assume that the rationale underpinning the shift of the child's age from the CPPG (Kingdom of Cambodia, 2003) to the LOP (Kingdom of Cambodia, 2011) is linked to the overarching desire to reduce the number of children in prison. Indeed, since the introduction of LOP (Kingdom of Cambodia, 2011), the official number of children in Cambodian prisons dropped by more than 50%. In the month following the passing of the law in December 2011, of the 71 children in prison, 17 were over the age of three. In 2014, there were just seven children in prison over the age of three. Yet, in contrast to official figures, children over the age of three continue to be in prison with their mothers, especially if no family members are willing to take custody. Furthermore, it is suggested that the overall number of has risen since the LOP (Cambodian League for the Promotion and Defense of Human Rights, 2021; Kingdom of Cambodia, 2011). This Life Cambodia (2019) estimates that there are now at least 170 mothers living in prisons with their children, with a further 50 pregnant women currently detained. This rise has been attributed to increased government activities relating to illicit drug offending, which has been driving up trends in women's imprisonment for a couple of decades (Phnom Penh Post, 2019; Walmsley, 2017).

As per the Bangkok and Nelson Mandela Rules, the decision to allow children to stay with their mothers in prison should be based on full individual assessments and the best interests of the child, as per Article 3 of the United Nations Convention on the Rights of the Child (Cassidy et al., 2010). However, in Cambodia, there are no consistent guidelines in place for determining when it is appropriate for a child to live in prison, or how to remove a child from its mother when the child reaches the age of three. There appears to be no underlying rationale, or evidence, as to why the age of three is even identified – a one size fits all pivotal age, gives no ground for the range or spectrum of difference that underlies children and their development. Rather, the determining factors that underpin this appear more random and circumstantial, than coordinated. The geographical location, the presence of other adults at the time of arrest, the identity of the arresting authorities and the policy of individual prisons are all influential and determining elements that prevail over the wishes of the mother or the best interests of the child.

Some women interviewed by This Life Cambodia (2019) have reported that their child stayed with them in prison simply because they were together at the point of arrest and there was no one else immediately present to care for the child. Others explained that police actively prevented them from taking their young children with them to the police station, even if there was no alternative care in place (Cambodian League for the Promotion and Defense of Human Rights, 2015). In some prisons, children were allowed to join their mothers later, following a prisoner request to prison authorities but prison authorities also frequently denied such requests, without informing mothers or providing an opportunity for appeal. These simple disparities, in the way such cases have been handled, illustrate the nature in which women with children are treated and explain why some mothers have been able to keep their children in prison and others have not.

Profiling mothers and their treatment in Cambodian prisons is a difficult endeavor. Any attempt to investigate or assess the circumstances surrounding this distinct cohort is significantly and/or inconveniently inhibited by the lack of accessible information collected on them. In the absence of any concept of freedom of information, it is difficult to determine if this deficit of data is largely due to access issues or simple deficiency in administrative record-keeping. Wider issues associated with the institutional investment, capacity and/or competence may also be a mitigating factor. Furthermore, whilst international rules (e.g., the Bangkok Rules) and domestic rules (Kingdom of Cambodia, 2003), require mandatory recording for prisoners, it is difficult to find any evidence of organized public records that account for the number of children affected by parental incarceration.

The Courts: Cambodian Law and International Human Rights

During sentencing, judges are required to consider the personal circumstances of a suspect, before ordering pre-trial detention. This specifically relates to those who are either pregnant and/or have young children. Aligned with this, the Bangkok Rules are clear, that non-custodial measures are preferable particularly for pregnant women and those with dependent children. However, given the pervasive use of pre-trial detention in Cambodia (see Chapter 1), when mothers are unable or unwilling to have their children accompany them in prison, hundreds of children are unnecessarily removed and separated. A penalty that unfairly impacts women's mental well-being explicitly, as well as both the short-term needs of the mother and long-term outcomes of an otherwise innocent child (Goshin, Byrne, & Blanchard-Lewis, 2014; Krisberg & Engel-Temin, 2007).

The Code of Criminal Procedure of the Kingdom of Cambodia (2021) states that pre-trial detention should only be ordered in exceptional circumstances. The Ministry of Justice guidelines categorically state that investigating judges should always collect relevant information surrounding an accused individual, before determining the use of pre-trial detention. The guidelines are also clear that if a woman is pregnant, or if she has children, and there are no suitable alternative care arrangements, pre-trial detention should not be imposed unless absolutely necessary. Unfortunately, it is all too common to find that the welfare of the child is ill-conceived or not even considered at the time of the arrest. In many regards, it simply does not feature as an important factor throughout the whole judicial process (Phnom Penh Post, 2019). The net result of this custom and practice is that pre-trial detention is now proactively driving the overcrowding of prisons and more importantly, becoming the norm (see Table 1, in Chapter 1).

Legal Literacy and Prisons, an Unnecessary Evil

For the most part, it would seem reasonable to presume that people understand and recognize that the freedoms they enjoy, are subject to the rules that underpin law and order. With freedom comes responsibility, to coin a familiar phrase. Freedom therefore can be seen as a precious commodity, held on license, and contingent on the fair and reasonable conduct of the individual. Naturally, perhaps, we recognize that if we break the law, then we run the risk of losing our freedom. However, as with many other places, not everybody in Cambodia enjoys what might be understood as a reasonable degree of legal literacy. This begs the question, if you do not, or cannot fully understand or interpret the fundamental nature of law, is it reasonable for you to be held responsible for any actions that occur should you breach them?

One could suggest that people innately understand what the law fully entails and encompasses and that all people, somehow, can articulate what is right from wrong. However, this is not so clear cut. This Life Cambodia (2019, 2021a, 2021b) routinely identifies people (adults, children and young people) who do not possess these levels of legal literacy and do not fully comprehend the implications of the law at all. It is worth highlighting that not everybody in Cambodia has completed what most, in mature economies, might consider a basic formal education. For example, 23.6% of young people complete upper secondary education in Cambodia which is further set within the context of an education system where only 34.5% of teachers are qualified, according to national standards (CESP, 2019).

Given these mitigating circumstances, it is not difficult to conceptualize how and why so many Cambodians find themselves in conflict with the law. Furthermore, it can be argued that both the legal system and the media do little to openly educate or communicate its evolution to the wider public sphere (Freedom House, 2017; Gover & Aalders, 2014, 2016). This Life Cambodia's (2021b) research has found that a lack of legal literacy, in conjunction with extreme poverty (an extension of undereducation), often results in people becoming involved in the criminal justice system. Acts of desperation, such as the theft of small quantities of food is an example in point. In this sense, we can begin to understand why so many people, often from multiply deprived communities, find themselves in conflict with the law and imprisoned.

Prisons as Settings for Inequality

Set against these discussions, and perhaps of most importance, is the existence, provision and material reality of prison facilities – the tangible means and mechanism by which the legal system sees fit to isolate and deprive an individual of their freedom and liberty. Cambodia operates 24 prisons and 4 additional, social/correctional related facilities. As noted in Chapter 1, these facilities are grossly over capacity (Amnesty International, 2020a).

Prisons represent the sharp end of the law, the place and settings where the criminalized exchange their freedom and liberty for fixed periods of detention. However, that is not the only exchange that takes place. We know, via Sykes (1958) and Goffman (1961) that prisons, like state facilities, depersonalize and stigmatize prisoners in several ways. However, a range of additional, bundled risks and toxic elements, also exist, above and beyond the loss of liberty – which is the only legal penalty that a convicted sentence fundamentally demands (Scharff-Smith, 2016). Overcrowded prisons are often violent and unhealthy settings and pose numerous challenges to international human rights standards, with particular emphasis on mental and physical health (MacDonald, 2018). Research in Cambodia has found the prevalence of mental health issues is common behind prison walls. Disease and infection control is deficient, with a flow of negative consequences impacting prisoners, families and wider communities when prisoners are released (Puthy, Richter-Sundberg, Jegannathan, Edin, & San Sebastian, 2020, Stürup-Toft, O'Moore, & Plugge, 2018). The problem of disease control is especially concerning, given the unprecedented transmission of Covid-19 within Cambodia's prisons. The provision of prison food and subsequent poor nutrition has also been cited as a critical element of punishment that affects both the physical health and mental well-being of the individual (Smoyer & Lopes, 2017). In Cambodia, the amount allocated for food per prisoner per day has been reported to be circa KHR 3,500 or 75 US Cents (Penal Reform International, 2020).

Empirical research clearly shows the negative effects of separating (small) children from their parents (Lamb & Kelly, 2009). Here, the evidence suggests that the detention of a mother is probably more serious for children than when the father is in custody (Kury, 2021). Beyond this employment opportunities invariably dwindle, as criminal stigma follows the prisoner throughout their life (Couloute & Kopf, 2018).

This Life Cambodia

In Cambodia, like many other countries, there is a lack of robust programs that address the specific needs associated with juvenile justice or the challenges associated with women who reside in prison, either accompanied by or separated from their children. However, This Life Cambodia does have targeted programs for supporting both.

This Life Cambodia is a community development driven Non-Government Organization (NGO), that places dialogue at the center of development. Using this approach, This Life Cambodia discovered a depth of community concern, relating to women and young people in conflict with the law. It learned and recognized that women and young people spend disproportionately long sentences in prison, for non-violent and/or misdemeanor type infractions. As such, This Life Cambodia conducted a primary research project and attempted to perception-test the value of diversion – which refers to community-based programs of action, that are used as alternative pathways for children, young people and adults facing detention for minor, non-violent offenses. At the outset, This Life Cambodia thought that the research would reveal a lot of objections to this concept, but, in fact, there was virtually no resistance to this at all.

The research recognized the key drivers of youth crime. Engagement with drugs, to generate income and for recreational use, was a primary root cause. Theft was often opportunistic, linked to drug-related addiction, poverty and personal desperation. Young people from poorer families, and those who already had an incomplete education of some sort, were extremely vulnerable to these types of activities and therefore, prosecution.

In terms of women, 57% of all prisoners in Cambodia are held on drug-related charges but 73% of all women prisoners are incarcerated on drug-related charges. Amnesty International (2020a, 2020b), reported that between January 2017 and March 2020, at least 55,770 people were arrested in Cambodia, specifically on drug-related charges, as part of the Government's anti-drugs campaign. Inherent to this, young women, with low earning capability, and who otherwise perceive themselves living out their foreseeable lives in poverty, disproportionately engage in the wider drug supply chain. Acting as couriers, or other low-ranking, low-paying, high-risk positions this, in turn, makes them especially vulnerable to prosecution.

Working with Women and Children in Prison

This Life Cambodia has also researched why women choose to have their children accompany them in prison, finding that both personal, family and community factors largely influenced this distinctly double-edged decision. Personal factors included: whether a woman was pregnant at the time, the age of the child, as well as the presence or absence of trusted family members who had the means to provide safe alternative care options. Other factors included the belief that a child may have more opportunities, if they did not stay with their mother in prison, such as access to education. Community factors included: access to legal advice as well as social norms, including stigma and neighborhood perceptions of a mother being in prison. The following anonymous case study example brings together many of the circumstances and drivers that collectively serve to disproportionately criminalize women in Cambodia.

Tola, a 38-year-old woman, had migrated from her rural home, in a northern province in 2018, to find new employment opportunities in a nearby city. With strained family relations and financial insecurity, Tola was convinced that she could find new employment opportunities, working in either hotels or the numerous restaurants that served the city. After all, Siem Reap was a big tourist city. On arrival, she lived in a small, rented room with her husband and three children. The family included a six-year-old daughter, a two-year-old son, and a three-month-old baby boy. Tola quickly found a job reselling fruit on the roadside, and her husband secured work on a construction site. The family developed a new network of friends and an especially good relationship emerged with their neighbor. However, with the move and the long hours of work, Tola began to lose contact with her family, who lived in a distant rural village.

To supplement her income, Tola also began to sell vehicle fuel in soda bottles informally on the roadside. Later, she also used her roadside business to distribute drugs. Tola never used drugs, but understood that if she occasionally helped sell them, she could make a few more dollars for her family. For several months, this arrangement enabled Tola to house, feed, and clothe her family. Whilst they were not living a life of luxury, they were content, because they were not struggling in the same hopeless way, as when they lived in the countryside.

In August 2018, Tola's life changed. As a result of her drug-related activities, the police arrested and charged her with drug offenses and detained her in Siem Reap prison. Given the circumstances, her husband looked after the older children and Tola decided to take the infant into prison with her. In due course, Tola was sentenced to 30 months in prison. By December 2018, Tola had spent three months in jail, when she learned that her husband had found a new partner, moved to Sihanoukville and had left the two children with her neighbor. The neighbor's family were worried about the situation, and in discussion with the father, had agreed to look after the two children, in addition to their own four. During the recording of this case study, Tola described her situation and circumstances:

> I didn't want my boy to be here, it's a nightmare (in prison), but I had no choice, what could I do? He was only seven months old when I was arrested. I didn't want to involve my family as they live so far away … if they told the truth, they couldn't help either, they are so poor … I just didn't want to involve them after being away for so long. I also didn't want to put any more pressure on my neighbor, since they are already helping my two elder children, and they are not even my relatives. I am so blessed to have stumbled on such good people (neighbors), I don't know what would have happened without them, but I also constantly worry about my baby. My mind never stops, it just never stops spinning.

In late February 2019, a Prison Official alerted Tola's case to the This Life in Family (TLIF) program. Following initial engagement meetings, Tola enrolled on the program in mid-March 2019. Tola showed both a desire and hesitance to resettle her infant outside of prison. She was adamant that her family should not be called upon to assist. She was ashamed and reluctant to consider her neighbor, given the existing burden, albeit that her neighbor was willing to look after the baby, in addition to their own family.

In September 2019, after seven months of participating in the program, Tola's husband returned. He re-established his responsibility as a father and began to look after and care for the elder children again. After a range of supported discussions between Tola and her husband, the time appeared right for Tola to make a final decision regarding her baby. In November 2019, she sent her small child home, into the care of the father, with agreed support from her neighbor.

The TLIF Program ensured that Tola's family received a range of support packages, including long-term social work case management, emergency packages, health support, monthly in-prison visitation, and educational support for her two children. The program also extended support to her neighbors, in terms of financial assistance, to help them generate extra income by growing vegetables and raising chickens. TLIF also created a comprehensive care plan that helped Tola during her remaining months in prison. This was extended to cover several months after Tola's release.

In February 2020, Tola was released from prison and planned to live with her husband and raise their family. During this period, Tola received support to help her resettle, reintegrate, and overcome the long-term psychological impact of prison. Tola managed to strengthen her family ties and continues to live with her husband, raising her three children.

Whilst Tola's story illustrates a range of factors and drivers that are worthy of individual discussion, it should be highlighted that they often combine to deliver familiar and predictable outcomes. A young couple under pressure to raise a family in a subsistence-based rural economy, choose to migrate and pursue a better life. For Tola, improved quality of life meant leaving her family and community behind. With her unskilled partner adopting fixed-term laboring contracts, they engaged with formal, informal, and shadow based economic activities, cheek and jowl, to gain traction on their evolving circumstances. Together they shifted their family's quality of life from subsistence to meager modesty. With limited skills and educational achievement, or industrial experience, this approach to daily life is common in Cambodia. Not only is it common, but it is also visual, it is copied, it is customary and it is accepted and acknowledged as normal.

Set against the example of Tola are other important questions. In circumstances where whole systems have broken down, or may not even exist, how are families expected to solve the everyday challenges associated with basic human provisioning? As has been described elsewhere, at the periphery of an affluent society, poor, disadvantaged and multiple deprived people routinely adapt, using the skills, knowledge and resources they have to hand (Latouche, 1993). The role undertaken by Tola's neighbor is central to this. Alongside embedded respect for human values and sentiments, the informal and shadow economies represent and provide important methods that replace, and often eclipse, the promises and absence of a free, open and accessible market economy (Banks, Lombard, & Mitlin, 2020). In this regard, street vending in all its guises can simply be regarded as a common, popular, if not primary choice amongst the poor, who lack both plans and capital (Truong, 2018).

In line with Tola's story, This Life Cambodia continues to deliver subject-specific community programs that address the wider reality of the socio-economic circumstances of prisoners and their families.

Community Programs

This Life in Families (TLIF) is a specific program that works within this prime context, supporting and helping mothers in conflict with the law to stay together, by reducing family separation, when families experience poverty shocks and have insufficient support or coping mechanisms. As a result of a range of factors, including the imprisonment of a parent, many children in Cambodia become unnecessarily separated from their families and communities. The use of institutional care in Cambodia has become increasingly common, because of a wide range of factors, including household conflict with the law. Some published studies in 2017 estimated that nearly 1 in 100 children were residing in residential care (Stark, Rubenstein, Pak, & Kosal, 2017). In these circumstances, TLIF supports and preserves vulnerable families at risk. This Life recognizes that separation invariably creates both instability and an entrenched and lasting sense of disconnect amongst family members. This is often because family members who consequently adopt unplanned caring obligations do not always have sufficient time, means or desire to sustain the obligation. Extended family members in poor rural areas may not in truth have the financial security to sustain the entirety of the obligation – the feeding, clothing, schooling, and funding of prison visits to reunite and maintain conducive relations.

This Life Cambodia is a recognized NGO in Cambodia, specializing in programs dedicated to upholding the human rights of prisoners and their children, addressing needs and preventing the unnecessary impact of mother, child and family separation. With an emphasis on family preservation and community-based care options, concerted efforts are made to ensure that as many targeted children are supported to remain within, or able to return to their families and communities.

Critical in the initial stages of the TLIF program is family preservation. This involves collaboration and partnership work, with local level government stakeholders, to secure approval and authorization for joint family engagement. This includes working in partnership with the Police, when mothers, accompanied by children, come into conflict with the law. At the point of arrest, detention is common. Therefore, This Life Cambodia provides legal advocacy and representation, and upholds the rights of the individual and the interests of the family, following legislative frameworks.

TLIF also involves family support, which translates into the provision of support and assistance to the children of parents already detained within a prison. Family support ensures that a mother and child's fundamental needs are met and that the child's safety, stability, and developmental concerns are recorded, addressed, and maintained throughout their parent's incarceration. Working in close conjunction with prison officials, families entering the program are selected following key criteria, which include sentence length, time remaining on the sentence, (in)frequency of visitation, the risk of siblings starting/dropping out of school, and the socio-economic circumstances of the family. Family Support Case Managers work closely with the primary caregiver of children, which is often the other parent, a family member or a friend. In this context, case management relies on the prisoner and their family setting mutually beneficial goals that all parties can work toward. For the most part, the prisoner is largely responsible for determining the outcomes, whilst the Family Support Case Manager is responsible for supporting the processes that involve the family.

This approach to personal support places the mother in control of determining the best interests of both her and the child. The nature of this family support can last for up to two years, depending on the individual and the impact of the prison circumstances.

Looking Forward

Combining both our program and research activities, This Life Cambodia recommends the immediate use of non-custodial sentences for both juveniles and women with children, who have committed first time, non-violent offenses. In keeping with a diverse range of theories (McCarthy, Schiraldi, & Shark, 2016), there is a strong belief that community-based diversion programs can arrest and prevent that range of harmful and lasting factors that impact those who are incarcerated in overcrowded prisons. We also believe that this is a practical and meaningful way to learn, manage, and reduce prison populations (Garside, 2021; Farrington & Welsh, 2005; Schlesinger, 2018). Furthermore, we believe that this approach helps reduce the incidence of family separation, which is of critical importance when considering the long-term interests of children and their mothers.

Our position resonates with local people and provides an opportunity to further explore new opportunities in which the Cambodian community can play a proactive and directive role. As we move forward, This Life will embrace the new opportunities that we have created to date and form a new research prospectus that can deliver strategic partnerships that help bridge the gap in coordinating key activities between the central government and provincial-based authorities.

In Siem Reap, we are proud to have produced and presented both credible evidence and practical plans that have subsequently secured an official mandate to deliver a new Juvenile Justice Diversion Program. We will use this opportunity in the first instance, to target young people in conflict with the law. We intend to deliver this program in 2021 and explore supplementary pathways with neighboring authorities. This gives rise to further opportunities to develop parallel plans that involve women with children, and eventually the wider adult population.

In this context, This Life Cambodia sees an optimistic future in which ambition, change, and development are central to the aspirations of the communities that we support. We recognize that it can seem difficult to see change unfold daily. However, by working in partnership and amplifying the voices of those in need, new innovative and practical opportunities can be developed that help deliver inclusive prospects for those most vulnerable members of society.

Chapter 5

Catching Flies: How Women are Exploited Through Prison Work in Myanmar

Myanmar Research Team

Abstract

This chapter explores the work tasks assigned to women prisoners in Myanmar. The official intention of such tasks is to help rehabilitate women in prison by providing them with skills to enhance their future employability outside the prison. The chapter critically inspects this proposition based on an ethnographic case study involving interviews with previously incarcerated women. The women's narratives allow us to juxtapose the actual practice of prison work with the aims of rehabilitation and to critically examine the connection between the types of work tasks given, the distribution of tasks to different kinds of prisoners, and the potential of such work to enhance employability post-release. We find that while prison work is provided ostensibly to prepare and equip women with skills as a form of vocational training, in fact, it rather serves the interests of private companies and the Myanmar Prison Department. We argue that the types of work are intentionally and unintentionally exploitative. The challenges faced by women concerning prison work are highlighted, and the authors propose that the Myanmar Prison Department must commit to more genuine livelihood training options that are not exploitative, but meaningful and orientated toward the employability of women prisoners upon their release.

Keywords: Women; prisoners; work; skills; employment; Myanmar

Introduction: Issues and Challenges

This chapter examines the work tasks and training activities available to women prisoners in Myanmar. Worldwide, there are many types of programs that

Gender, Criminalization, Imprisonment and Human Rights in Southeast Asia, 59–75

Copyright © 2022 by Myanmar Research Team

Published under exclusive licence by Emerald Publishing Limited

doi:10.1108/978-1-80117-286-820221014

prisoners are offered or obliged to undertake. Dominant approaches include education (from basic literacy to higher education), health provision, offender behavior programs and counseling, as well as vocational training and work. In Myanmar, prison work and vocational training comprise diverse and frequently gendered activities including, for example, carpentry and masonry for men and sewing classes for women. Apart from formal work and training programs, prisoners are also tasked with other kinds of work intended to enhance their employability skills. According to the Myanmar Prison Department, such tasks intend to help reintegrate the "offender" via the provision of skills to enhance future employability outside prison (Myanmar Prison Department, 2020). Yet, as we argue below, work and training programs for women prisoners are based on a crude and traditional approach to gender and imprisonment and are highly unsatisfactory from the women's point of view and a human rights perspective. As seen below, in the experiences and stories shared by the women that we spoke to, while work is provided ostensibly to prepare and equip prisoners with skills to benefit their reintegration, these tasks and approaches rather serve the interests of private companies and the Myanmar Prison Department. Thus, we argue that the programs are intentionally and unintentionally exploitative. This point is illustrated by analyzing four main areas of work that women prisoners are engaged in: administration, maintenance, training, and labor in special camps. We begin by looking at some of the pertinent issues raised in the extant literature about women and prison work.

Women and Work in Prisons: Punitive, Pragmatic or Positive?

Work is a salient feature of most prison systems around the world. From the perspective of prison managers, this work has multiple purposes: it helps control prisoners and maintain order, it can be used to punish prisoners, and it may change the behavior of prisoners and help to rehabilitate them and facilitate their reintegration into society. Thus, prison work plays a key role in both maintaining prison order and supporting prisoners' reintegration prospects by enhancing post-release employability and reducing the risk of re-imprisonment (Alos, Esteban, Jodar, & Miguelez, 2015).

According to Alos et al. (2015), when prisoners are kept busy and obliged to work, the amount of misconduct is reduced significantly which is of benefit to prison staff. Work programs give prisoners something to do, make the days go faster, alleviate boredom, overthinking and stress (Jeffries et al., 2020, p. 15). In addition to the social and psychological benefits of work, there are also financial and managerial benefits because prison work often helps to reduce the cost of running prisons, especially when prisoners perform a considerable part of the basic operational tasks (like cleaning and cooking). Yet, prison work is not just beneficial and practical. It may also be central to prisoners' punishment – either as a means to repay a debt to society through low or unpaid labor or by adding an afflictive and harsh dimension to the deprivation of liberty in the form of hard labor (like quarry work) (Bushway, 2003). This is in direct contradiction of the recently updated United Nations Standard Minimum Rules for the Treatment of Prisoners commonly referred to as the Nelson Mandela Rules, which states there should be "a system of equitable remuneration of the work of prisoners" (Rule 103 (1) (United Nations General Assembly, 2016).

Finally, prison work is also supposed to be central to the rehabilitation and reintegration of prisoners by building skills that would enable prisoners to gain employment after their release (Crittenden, Koons-Witt, & Kaminski, 2018). Work programs have been seen as an important aspect of rehabilitation and reintegration in prisons for the past 150 years (Moses & Smith, 2007) and the most obvious response to the fact that most people in prison have little education, few formal vocational skills, limited employment prospects, various social problems, debt, limited family support and so on. Yet, the more pertinent question to ask is "what works" for women in prison? In the United Kingdom, Hunter and Boyce (2009) have examined whether or not training and work programs for women prisoners are beneficial to employability post-release. They found that there is a lack of support for prisoners to find jobs when they return to the community. Similarly, a recent study undertaken in Thailand exploring prisoner re-entry found that women faced numerous challenges in securing post-release work. The social stigma associated with being formally imprisoned restricted women's ability to find stable adequately paying employment and there was little support available to connect them with post-release work opportunities. Dubiousness was also expressed about the transferability of prison-based vocational skills/work to the outside world (Jeffries et al., 2020, pp. 20–21). This raises the question of the benefit of training if jobs are unavailable in the community or if in-prison training is irrelevant to post-release employability. To be properly meaningful and to avoid exploitation and corruption, prison work should be carefully regulated and provide a way to develop marketable skills.

A key problem, when it comes to women's work in prison, is that the kinds of work that are assigned to women are based on gendered stereotypes that limit women's ability to secure well-paying post-release employment. The institutional distribution of work based on gender stereotypes is an indication of the limited opportunities given to women. The assignment of work to women including food preparation, janitorial service and laundry are low-skilled, underpaid and less valued than traditional men's work. The stereotyping makes prison work even more humiliating, meaningless and exploitative for women during their imprisonment. Women are generally tasked with what is considered "appropriate" women's work, such as cooking or sewing, whereas men are tasked with public work or farming which will earn them money in prison and once they return to the community post-release (Crittenden et al., 2018). In Chapter 8 of this volume, Pravattiyagul observes that in Thai prisons while men are trained for metalwork and furniture making, women work as medical assistants in the prison hospital and receive training in embroidery, sewing, massage, cooking, hairdressing, handcrafting clothes, perfumery, baking, and knitting (Pravattiyagul, 2021). This gendering of labor is influenced by prison authorities' perception of women. They interpret women's needs from their cultural perspective believing that women should engage only in domestic work.

Similarly, Bermingham (1996, p. 361) shows that prisons in the United Kingdom, despite constant policy changes and reforms, continue to base educational programs on gender stereotypes. The findings suggest that

> the nature of courses offered to female prisoners stems from customary notions of the role of women as guardians of the home and family. The education and training for women prisoners remain disproportionately concerned with domesticity.

Thus, the traditional view of women as homemakers and dependents continues to be reflected in the work assigned to them in prison, limiting women prisoners' work to domestic service, clerical work, or cosmetology. Although such programs may be beneficial to lessen the pains of imprisonment, in contrast to men, this gendering of prison work reduces women's prospects of accessing meaningful, and adequate paying post-release employment (Schram, 1998). Education, including vocational training for women prisoners, has in practice been more about making sure women know their place in the gendered societal hierarchy than equipping them to develop as autonomous citizens with independent futures. The commentary to the United Nations Rules for the Treatment of Women Prisoners and Non-Custodial Measures for Women Offenders (the Bangkok Rules) calls for more individualized work programs that break away from traditional understandings and gendered stereotyping of women and genuinely build the skills and self-confidence of women. Accordingly, the Bangkok Rules also require that women should have access to a balanced and comprehensive program of activities, that take into account their gendered needs (see Bangkok Rule 42). Women should be able to choose their preferred type of prison work and not be discriminated against in their access to programs of employability because of their gender (United Nations General Assembly, 2010).

In some prison systems in Southeast Asia, work is important for basic survival, informal work more so than formal prison work programs. Informal work involves undertaking menial tasks (e.g., laundry, cooking) for prison officers or other prisoners who then provide remuneration (Jeffries et al., 2020; Park & Jeffries, 2018). For example, in Cambodian prisons, women do not want to work in formal work programs because the pay is low compared to informal work which is lucrative and beneficial (Park & Jeffries, 2018). The availability of appropriate work and training programs are not the only problems that the prison has to address to prepare prisoners for post-release. In Thai prisons, there are vocational training and work programs from which women can earn money but there is a lack of support from the prison department and labor ministry regarding post-release employment. Therefore, some women prisoners express a preference to be trained in setting up small businesses, because there is no guarantee of getting a salaried job after release, despite the training and work experiences in the prison (Jeffries et al., 2020).

So, work has important potential roles in prisons. Yet, research shows that prison work can be used as a tool to control prisoners, to limit women's role in society, and to promote business interests instead of providing prisoners with new skills that will help them to source meaningful and adequately paying work on release (Haney, 2010). Despite the stated aims of supporting rehabilitation and reintegration, work programs rarely lead directly to employment for women when they are released from prison. In what follows we look at the specific situation of women in Myanmar's prisons.

Women Prisoners in Myanmar

It is well documented that the rate of women's imprisonment has been increasing in Southeast Asia for the last two decades. According to Jeffries (2014), imprisoned women in the region are mostly first-timers, accused of non-violent crimes. The region's respective governments' "war on drugs" policies has been one of the major contributing factors leading to the increasing imprisonment of women in Southeast Asia, particularly in Thailand, Cambodia and the Philippines. The trend is aggravated by women's lack of opportunities, low economic status, limited education and knowledge of how to navigate criminal justice settings (e.g., police stations and courts). In our view, reform efforts that strive to keep women out of prison should be the priority, but once women are in prison their situation is in dire need of attention. Means to improve the situation of women in prison through opportunities that will benefit them post-release and empower them to lead lives without recourse to law-breaking should be sought. To contribute to such a development, prison authorities should provide viable programs – including meaningful work – that enable incarcerated women to learn new skills and gain relevant knowledge so that they can find proper and adequately paying work post-release. This would bring the authorities into line with relevant international human rights norms and standards, including the Nelson Mandela and Bangkok Rules both of which include provisions about prison work (United Nations General Assembly, 2010, 2016).

As outlined in Chapter 1 of this book, 12% of Myanmar's total prison population are women ranking it fifth highest, proportionally speaking, out of 221 prison systems worldwide. Furthermore, incarceration numbers in Myanmar have been growing. In 2001, there were 6,034 women imprisoned in Myanmar. By 2017, this had increased to 9,807 (see Table 2 in Chapter 1 and the World Prison Brief, 2021). It was this fact that inspired us to explore the issue of gender and imprisonment in Myanmar. Despite growing numbers, Myanmar does not have a women-only prison. Rather, all prisons across the country house both men and women (except the all-men prison at Thaton). Incarcerating women in male prisons creates difficulties in accessing gender-sensitive facilities and work programs necessary for enhancing women's post-release employability skills. For example, if a woman wants to work to improve her skills in cooking, it is not possible because the cookhouse is occupied by men. Allowing men and women to come together in the same space poses a security risk that many prison authorities are unwilling to address. Thus, women are discriminated against in their access to work for their own protection. They are denied the opportunity to improve their employability skill-set while their freedom of movement and autonomy within the prison is curtailed. As already mentioned, research on women's experiences of prison work and vocational training shows that programs tend to be shaped by a very traditional understanding of women's role in society (Morash, Haarr, & Rucker, 1994). As we will show, Myanmar prisons are no exception. Myanmar prisons are not only highly traditional in their stereotypical gendered approach to work programs but also lack sensitivity regarding what women need to develop their work experiences so that they can make a reasonable living post-release.

In Myanmar, almost every prisoner will participate in different kinds of work tasks assigned to them by the prison department depending on their status, sentence, time served and so on. The work can be voluntary and involuntary. According to the law, "...they [detainees] shall not be required to clean their own latrines, or to perform any other degrading work" (Burma Jail Manual, 1969), though it is not specified further what "degrading" work is, and, according to data we cite later, they do in fact clean their own latrines.

Formal or official work can be classified into four categories: administrative; maintenance and production; vocational training and educational activities; and prison industries. Apart from these, prisoners may also engage in unofficial work such as cooking for each other, massage and laundry. Formal work refers here to any assignment given by the prison authorities, while informal work includes the myriad of routine and ad-hoc tasks that are organized (more or less voluntarily) between prisoners themselves in exchange for money and services. Even though prisoners are supposed to get paid for formal work, in reality, remuneration is rarely forthcoming. Only those who work in labor camps are paid, though very minimally, and only upon release. Administrative work involves prisoners directly in the smooth running of the prison via the delegation of authority. Maintenance work includes cleaning the prison compound and facilities. In production workshops, prisoners make artificial flowers, incense, cigarettes, and other items. Vocational training includes sewing classes, training in making decorative items (banners, flags, etc.), and cosmetics training. Educational activities include classes for literacy, matriculation exams, and university enrollment. In practice, some tasks overlap. For example, the making of decorations and paper flowers can be classified as production work as well as vocational training. Additionally, women prisoners serving long sentences may do farm work and crush stones in designated agriculture and quarry labor camps that comprise what we might term prison industries. Not all these types of work are available to women in every prison. Out of the prisons we visited, only Mandalay prison, which is one of the largest prisons in Myanmar, provides almost all these types of work or training. Since there are no women-only prisons in Myanmar it is difficult to ensure women's access to the facilities needed to improve their possibilities while in prison and upon release.

Methodology and Field Sites

Our analysis draws on a qualitative study, which explored the gendered nature of imprisonment in Myanmar. The study sought to uncover research participants' interpretations of their experiences in prison. Information about different types of work was gathered to examine the connection between work tasks, their distribution to different kinds of prisoners, and their potential to enhance employability after release. The research team took three trips to prisons in Mandalay, Taunggyi and Myeik. In addition, we visited two labor camps in Mandalay and Myeik. These prisons were chosen through dialogue with a network of lawyers, activists and local professionals about the feasibility of interviewing former prisoners. In the field, the research team largely depended on key members of these local networks for access. They introduced us to former prisoners and took us to visit prisons, prison administration offices and labor camps. During these field trips, we took extensive field notes including observations of prison life as it unfolded.

The primary source of data comes from interviews with 14 formally imprisoned women and two prison superintendents. Before going into the field, we designed semi-structured interview guides to examine the different work programs in prison. In interviews, we asked about people's professions and work experiences before and after imprisonment. Interviews were conducted in private; sometimes one on one interviews, sometimes two researchers with one ex-prisoner. While all the ex-prisoners allowed us to record the interviews, we were unable to record the conversations we had with prison superintendents. Instead, extensive and detailed notes were taken. In the same way, notes were taken when we visited labor camps. The length of interviews was about one to one and a half hours.

The interviews and notes were processed in two stages. Firstly, interviews were transcribed from Burmese to English and, secondly, the research team jointly identified key themes, issues and ideas, including labor and prison work which we discuss in detail below.

Types of Prison Work for Women in Myanmar

All prisons and labor camps across Myanmar house both men and women, except Thaton Prison which is a men-only prison. This means that women share most of the important facilities with men such as the kitchen, sickbay, visiting room etc. These important facilities are typically located in men's wings and often only accessible to women in limited ways, during limited times or not at all.

Across the significant differences in size, placement and security categorization, all prisons are expected to follow the same rules and regulations set by the central authority in Nay Pyi Daw, Myanmar's capital. Prisoners are subject to strict discipline in an authoritarian military-style; prisoners may not question the authorities, look into the eyes of staff and must always display obedience and submission. Daily routines and the organization of prison life are highly structured and follow strict command hierarchies. However, rules are also broken and adapted to local contexts – especially in smaller rural prisons and camps, where some prisoners and staff can be both more relaxed and more exploitative than the formal rules demand. Staff delegate a significant share of their power to selected prisoners, who subsequently manage their fellow prisoners and allocate work tasks to each prisoner depending on their background, sentence and security status. As mentioned, the work that prisoners are assigned can be classed into four categories: administration; maintenance and production; vocational training; and prison industries. Work tasks are to some extent distributed according to prisoners' abilities and needs. For example, pregnant women would typically be assigned to lighter work such as cleaning rice, whereas prisoners with professional skills might be assigned to do administrative work. Other prisoners attend work training, while prisoners with short sentences are made to do maintenance. However, all decisions on these assignments come down to the discretion of the prison authorities and by delegation to prisoner leaders. It is also very common that more wealthy prisoners can pay to avoid certain tasks or access lucrative and light work.

Helping the Administration

Administrative work is the most sought-after job among prisoners because it gives opportunities to serve as representatives of staff and as messengers to peers and is not physically demanding. The "prisoner clerk" is a well-known role in prisons. But administering prisons is not only a clerical task and, in Myanmar, prisoners are also "employed" or delegated responsibility in ways that go beyond paperwork. Other administrative work includes tasks where prisoners serve as a focal point for the daily operation of prisons, for instance, to ensure that the scheduled time for waking and sleeping is strictly followed. Even among this privileged group of prisoner leaders, who are also known as "convict officers," tasks are divided by rank. For example, the Tan-zi[1] is responsible for the overall operation and management of a prison ward, whereas the lower-ranked discipliners[2] maintain order. The primary administrative task of "convict officers," is to help the prison department govern the prison, that is to organize, regulate and keep order. In that capacity, this group of prisoners help staff with the registration of new prisoners and with keeping records of who goes in and out of the prison. They make lists of detainees who are called to attend court, and they body-search newcomers or prisoners returning from court, a practice which is highly problematic from a human rights perspective. The most sought-after administrative jobs are those in the common areas of the prisons, which is light clerical work with many opportunities to move around, to build relations with staff and to initiate exchanges and do deals. Yet, even though almost all prisons house both men and women, the most attractive "convict officer" posts are all occupied by men. Due to the strict separation by gender, women are only permitted to perform administrative tasks in the closed-off women-only sections of the prisons, hindering the enhanced mobility enjoyed by men in these roles.

"Convict officers" begin the day by assembling prisoners for headcount, after which they receive instruction from senior staff about daily tasks which they then assign accordingly. This system is locally known as "Lu ko lu kah Pyan oak choke," or "rule of man by man," as a prison manager said with pride in Taungyi.

---

[1]Tan-zi is a convict officer appointed to oversee day to day operation of a prison ward.
[2]Discipliners are also convict officers but are ranked below Tan-zi in the hierarchy.

The system dates to the colonial period when the prison department did not have enough resources to hire staff as required by the law. The appointment of "convict officers" to oversee fellow prisoners is mentioned in chapter VI of the Prison Act, 1894 (Burma Jail Manual, 1969).

In exercising their powers, "convict officers" are supposed to bring about absolute obedience from other prisoners. Although the director told us that "convict officers" are selected based on qualities such as good behavior, organizational skills, and the ability to lead other prisoners, our research shows otherwise. In most cases, their power and authority are legitimized through coercion, intimidation, and violence. An ex-prisoner reported being brutally thrashed by a "convict officer" because she could not remember her prison number or the proper sitting position.[3]

One former prisoner that we interviewed was appointed both as "Baryar"[4] and "Water Board Holder."[5] Her job was to distribute water among prisoners and make sure that the women prisoners did not fight. But it is "hard to keep order," she claimed. When prisoners did not follow orders, she often used foul language to intimidate them. To some, one person controlling water distribution is unfair; a former prisoner from Myeik complained that she had to pay the water board holder for laundry:

> We pay them 7000 Kyats [approximately 4 USD] in a month, [so that we] can wash our clothes but the convict officers don't give us water. They only give water to the washerwomen. I think that is unfair.

Because of the strict control of water, the water board holder can in practice monopolize the distribution of water, appoint washerwomen and allow them privileged access to scarce water resources. The other prisoners must then get their laundry done by the washerwomen, generating income for the water board holder – and, in turn, the Tan-zi or staff, who appointed her. This illustrates the potential for conflict and exploitation when prisoners are delegated to administer the prison.

Moreover, the "convict officers" act as channels through which the prison staff and this privileged group of prisoners can make money or acquire other resources. Since the power to run the prison is delegated to them, "convict officers" can, for instance, control sleeping arrangements. Most prisons in Myanmar are designed with large dormitory-style wards and almost every prison is overcrowded. In this

---

[3]Prison postures are called "Pone-san." In Myanmar prisons, prisoners are required to sit or stand in specific postures in response to different circumstances. For example, when the superintendent comes, prisoners have to sit down with their legs crossed and hands folded with their heads down. They must not look up.

[4]Baryar is the title for "watchmen," who oversee ward security as a main part of the administrative team of "convict officers."

[5]Water Board Holder is responsible for distribution of water in the prison.

context, the "convict officers" are responsible for arranging the sleeping spaces of the entire ward, which often involves the exchange of money (or coffee mix which is the common prison currency in Myanmar). Those who cannot afford to pay sleep beside the toilets. Even when poor prisoners have served considerable time in prison and are eligible to be regarded as senior prisoners with ensuing privileges, they are moved from place to place if they cannot afford to pay. As an ex-prisoner reported, "I had to move to another space every night because I could not buy any space to sleep."

Almost every activity in the prison requires payment. As mentioned, the allocation of work is assigned by both "convict officers" and staff. If a prisoner wants to change her work or assignment, she must pay. A portion of the payments is fed up the system from "convict officers" to staff. Additionally, "convict officers" can get extra remission, that is days reduced from their sentence. Our interviews suggest that the "convict officers" role is both to make a profit, keep order, subject prisoners to deplorable conditions and keep prisoners from escaping through the use of intimidation and violence. This is a form of administrative work that involves controlling and supervising prisoners and distributing work tasks. It is not what we might typically think of as prison work or training, but the fact that prisoners fulfill roles we might normatively expect to be filled by staff is a core aspect of prison life in Myanmar. It is also an important contextualizing factor for understanding the other types of work and training that are available. For the "convict officers" themselves, this practice of supporting the administration does not help their future post-release employability prospects. It only serves the interest of the prison department and the individual prison staff and helps the "convict officers" get a slightly shorter and potentially easier time in prison at the expense of their fellow inmates.

Maintenance Work

Proponents of prison labor argue that institutional maintenance performed by prisoners helps to keep them active and productive. However, opponents argue that obligatory and meaningless maintenance work is exploitative (Nasr, 2017). In the following, we explain what kinds of maintenance tasks are given to women in Myanmar prisons.

Maintenance works are often assigned to women prisoners who are not qualified for vocational training. For example, short-termers or people with less than six months prison terms are not considered worth training, because proper skills take time to learn. A former prisoner in Taunggyi said, "I didn't join the vocational training provided by the prison. I was sentenced for one month so that I could not learn these training well." It is common practice that every new prisoner goes through a vetting process, where their work experiences outside of prison, education, and offense are assessed. This vetting process determines what kinds of tasks or assignments a person should perform in the prison. "During imprisonment, every prisoner had to tell what kind of profession they practice or vocational training they attended or developed skills before the prison," said an ex-prisoner. After this examination of the prisoner's background, she is assigned to a work task that the responsible staff and "convict officer" consider "appropriate." If the prisoner wants to move to another job, the "convict officer" and the staff might consider it but there are no guarantees unless she can pay, in which case she may even be able to get transferred to another prison closer to her home.

The maintenance activities available are fairly limited in the women's section of prisons. Maintenance work that has the potential for substantial skills development is only applicable to men. Carpentry, plumbing, mechanical and electrical maintenance are for instance not considered to be women's work, which is limited to very basic manual tasks like cleaning, water distribution, gardening or, as we will see below, catching flies. On the face of it, such tasks seem to be quite trivial and minimal. But, in reality, they can be exhausting because of the imposition of massive quotas and strict timelines. The failure to meet quotas or deliver on time might result in disciplinary actions or the payment of a fine.

One of the best examples of this is catching flies. The task of catching flies is assigned to women who do not meet the criteria for production work or vocational training, and who cannot be sent to labor camps for reasons such as health issues, being under trial or serving short sentences. These women are obliged to catch flies "to improve hygiene." In fact, such tasks are more about discipline and control than doing meaningful work. Some former prisoners reported that they would have to catch 50 flies, others said that had to catch 100 flies per day.[6] Speaking about her fly-catching experience, an ex-prisoner said:

> I have done many jobs such as catching flies. If I did not catch 50 flies, I would have to stand under the hot sun. I have also cleaned the toilet baskets and fetched water for the toilets. Rich prisoners did not need to do these jobs. The toilet water was never filled up [for the rest of us], because the rich prisoners often came to use it [up first and for themselves].

Being fearful of the consequences of failing to meet the required fly catching quota, many women prisoners ended up buying flies from more experienced prisoners, who caught more. In this way, they could present the required flies to the "convict officers" – and the experienced old-timers, who had taught themselves to catch flies could earn money catching flies for newcomers.

As stated above, every prisoner is involved in work of some kind. Even women with newborn babies are not spared. They must also engage in maintenance work in the prison. A woman who had a child in the prison said that she was always busy with cleaning the floors and taking care of her child. This is a typical example of how Myanmar prisons discipline prisoners without gender sensitivity.

In some prisons, access to drinking water is limited. In Myeik prison, men are tasked with the delivery of drinking water to the women's section, but they are not

---

[6]An interesting parallel is to the practice of rat-killing in Myanmar prisons in the late nineteenth century reported on standardized forms by colonial prison administrators to HQ in London.

allowed to enter the section, and the drinking water is left in front of the gate. The women prisoners must then fetch the water and fill their respective cans:

> Some prisoners carried water bottles to fill the water bowls of other prisoners. For instance, if I don't want to do it today, I would give a coffee package to a fellow prisoner to do my tasks,

said a former prisoner in Myeik. Although there is no involvement of staff or "convict officers" in this case, even the small task of carrying water leaves room for prisoner exploitation, due to lack of facilities and access to necessities.

Maintenance work involves basic tasks such as cleaning and water distribution that exploits low-status prisoners. But maintenance is also a market, where wealthier prisoners can buy themselves out of these tasks, poorer prisoners can work for others (washing clothes, cooking, massaging) or take other's work (catching "their" flies) to make money. Mopping floors, catching flies and cleaning toilets are tedious and unattractive jobs in themselves and they do not offer any opportunities to women prisoners on release.

Vocational Training

An area where women prisoners seem to face especially stark disparities is vocational training. Interviews with women ex-prisoners reveal that opportunities and access to training are minimal compared to men. In the men's sections of the prisons, there are varied programs, although their effectiveness is questionable considering the limited resources and rampant corruption. But during an interview, one senior prison official proudly claimed that many (men) prisoners have become masons and carpenters after their release and are now earning a decent income. Mandalay prison has a range of vocational training programs such as cigar making, recycling of plastic bags, incense making, tailoring and so on. But few of these programs are available in smaller, rural prisons like Myeik and Taunggyi.

More fundamentally, the gender stereotypical programming entails that vocational training is not pursued according to the women prisoners' needs. Firstly, training is arbitrarily assigned and thus unlikely to teach skills and impart knowledge perceived as relevant. Moreover, the already skilled prisoners are picked out and assigned tasks within their established professional areas of work, while unskilled prisoners in real need of training, are assigned to work that does not require qualifications:

> If the person can do tailoring, then [she is] included in tailoring group. If the person will stay for one year, then she is included in making festival decoration material. The person who serves a longer (sentence) would be included in handicraft of making animal picture on pieces of cloths. There was not actual liberty to choose the type of work.

Upon examining actual work available in the prison, we found that the vocational training programs were not introduced so that the women could acquire knowledge and skills, rather to serve the interests of private companies and the Myanmar Prison Department. The companies bring raw materials into the prison, and the prisoners produce or complete the products. One of the former prisoners from Mandalay prison reported being given paper and plastic to make flowers for festival decorations. Likewise, each prison has its own business with private companies. In Myiek, one former prisoner reported, "I had to make fake eyelashes and fake hair. After finishing these products, the prison staff exported them to the company to get money." In Taunggyi, incense making is the most common work that makes money for the prison. Aside from these, there are also many other industries such as cigarette, construction and agricultural companies that use Myanmar prisons to capitalize on women prisoners' labor.

Unsurprisingly, none of the interviewees had gone to the companies they had worked for in the prison, to look for a job after their release. Almost all of them had gone back to their previous profession. Others had changed their profession because of the risk involved in going back to their former jobs, especially for former sex workers due to the danger, they said, of being arrested again, bringing shame to the family and being ostracized.

In the west, many ex-prisoners are denied jobs because of stigma a situation that is also noted to exist in Thailand (Jeffries et al., 2020; Visher, Debus, & Yahner, 2008), whereas the Myanmar ex-prisoners we interviewed seemed able and willing to pick up their former professions. This is likely because most of the women were farmers, self-employed small business owners, sex-workers or private company employees. Additionally, some of the barriers to returning to the job market found in other countries do not exist in Myanmar. For example, background checks on prospective employees are rare and information provided on previous convictions is uncheckable. The ex-prisoners we interviewed did not wish to work for the companies that they had worked for in the prison because of low pay and they typically found that their previous professions were more attractive and profitable than the jobs that companies involved in prisons could offer outside.

Tailoring seems to be the most common vocational training in all the prisons studied. Tailoring has two purposes; to produce prisoners' uniforms and mend prisoner and staff clothing, and to provide services to private companies. A former prisoner who worked as a tailor said,

> During life in prison, we had to work as tailors, and had to make prison staffs' attire and mend buttons on their uniforms. In meantime, they (staff) could earn some money from sewing [for outsider customers] as prisoners could sew various forms of design of clothes and pants.

Another form of work that women prisoners do is the crafting of baskets, bags, mats etc. out of old plastic bags which are given as souvenirs to visitors and displayed in the prison shop. One of the ex-prisoners said that, although the crafted bags are really beautiful, it is not easy to make money out of them after release and build a business around that, because they demand a lot of time and labor to produce. Prisoners were therefore mainly engaged in making bags to simply pass time and it is not in any way believed that they could make a profession out of it.

Even in the so-called training programs, be it sewing, making flowers, bags or decorations, every women prisoner must meet quotas, which some often fail to do. In these cases, newcomers often hire experienced and skilled prisoners to help them out or do the work. Some prisoners resist participating in work activities because they do not think that it will benefit their future employment or enhance their skills. Additionally, many women already have experience of traditional women's work and are therefore unlikely to learn anything new. Instead of training prisoners and admitting them into relevant work programs, women prisoners' labor is mainly to the advantage of the Myanmar Prison Department because the prisoners are not paid for the work they have done, the work and skills do not improve post-release opportunities and the products and profits only benefit the prison department and the involved companies.

Prison Industries

Although harsh criticism of penal labor camps has led to the abolishment of individual camps in many parts of the country, the labor camps continue to exist in Myanmar's penal system today (Swe Win, 2016). In 2018, the award-winning *Myanmar Now* journalist, Swe Win (2018) reported widespread corruption and human rights abuses in these camps, such as continuous shackling and beatings across all 48 prison labor camps, which hold some 20,000 prisoners. During our field trip, we visited two labor camps in Mandalay and Myiek. The agricultural camp in Myiek only housed men who were growing rice. We were not able to visit a labor camp in Taunggyi, where women were housed, but have interviewed former detainees.

Mandalay and Taunggyi labor camps have agricultural activities and animal breeding. In quarry camps, rocks are extracted from the mountains by blasting boulders off the cliffs with dynamite and then using iron bars and hammers to manually crush the boulders to stones and gravel. After the rocks are extracted, they are processed into fragments. The smaller pieces of stone are then sold off and transported to different places according to size and usage. This work is done by men only. These quarry camps are established with the stated purpose of supporting national infrastructure projects such as building highways and bridges. During a conversation in Mandalay labor camp, we learned that private construction companies also buy these stones and that the labor camps are part of a big and established private business (Swe Win, 2019).

Women's tasks in the labor camps are to pick up the stones that the men have crushed, process them, and load them onto trucks for transportation. In the prison, prisoners work individually to meet their quota, but in the labor camps, women are grouped to meet quotas. Senior prisoners can use their status to work not out in the open sun, but in a tent where the stones are broken into even smaller pieces:

> There is also a place that is kind of tent in the labor camp, if you don't want (to) carry the stone then you have to approach the

authorities and break the stone to smaller one in the tent. But you cannot directly ask to work in the tent, the first month you have to carry the stone. Then the following month if you cannot do that then you can request to work in the tent. But you have to buy from the authorities to work in the tent, it cost around 2-3 lakhs (100 to 150 USD).

Unlike prisons, labor camps have a functioning payment scheme whereby prisoners are paid for their work. Still, the pay is extremely low – 200 kyats per day which is equivalent to about 00.15 USD in 2021. These camps are extremely dangerous for women's health and physical safety (Swe Win, 2018). Because of the heavy work, women are exhausted: "most of the (break) time we sleep because we were so tired," one interviewee told us. Despite the well-known dangers, safety measures are almost non-existent. And prisoners often experience this danger very directly: "Labor camp is very dangerous and we work very hard and it is tiresome. We often experience minor injury because of pieces of stone and rock," an interviewee said. The only safety measure discovered was where some staff and "convict officers" would "look-out" for where the rocks are cracking and falling and warn working prisoners. The effectiveness of such systems is seriously questionable. There have been reports of casualties resulting in deaths and serious injury while working in the labor camps. The Assistance Association for Political Prisoners referred to the labor camps as, "killing fields" (2008) during the military dictatorship in the 1990s and early 2000s. Furthermore, the prisoners have little time to look out for their safety because of the quota system. Reflecting on her time in the labor camps, a woman said:

> I have memories of collecting stone rushing because we had quota to collect the stone set for us (by authority) and we have to fulfil it. Those who complete first would return to the room earlier. After breaking the rock with dynamite, we had to rush and collect the stone. The group who complete the quota first are rewarded with juice and soap by the authorities. When I was there for the first time at the site, I do not understand why people are rushing for that, but later I realized the nature of work and worried that I may not be able to fulfil the quota. It was very tiresome because we moved the stones from one place to another and the ways were full of up and down. Since it was every day we become very tired.

When women approach the end of their sentences in the labor camps, they are sent to do lighter work in a more relaxed environment with minimal security checks because the staff presume that they would not escape and risk facing a new longer sentence if caught. In the labor camp, the prisoners approaching release would be sent to the agricultural section of the camp, where they would work with gardening, cutting grass and weeding.

The camps also feature agriculture and livestock-rearing but when it comes to work tasks in the piggery and the poultry section, women are excluded. In Mandalay and Taunggyi, these positions were all given to men, who again solely benefitted from gaining relevant skills. Though they offer no benefit to the women prisoners post-release, the labor camps continue to exist because the production of stones serves the prison department and corporate interests.

Concluding Remarks

In this chapter, we have explored four types of work available to women in Myanmar prisons. Prison work is supposed to enhance skills, knowledge and facilitate women's employment opportunities upon release. Analysis of these work tasks and programs suggests, however, that these function more as a form of social control than a means of rehabilitation or a route to reintegration. Education and training for women prisoners are focused on domesticity and their labor-power is utilized for profit. Our analysis also emphasizes the prevalence of gendered approaches to women, imprisonment and work, and shows that work meaningfully associated with future employment is limited for women prisoners compared to men. In addition, the findings suggest that the way that work is assigned to women creates fear and stress. Most of the interviewees felt frustrated with the system because they knew the work and tasks were not designed for their benefit. Some of the work that prisoners engaged in – like catching flies – simply does not exist in the outside world (Schram, 1998).

We emphasize that prison work for women is assigned without much benefit for prisoners themselves. The Nelson Mandela Rules state that prisoners should not be held in slavery or servitude and that work should be given to prisoners to enhance their skills and be utilized after their release (Rules 97 and 98). Furthermore, Bangkok Rule 42 is clear that women shall have access to a balanced and comprehensive program of activities that take into account their gender-appropriate needs. The lack of specific work programs in which women prisoners could be engaged meaningfully to enhance their skills according to their needs is a serious matter. Rather than empowering women prisoners by enhancing their work skills and level of education so that they have a better chance of rebuilding their lives upon release and staying clear of crime and the claws of the justice system, their labor is exploited by the prison department and the private businesses that earn money on the gravel, the paper flowers, the incense, etc. that incarcerated women are forced to produce. To support these claims, we have offered a critical, ethnographic exploration of the women's own experiences and perspectives on working in prison administration, maintenance, training, and labor camps. We have shown that educated, skilled and affluent people are likely to get positions in the "prisoner" administration, which controls poorer prisoners' activities and distributes disciplinary power, sleeping places and labor positions. Working as a "convict officer" might offer immediate benefits (often at the expense of others), but even this attractive job does not help these prisoners' future employment post-release.

We have also emphasized that women prisoners crushing stones in the camps are an integral but exploited part of the labor market in Myanmar. The vetting of prisoners is not a process to assess their needs for training, but a determination of their production value. Even the smallest and seemingly meaningless work task of catching flies is part of an exploitative prison economy. If a prisoner could not meet her quota of "50 flies," she might be fined or punished, which forces her to buy flies from other prisoners, more adept at the task. We thus conclude that fly catching vividly illustrates how women's work in Myanmar's prisons is in no way whatsoever designed, implemented, or intended to benefit them. The function of women prisoners' labor and work is to maintain discipline, underpin relations of dependency, fuel the prisoner leadership system, keep the prisoners busy for nothing, and reproduce gender stereotypes and patriarchal relations of domination.

Chapter 6

Experiences of Ethnic Minority Women Imprisoned in Thailand

Prarthana Rao, Min Jee Yamada Park and Samantha Jeffries

Abstract

To date, intersectional feminist criminological enquiry concerned with exploring junctions of gender and ethnicity amongst incarcerated women, has mainly come from studies undertaken in western nations. In this chapter, we present findings from research undertaken in Thailand that explored incarcerated ethnic minority women's backgrounds, situational contexts surrounding their criminalization and criminal justice system experiences, with particular attention paid to women's time in prison. Our purpose was to examine how gender and ethnicity intersected, impacting the lived experiences of criminalized ethnic minority women before and during their incarceration. Findings revealed the ways in which these women are marginalized inside and outside prison walls. On the outside, the women struggled with patriarchal systems of power, both within and beyond their communities. They were subjugated as women and by discourses of ethnic othering. Under-education, poverty, living with state, community, familial and intimate partner violence, trauma, and other adversity were key aspects of the women's pre-prison lives and created the contexts from which they came into conflict with the law. The women faced challenges in accessing justice and, once imprisoned, gender and ethnicity intersected in several domains, to impact their carceral experiences.

Keywords: Women; ethnic minority; Indigenous; prison; Thailand; Bangkok Rules

Gender, Criminalization, Imprisonment and Human Rights in Southeast Asia, 77–92
Copyright © 2022 by Prarthana Rao, Min Jee Yamada Park and Samantha Jeffries
Published under exclusive licence by Emerald Publishing Limited
doi:10.1108/978-1-80117-286-820221005

Introduction

The United Nations Rules for the Treatment of Women Prisoners and Non-Custodial Measures for Women Offenders (the Bangkok Rules) (United Nations General Assembly, 2010) provide gendered directives to policymakers, legislators, sentencing authorities, and prison staff around prison management, allocation, admission, classification, hygiene and healthcare, safety, security, well-being, rehabilitation activities and programs, contact with the outside world, and the special or additional needs, of particularly vulnerable women. As outlined in Bangkok Rule 54, "prison authorities shall recognise that women prisoners from different religious and cultural backgrounds have distinctive needs and may face multiple forms of discrimination," and Bangkok Rule 55 directs that "pre and post-release services shall be reviewed to ensure that they are appropriate and accessible to indigenous women prisoners and women prisoners from ethnic and racial groups." Directions are also provided to reduce the disadvantages created by language barriers (Bangkok Rule 2[1]) and geographical distance, that is when women are housed in prisons that are a long distance away from their families and communities (Bangkok Rule 26). The feminist notion of intersectional disadvantage is implicit here.

Within a male-dominated social structure, all women will face oppression because of their subordinated place in the gender hierarchy, while women from ethnic minority groups sit at the crossroads of patriarchy, racial and other subjugations. It is at this junction that intersecting systems of gendered and racialized power meet, shaping women's life experiences, and situating them within multiple hierarchies of oppression (Burgess-Proctor, 2006). In this chapter, we utilize a feminist intersectional approach to explore axes of gender and ethnicity in the lived experiences of women imprisoned in Thailand, pinpointing how traversing intersectional systems of power impact lived experiences of criminalization and incarceration.

To date, intersectional feminist criminological enquiry concerned with exploring junctions of gender and ethnicity amongst incarcerated women has mainly come from studies undertaken in western nations. This research has either focused on Indigenous women imprisoned in settler-colonial countries, such as Australia, New Zealand, Canada and United States (e.g., Bissen, 2020; George & Ngamu, 2020; Kendall, Lighton, Sherwood, Baldry, & Sullivan, 2020; Martin, Buxton, & Smith, 2012; Ogden, 2020), or incarcerated ethnic minority women (often also foreign nationals) in England, the United States and Europe (e.g., Ballesteros-Pena, 2020; Hales & Gelsthorpe, 2012; Joseph, 2006; Kruttschnitt & Hussemann, 2008; Matos, 2016; Ruiz-García & Castillo-Algarra, 2014). Beyond Europe, Australasia, and North America, there are only two published studies. The first was undertaken in Bangladesh (Mehta, 2016), and the second in Cambodia (Park & Jeffries, 2018). Overall, this research shows that while all women in prison experience difficulties, ethnic minority women encounter additional hardships. Prison systems are not only established and designed by men for men, but also for the ethnic majority group (Joseph, 2006, p. 151).

Gender and ethnicity structure the social world and converge to impact women's criminalization and carceral experiences. We know that women's imprisonment is impacted by the clustering of adverse life factors, which include: under-education, poverty, familial caregiving, problematic interpersonal relation-ships with men, gendered violence and victimization, associated trauma, and problems with mental and physical health, including substance misuse (e.g., see Daly, 1994; Owen, Wells, & Pollock, 2017) . We also know that under-education and poverty can limit women's capacity to access justice (Park & Jeffries, 2018).

Ethnic minority women experience the above aspects differently, and perhaps more acutely, than their more privileged female counterparts. For example, eth-nic minority women tend to have lower levels of education, higher than aver-age poverty rates, and are more likely to be the victims of gender-based violence (Minority Rights Group International, 2009). Then, of course, these women face additional problems, including systemic racism, historical legacies of racial oppression, other acts of violence, and in some cases, precarious citizenship sta-tuses (e.g., Ballesteros-Pena, 2020; Bissen, 2020; George & Ngamu, 2020; Hales & Gelsthorpe, 2012; Joseph, 2006; Kruttschnitt & Hussemann, 2008; Matos, 2016; Mehta, 2016; Ogden, 2020; Park & Jeffries, 2018).

Behind prison walls, gender intersects in several ways with ethnicity to exac-erbate the pains of imprisonment. Familial disconnection, as well as isolation from community and culture, can be especially difficult. Language and cultural barriers can result in ethnic minority women feeling confused and anxious about prison regimes. This group of women are often disadvantaged in their ability to access information, legal support, healthcare, and educational and vocational training programs. They may be confused around systems of justice, face prob-lems associated with their immigration status and a lack of cultural compe-tency within the prison can result in them being treated disrespectfully, and in racially discriminatory ways (Ballesteros-Pena, 2020; Cox & Sacks-Jones, 2017; Hales & Gelsthorpe, 2012; Jefferson, 2019; Joseph, 2006; Kendall et al., 2020; Kruttschnitt & Hussemann, 2008; Martin et al., 2012; Matos, 2016; Mehta, 2016; Park & Jeffries, 2018; Ruiz-García & Castillo-Algarra, 2014).

In this chapter, we present findings from a study undertaken in Thailand that explored incarcerated ethnic minority women's backgrounds, situational contexts surrounding their criminalization, and criminal justice system experiences. More specifically, this research has focused on women from five ethnic minority groups: the Akha, Hmong, Lahu, Lisu, and Shan. However, before discussing this study in more detail, we locate our research participants within the broader social context.

Positioning Ethnic Minority Women in Thailand

Despite distinctive cultural identities and histories, the Akha, Hmong, Lahu, Lisu, and Shan are officially constituted by the Thai government as "hill tribe" ("chao khao") peoples because of their geographical placement in the upland border regions of Northern Thailand (Laungaramsri, 2003, p. 164; Morton & Baird, 2019, p. 12). The population of these officially designated border-dwell-ing uplanders in Thailand is estimated to include a little over one million people (Morton & Baird, 2019, p.12).

The separation of lowlander Thais from upland minorities by referring to these ethnic peoples as "chao khao" has discursively constructed them as "other"; being opposed to real "Thais" or "chao rao" (Morton & Baird, 2019, pp. 10–11). As outlined by Laungaramsri (2003, p. 163),

> one literal translation of chao khao is people of the hills. However, the term chao khao apart from meaning hills or mountains, is also a third-person pronoun, connoting the other. When contrasted with chao rao, literally those of us, or we people, the expression falls into opposition to us.

"Hill tribe" peoples have, at numerous points in history, been constructed within narratives of threat. Namely, as less civilized than ethnic Thais, borderless migrants lacking any loyalty to the Thai nation, the primary producers of opium and other drugs, and destroyers of the forest due to "irrational" and "destructive" agricultural practices (Laungaramsri, 2003; Morton & Baird, 2019). These official discourses of dangerousness have been used by the Thai state to legitimize control through the surveying, demarcating and over-policing of "chao khao." "Hill tribe" peoples have been "dispersed" from their lands, and attempts have been made at "re-education" to culturally assimilate them into mainstream Thai society (Laungaramsri, 2003; Morton & Baird, 2019). This assimilation agenda is noted to be fragmenting traditionally close-knit communities by impeding the intergenerational transmission of traditional languages, cultures, and traditions (Asavasaetakul, 2019, p. 3).

Ethnic "hill tribe" peoples exist at the margins of mainstream Thai society. Around 38% are without Thai citizenship, despite being born in, and residing within Thailand's borders. An estimated 380,000 "chao khao" possess one of several color-coded "hill tribe" identification cards issued since the early 1990s. These cards mark their holders as partial Thai citizen-subjects, whose rights to mobility beyond districts of residence are severely curtailed (Morton & Baird, 2019, p. 11). This has been described as "Thai-style apartheid," and situated "hill tribe" peoples on the periphery of policies and practices created for the welfare of "Thai" people (Kemasingki, 2016). Access to the most basic of human rights, such as education, health care, land tenure, education, freedom of movement and political participation is severely curtailed (Morton & Baird, 2019, p. 11). Unsurprisingly, many "hill tribe" peoples live with poverty and suffer poor physical and mental ill-health, including problems with substance misuse (Apidechkul et al., 2020; Chomchoei et al., 2020; Diamond, 2011; Park, Tanagho, & Weicher, 2009). Discrimination and ethnic vilification in their everyday lives are common. They are often perceived as ignorant, uncivilized, rural "others" who threaten legitimate "Thai-ness" (Draper, Sobieszczyk, Crumpton, Lefferts, & Chachavalpongpun, 2019).

"Chao khao" women are especially vulnerable because they are subjugated at the intersection of gendered and ethnic oppression. As noted by Physicians for Human Rights (2004, p. 27), Thai women, overall, have lower status than men, and "hill tribe" women endure a particularly low status among women, both in mainstream Thai society and, oftentimes, within their communities. Some ethnic minority communities are especially patriarchal. Here, women hold no decision-making or political power, and are expected to fulfill defined gender roles. They are construed as male property and relegated to life within the private familial sphere. There is no freedom to choose an intimate partner, and they can be forced into marriage and out of school at a young age. Even in matrilineal ethnic minority communities, where women have historically enjoyed more power, the Thai state's arguably patriarchal assimilation project is noted to be fragmenting traditional values to the detriment of women (The Indigenous Women's Network of Thailand, 2011)

Overall, socioeconomic indicators paint a picture of severe disadvantage. Language and cultural barriers, geographical isolation, poverty, patriarchal community, and family structures coalesce to keep women out of Thai state-run education. Unsurprisingly, poverty then features in the lives of many. These situations are exacerbated and intertwined with "hill tribe" women's tenuous citizenship statuses. The Thai education system, for example, is difficult to access without citizenship, but this education is needed to meet the Thai language requirements of citizenship. Research shows that in ethnic minority communities, men are more likely than women to possess citizenship (The Indigenous Women's Network of Thailand, 2011).

State and community-based violence is common, and gender-based abuse occurs both within and outside of "hill tribe" communities and families (Dhongchai et al., 2005; Hongladarom, 1999). Ethnic minority women are noted to be especially vulnerable to human trafficking, domestic and family violence, sexual exploitation, and abuse (Dhongchai et al., 2005; Diamond, 2011; Panjaphothiwat et al., 2021; Physicians for Human Rights, 2004; The Indigenous Women's Network of Thailand, 2011). Finally, the adversities and acts of violence endured by these groups of ethnic minority women can result in compromised physical and mental health, including substance misuse (Apidechkul et al., 2020; Chomchoei et al., 2020). In the following sections of this chapter, we overview our research methodology and findings.

Methodology

Semi-structured in-depth interviews were undertaken with 29 ethnic minority women imprisoned in 4 Thai prisons: (1) Central Women's Correctional Institution, Bangkok, (2) Fang District Prison, Chiang Mai, (3) Chiang Rai Central Prison, Chiang Rai, and (4) Chiang Mai Women's Correctional Institution, Chiang Mai. The purpose of these interviews was to explore how gender and ethnicity intersected, impacting the lived experiences of ethnic minority women before and during imprisonment. The interview schedule covered four broad areas: (1) background characteristics and life pre-imprisonment, (2) offense characteristics and situational context, (3) experiences with police and courts, and (4) experiences of imprisonment. The results are presented below.

Background Characteristics and Life Before Imprisonment

Women were aged between 20 and 60 years. Twenty-one had Thai citizenship; 14 at birth, and 7 were naturalized later in life. The latter had existed for a substantial part of their lives as stateless persons (i.e., not citizens of any country). Nearly all the remaining women had been stateless throughout their lives, but only a couple were, under Thai law, "illegal immigrants."

As previously noted, the women came from five different ethnic groups. Their communities were dispersed across the Northern Thai border regions, described as small-sized remote rural villages, surrounded by or located in the mountains. As children, the women reported that their caregivers were usually subsistence farmers, and struggled to scrape by financially. Having parents, relatives, and friends involved in illicit drugs was common. Drug dealing by caregivers presented as a viable way to escape poverty.

During adulthood, most of the women continued to live in poverty. Geographic isolation alongside precarious citizenship statuses, restricted mobility, education, and in turn, life opportunities. The women were generally under-educated (see Table 3), and over half had resultant low levels of Thai literacy. The women generally worked in low-paying occupations, for example, farming, factory, and construction work. Only two women participated in relatively better-paying employment, and both had attended university.

Table 3.   Women's Education Levels.

Education Level	Number of Women
None	10
Elementary	8
Lower secondary	6
Upper secondary	1
University	2
Informal school	2

Living in remote villages meant that there were often no schools within commuting distance. This was particularly true for older interviewees. Also, poverty and traditional patriarchal cultural values coalesced to exclude women from education. In families where money was scarce, decisions were made about who would most benefit from education. In contrast to boys, girls were viewed as being destined for marriage and familial caregiving. Zhong, for example, explained

> two of my brothers attended school [but not me] because according to my dad, boys have to learn and take care of the family [financially]. Girls just go and get married and live with their husbands.

Boys would be sent to school, while girls would be directed into work to help support their families, including the education of their brothers. Patriarchal gender roles also meant that early marriage and motherhood were common, another contributing factor to school dropout. Several women reported getting married in the "traditional" way and having children as teenagers. By the time they were incarcerated, nearly all the women were mothers.

Many of the women described problematic intimate relationships with men, including intimate partners using or dealing drugs, and struggling with addiction (alcohol, drugs, gambling). Living with domestic violence was common. While some women reported being able to escape these relationships, others described being trapped. Family members told them to stay with their abusers because "it's [domestic violence] normal ... when two people can't get along well, sometimes there would be some fights" and "it's better not to get divorced."

As stated previously, most of the women (21/29) had Thai citizenship, but this was not always the case. Previously, they had held "highlander" or "stateless cards," which recognized "hill tribe" residency in Thailand, but restricted freedom of movement by only allowing the women to live and work in designated areas, often within the district or provincial boundaries of their remote communities. Those seeking to leave their communities to find employment, access education, health care, and so on, needed to apply and receive permission from the Thai Government. Permissions then needed to be renewed regularly. These applications and renewals cost a significant amount of money (see Aei's story below). Expired permissions that were not renewed promptly could result in the person being charged with an immigration offense.

Offense Characteristics and Situational Context

Every woman was in prison for a drug offense involving methamphetamine – mostly Yaba (tablets containing a mixture of methamphetamine and caffeine), and sometimes Ice (crystal methamphetamine). Sentence lengths ranged from just over two years to life and the death penalty. Aei was convicted of both a drug and immigration offense. She had held a stateless Thai identification card since she was a child. This card needed to be renewed every five years for 10,000 THB (approximately 315 USD). Her card had expired when she was arrested for drug possession, and this resulted in an additional conviction for an immigration offense. Aei was uncertain about what would happen to her post-release. Normally, foreign nationals are placed in an immigration detention center or deported back to their country of citizenship, but for a stateless person, there is no country to be sent back to. As Shan, Aei said that she may be taken across the border into Myanmar, even though her family, community, and life were in Thailand. The Shan primarily reside within Myanmar and along the Thai border region.

Overall, the situational context surrounding the women's drug offending was not a single event, but rather, a combination of life experiences. Precarious citizenship statuses and gendered cultural expectations restricting women to the private sphere coalesced in low levels of education, limited employment opportunities, and associated poverty. Unsurprisingly, given ethnic group socioeconomic marginalization in Thailand, many of these women, including Aei (above), lived in communities and families reliant on the illicit drug trade for survival. They witnessed violence in their communities, and their loved ones and other community members coming into conflict with the law, being imprisoned and subjected to state violence. As primary familial caregivers, the women recounted needing to support their children against backdrops of poverty and problematic, oftentimes abusive, intimate relationships with men. All these adverse and arguably traumatic life experiences created emotional distress, and for some, led to substance abuse. These themes are explored in more detail below.

For some women, drug offending was narrated as a reasonable avenue for earning a living within the context of financial insecurity. They observed other people in their families and communities "making a good amount of money" through drug selling. Amima grew up with a father who sold drugs,and witnessed the perpetration of state violence against him and others. Amima's father was shot by the police when she was 14 years old. Her two brothers were addicted to drugs and alcohol. When she got married, Amima learned that her husband also made "a living" selling drugs. Her husband was arrested and imprisoned soon after they were married. She began working as a drug courier. She later had two more marriages. Husband number two was shot dead by the police during a drug arrest, and her third spouse abused drugs and alcohol. Amima was her family's main financial provider, and sold drugs to support them.

Like Amima, Hu-Bo grew up with family members in the illicit drug trade. Her father was imprisoned for drug offending and her mother sold drugs in nearby villages to support the family after he was incarcerated. Hu-Bo's mother was murdered one day during a drug-related conflict in her community. From the age of 15 years, she earned money as a domestic worker in Bangkok and sent money home to support her family. However, Hu-Bo's father, now released, used her money to support his drug habit, and was soon back behind bars, and Hu-Bo had her child to support. This placed a significant financial strain on the family. Amidst this financial crisis, a group of friends from Hu-Bo's village suggested that she help them to deliver drugs. She explained that,

> at the beginning I refused. I said I am afraid of doing this, but I also needed some cash to feed [my] child. At first, it [delivering drugs] was very peacefully successful. I earned 20,000 THB (approximately 630 USD) in only one night. So, I started to think that it's a good source of income.

For other women, intimate relationships with men underscored their drug offending, either through love, fear, or guilt by association. For example, Gao-Jer's husband threatened her with a knife and said that he would kill their daughter if she did not help him to sell drugs. Nado was imprisoned because she delivered drugs for the money to bail her boyfriend out of pre-trial detention on a drug use charge. Two other women explained that they had been arrested alongside their husbands, who had committed the offense; they were unaware of what their husbands were doing. Other women explained that they happened to be accompanying a family member or a friend who was carrying drugs, and were subsequently arrested as an accomplice.

Less than one-quarter of the women reported ever having used drugs. In these cases, the women were introduced to drugs by friends and family during their teenage years, and eventually developed what they described as an addiction. At certain points in their lives, they would stop using drugs, but when confronted with trauma or other life adversities, would self-medicate as a coping mechanism. These women explained that they would turn to drugs to deal with a myriad of emotional stressors stemming from their intimate relationships, including domestic violence, infidelity, and abandonment, as well as the anxiety associated with impoverishment. Drug use in these cases eventually led to drug selling to support their addictions, themselves, and their families.

Access to Justice: Police and Courts

The women articulated that coming from an ethnic minority background made it more difficult for them to access justice due to under-education, language barriers, and few financial resources. For example, one woman explained,

> I think being ethnic minority affected me [accessing justice]. I was not educated and did not know about the justice system. I did not have a good lawyer. I felt that the court or police didn't listen to me.

The women recounted problems communicating with criminal justice actors, police misconduct, inadequate legal representation, general confusion, and lack of understanding around the process, ethnic bias, and not being informed about their right to appeal.

Around one-quarter of the women explained that they found it difficult to communicate with police because they had limited or no capacity to speak or understand Thai, but only one received help with translation, although not from a professional interpreter. Rather, a police officer who happened to understand her native language was utilized. One-third relayed having been asked, tricked, or sometimes even forced, to sign their charge sheets, statements, and other papers by police, when they did not know what these documents contained. This documentation was then used in the court by police as evidence, and to invalidate any contrary verbal evidence provided by the women.

For example, Asuema (who had no Thai literacy) had been told by a police officer that if she signed the paper, she would be released. She was arrested together with her sister-in-law and friends for being in a car containing drugs. Asuema narrated being unaware that the drugs were in the car. As such, when the police told her not to "worry" and to just "sign the paper," she took this to mean that she would not be charged. She said, "I thought I will be released by the next morning," but instead, Asuema was charged, convicted, and eventually sentenced to 33 years in prison.

Two women mentioned being physically abused by the police. Zhong described her experience at the police station following her arrest as follows,

> There were a lot of documents that they [the police] asked me to sign and they didn't read them to me, and I didn't know what it meant. ... If I didn't sign, they would just slap me. After they hit me, whatever they asked me I just did it because I didn't want to get slapped so many times.

Kajsiab explained that, rather than going to the police station, she had been taken to a private house for questioning,

> At the house, the police pointed a gun at me and forced me to plead guilty [sign a document confessing to the crime]. They said if I don't plead guilty, they will kill me, and I was so scared.

In court, nearly one-third of women reported being without legal representation. They either thought it was unnecessary because they were pleading guilty or legal representation was not offered. For those women with legal representation, half had a public defender. Some said that public defenders were generally "trying to be helpful" and "gave advice." Others felt disillusioned, expressing that they "didn't care and only showed up in court," were "not reachable," "never advised anything but only said to plead guilty," and "seemed like [they were] just doing a routine job." Furthermore, those women with limited language skills reported being confused about what was happening in the courtroom. Naphe said that in court, "they asked me something, but I didn't understand what they said. Then they never talked to me again." The provision of a court interpreter for those women who struggled with Thai was rare.

Many women expressed angst around being sentenced to lengthy imprisonment terms after only a brief trial. They felt that they had neither the time nor the ability to explain themselves to the judge. These women articulated not being "completely sure of what the court said," and "felt that the court was not really listening to me but only listened to the police and their reports." Some women believed this judicial negligence was rooted in ethnic biases that positioned "people living in the mountains" as deviant/drug dealing "others." Hunb was arrested alongside her husband on drug possession charges. She explained that her husband had been selling drugs without her knowledge. The police discovered the drugs in the family home. She felt that "the court [and police] thought I am the drug dealer also just because there are a lot of Hmong involved with drugs." Similarly, Hu-Long had been arrested with her boyfriend in his car. Like Hunb, Hu-Long expressed being unaware the drugs were there. However, she felt the courts had "already judged me, they didn't listen to me. ... Because I came from the mountains, they have this sort of bias. They think I definitely was involved in drugs."

Several women also reported that they did not file appeals even when they thought the verdict of the first court was unfair because "nobody told me about the appeal," "nobody helped me do it," or they were afraid that, "it'd cost a lot to hire a lawyer and I didn't have money." One woman was told that she would need to pay a fee for filing an appeal, which is contrary to Thailand's Criminal Procedure Code.

Experiences of Imprisonment

Once in prison, the women reported experiencing several challenges at the intersection of gendered and racialized subjugation. Many of these issues arguably constituted breaches of the Bangkok Rules, and can be grouped under the following headings: admission, registration, and prison orientation; familial connection; healthcare; prison programs and work; everyday interactions with prison staff and inmates. We discuss the themes that emerged under each below.

Admission, Registration, and Orientation

Bangkok Rule 2 directs that during prison admission, registration, and orientation, all information must be provided to women in a language that they understand. However, no specific guidelines existed within the prisons regarding the endowment of language assistance. Instead, this generally rested on the altruism of staff within the individual prisons because formal interpretation services were not being used as a matter of course. For those women not proficient in spoken Thai, other prisoners who spoke their native languages were sometimes utilized as interpreters, creating an ad hoc, luck-based system with unequal access.

Familial Connection

It will be recalled that most of the women were mothers. As primary caregivers, separation from family, especially children, through incarceration can be especially distressing for women, and we know that familial connection is crucial to re-entry success (e.g., see Jeffries, Chuenurah, & Russell, 2020). Thus, prison systems that support the preservation of relational bonds are crucial to the well-being of women both during and post-incarceration. This gender-specific need for familial connection is clearly articulated in Bangkok Rule 26, which states that,

> women prisoners' contact with their families…shall be encouraged
> and facilitated by all reasonable means. Where possible, measures
> shall be taken to counterbalance disadvantages faced by women
> detained in institutions located far from their homes.

In Thailand's prisons, there is no access to public phones. Maintaining familial contact takes place through written correspondence and visitation, but both posed challenges for the women in this research.

First, they explained, that to write a letter, you must buy an envelope and stamp. This costs money that they found difficult to source because they simply did not have it. Some prison authorities, where possible, attempted to address this via the provision of financial support for buying stamps and envelopes. However, this was ad hoc and dependent on prison funds being available. Depending on the rules inside their institutions, the women were permitted to write letters once or twice a week. Practically, facilities with larger inmate numbers needed to restrict written correspondence to once a week. For security reasons, all letters must be screened by prison staff. Twice per week letter writing becomes untenable for staff working in prisons with larger inmate populations. Security screening also creates a specific set of problems for ethnic minority women because all letters must be written in Thai. Recall that few women had Thai literacy, and neither did their family members. It was therefore incumbent on the women to find a way to write or translate their letters into Thai. Typically, the women found a friend or cell-mate to help. For some, this peer assistance was given freely, but other women reported having to remunerate Thai inmates for their help, which they could ill-afford. Also, some women explained they could not send letters home, they did not know the address, or their houses were in remote highland areas without an address. Receiving letters could be as challenging as sending one. For example, one woman told us that even if she sent a letter, her family would find it very difficult to write back, since nobody in her family knew how to write.

Second, the women reported that visitation occurred during designated days of the week for 15 minutes per visit. Screens divided women from guests, and communication occurred through a telephone. All the women reported having received at least one visit from a family member during their incarceration. However, poverty, and the vast distances families needed to travel to reach the prisons, created barriers to more frequent visitation. For example, Hu-Long relayed that at one point she had only seen her family once in two years. This was particularly difficult because Hu-Long was serving a life sentence and had aging parents who she worried about. Since being transferred to a prison closer to her community, Hu-Long's sister is now able to visit her "every month." However, the distance is still "too far" for Hu-Long's parents, who she has not seen because they "are very old, they cannot travel here. I don't want to put the burden on them for traveling here." In one prison with an especially high ethnic minority population, prison authorities were trying to address these issues via the provision of twice-daily visitation.

Healthcare

International human rights standards are clear that the healthcare of prisoners is a state responsibility, and in prison, healthcare must be of equal standard to that available in the community (see United Nations Standard Minimum Rules for the Treatment of Prisoners, the Nelson Mandela Rules), (United Nations General Assembly, 2016). The Bangkok Rules directs further consideration of women prisoners' gender-specific healthcare needs (see Bangkok Rules 6, 7, 8, 10, 11, 12, 16, 17, 18). The first step in meeting the healthcare needs of women is to ensure that they undergo medical examination on admission to prison (see Bangkok Rule 6). Most of the women reported having received this initial medical screening, but approximately one-third had not. Since 2001, Thailand has implemented a universal healthcare system for those with citizenship, including prisoners. While the women who were Thai citizens (either by birth or through naturalization) were able to access free healthcare, including on admission, the remaining women expressed experiencing some difficulties in accessing adequate healthcare throughout their sentence.

For example, Gao-Jer explained that she had to pay for treatment outside prison because she only had a "pink card" for migrants. She said,

> whenever someone who doesn't have a Thai ID gets sick or has a
> serious sickness, the doctor always says you are not Thai, so you

need to pay for yourself, and you have to contact your parents or your relatives to come and pay for the medical cost.

Aam spoke about the disadvantages faced by prisoners who did not have relatives close by, highlighting that if the prison "did not have the medicines [she] needed, [her] relatives would need to get them." However, if prisoners did not have relatives or had relatives who could not visit, this left women without medical treatment. This put ethnic minority women at a distinct disadvantage because, for most, families resided long distances from the prison, and/or could not afford to pay for medical treatment due to poverty.

Furthermore, some women had problems communicating with the doctor because of language barriers, and other prisoners were assigned as their interpreters. This is a serious breach of the right to medical confidentiality. Bangkok Rule 8 makes it clear that "women prisoners," just like people outside prison walls, have "the right to medical confidentiality" and Bangkok Rule 11 states that, generally, "only medical staff shall be present during medical examinations" but if the presence of others (usually prison staff, not prisoners) is "necessary," examinations need to be "carried out in a manner that safeguards...confidentiality."

Bangkok Rule 48 specifies the need for special medical care and free access to a "healthy environment" for pregnant women, breastfeeding mothers, and children who stay with their mothers in prison. However, some of the women expressed that being from an ethnic minority group and not having Thai citizenship limited their access to these gender and child-specific health care provisions. Ye, a highlander cardholder without Thai citizenship, gave birth in prison. When Ye was pregnant, she did not have regular check-ups with the doctor, extra nutrition, extra vitamins, or food from the prison. After giving birth, Ye's baby developed a skin disease that was not treated properly because the prison did not have the resources. As a result, Ye made the heart-wrenching decision to send her baby to stay with her sister and friend back in the community.

Bangkok Rule 12 recognizes the gender-specific mental health needs of women in prison, and directs that "individualized, gender-sensitive, trauma-informed and comprehensive mental health care and rehabilitation programmes shall be made available." Prison itself can be a traumatizing experience for women, and this pain may be exacerbated for ethnic minority women who experience familial, community, and in turn, cultural dislocation. Furthermore, given the women's life history experiences (see previous), the need for therapeutic support is likely heightened for ethnic minority groups. Nearly half the women said that mental health support was available in prison, but it was not consistent, and sometimes came from other prisoners and prison staff, instead of trained mental health professionals. Aam said that during her nine years in prison, a psychologist only came to visit once. Arema mentioned that while a psychologist visited "once every three months, they didn't talk much [and] only asked general questions."

Even though Thai law restricts "non-Thai" prisoners' access to healthcare, within the individual prisons, efforts were being made to solve this problem. In some cases, prisons established close relationships with local hospitals and relied on their charity to provide treatment to these non-citizens for free. In other instances, prisons created fundraising foundations to pay for healthcare. Ye, for example (see previous), explained that, despite only having a highlander card, she gave birth in a hospital outside of the prison at no charge. However, since there was no centralized set of guidelines, consistency in the provision of healthcare to women varied across prisons because it was contingent on the goodwill of prison staff.

Programs and Work

Bangkok Rule 42 directs that woman shall have access to a balanced and comprehensive program of activities that consider their gender-specific needs. According to the Rules, gendered support in women's prisons must account for life history experiences, and the challenges women face while imprisoned (also see Bangkok Rules 29, 40, 41, 42). Acknowledging the intersection between gender and ethnicity/race, Bangkok Rule 54 further highlights that detained women from different religious and cultural backgrounds should receive comprehensive programs and services to address their distinct needs, and Bangkok Rule 55 elaborates that "pre and post-release services shall be reviewed to ensure that they are appropriate and accessible" to Indigenous women and those from ethnic and racially marginalized groups.

Every woman that could speak Thai said that they were able to participate in all prison programs. However, not being able to speak Thai hampered participation. For example, Naduo stated that she was not able to attend cooking and bakery "because of my language limitation." Efforts were being made to address this problem via the provision of Thai language classes. However, many of the ethnic minority women needed to engage in prison work to earn money. Familial poverty and dislocation meant they were unable to rely on family to provide them with financial support in prison which they needed, for example, to pay for healthcare, and this meant work needed to be prioritized over attending Thai language classes. Aruma stated that,

> if I go to study [Thai language] and I don't do work, they will reduce the amount of pay that I should receive for my work. That's why no one [i.e. ethnic minority women] wants to study.

Similarly, Kajsiab expressed "I did not take the course because I have no time to study. I have to work."

The ethnic minority women made money from a wide range of formal prison work activities, including sewing, baking, cooking, accounting, and making dolls. Their earnings ranged from 35 to 1,800 THB (one to 58 USD) per month for cooking and 35 to 400 THB (one to 13 USD) per month for sewing. Nearly half of the women mentioned engaging in informal work for other prisoners or prison staff to make extra money, for example, washing inmates' clothes and dishes, ironing, giving massages. Informal work did not pay well. Gao-Jer, narrated "there was [informal work like] ironing, washing clothes but it was very low pay."

Another point of contention for the women was the prison library. Research shows that prison libraries can play an integral role in the education, well-being (e.g., easing boredom and stress), and thus, rehabilitation of prisoners (Finlay & Bates, 2018). However, limited literacy in Thai meant that the prison library was of little benefit to ethnic minority women. Nayo relayed that, in the library, "90 percent are Thai books, and the rest are English and Chinese books. No ethnic languages." The only book that was regularly provided in the women's ethnic languages was the bible.

Finally, there was a general lack of cultural activities available to women in the prisons. Only four women mentioned that their prison organized an "ethnic sports day," where they could celebrate their cultures, wear traditional clothes, sing, dance, and play sports together. There was a lack of cultural activities available to women. Disconnection from culture can compound the pains of imprisonment and the isolation already felt from familial and community detachment.

Everyday Interactions with Prison Staff and Inmates

Protecting human rights and supporting women's opportunities to benefit from their stay in prison means that we must create environments that value safety, respect, dignity, and emotional well-being. As demonstrated above, the ethnic minority women in this research faced discrimination within their prison facilities on several fronts. This discrimination also extended to everyday interactions. While close to half of the women said they were never treated badly by other prisoners, others expressed that if you were an ethnic minority woman with limited on no ability to speak Thai, you might have a different experience. For example, Naqi said that Thai prisoners would heckle ethnic minority women who could not speak Thai with names such as "uneducated people," and Hu-Song relayed "for ethnic people who don't speak Thai, Thai prisoners don't like [them] and sometimes just say or talk with bad words [to them]." Aei reported having heard ethnic minority women being called names that mean "dirty" and "filthy." Dawb told us that she had been called "Kon Doi" and "Meao," which both loosely translates to "underdeveloped mountain people."

Others explained that access to resources could be blocked by Thai inmates, and that there was a clear inmate hierarchy between Thai and ethnic minority prisoners. Aam spoke about how "when you take a shower to wash your face or wash clothes if an ethnic minority prisoner goes and takes water, Thai prisoners tend to shout at them." Aruma said that between 5.30 p.m. and 6.00 p.m., Thai prisoners could go to the toilet if they wanted to, but ethnic minority women's access could be blocked by their Thai cellmates. She also stated that ethnic minority women's sleeping spaces were constricted by Thai inmates with whom they shared a cell. She explained, "Thai [women] have more space to sleep but not for me as I was not Thai." Thai prisoners also made sure they were able to wash their laundry first.

Nearly all the women expressed being treated well by prison staff. Nayo did note that if ethnic minority women could not understand Thai, the staff would "scold them." Dawb said, the prison staff scold old ethnic minority people who can't speak Thai and can't count numbers, saying that how can you, mountain people count drugs when you can't even count simple numbers?

Conclusion

Ethnic minority women imprisoned in Thailand are marginalized inside and outside prison walls. On the outside, the women in this research struggled with patriarchal systems of power, both within and beyond their communities. They were marginalized as women and by othering discourses, positioning ethnic minority communities as less than, problematic, and potentially "dangerous" peoples from the "hills." Under-education, poverty, living with state, community, familial and intimate partner violence, trauma, and other adversity were key aspects of the women's lives, and created the contexts from which they came into conflict with the law. The women faced challenges in accessing justice and once imprisoned, gender and ethnicity intersected in several domains to impact their carceral experiences. Precarious citizenship, language barriers, poverty, and the women's status as "chao khao" culminated in disconnection from family, community, and culture, restricted access to information, healthcare, education, training, and other rehabilitative opportunities, and sometimes redounded in prejudicial everyday interactions with inmates and prison staff.

The adoption of the Bangkok Rules has led to widespread recognition that human rights within prisons require us to respond to women's gender-specific needs. However, as this research suggests, women prisoners are not a uniform group, and, as such, in the short term at least, human rights behind prison walls requires a change in policy and practice to address the disadvantages faced by incarcerated women living with intersectional discrimination and oppression. Nevertheless, prisons cannot stop women from being criminalized because of actions they have taken in response to their gendered and racial subjugation. Ideally, therefore, what we should be striving for in the long-term, is sweeping social change that advances us toward substantive equality for Thailand's ethnic minority women.

Chapter 7

Older Women's Pathways to Prison in Thailand: Economic Precarity, Caregiving, and Adversity

Tristan Russell, Samantha Jeffries and Chontit Chuenurah

Abstract

In feminist criminology, there is a growing body of research exploring gendered pathways into prison. However, to date, this scholarship has not considered how age and gender may intersect to impact women's criminalization experiences. In this chapter, the authors have consequently chosen to explore older women's (aged 50+ years) narratives of their journeys to prison in Thailand using a feminist pathways approach. Results show several common threads in the stories of these women. Most were criminalized for the first time in later adulthood, had lived with various childhood and adulthood adversities, including, but not limited, to victimization and financial precarity, and had familial caretaking responsibilities. Many also recounted problems with substance misuse. Additionally, two relatively distinct pathways to prison emerged from the narratives: (1) economically motivated, (2) adversity, emotional distress, and addiction. A third pathway – intersectional, diffuse and unique – was also identified. It included themes from the first two pathways and the story of one woman that could not be categorized elsewhere. While the imprisonment pathways found mirrored those from previous pathways scholarship points of difference are noted.

Keywords: Older women; feminist pathways; Thailand; poverty; victimization; criminalization

Introduction

In 2003, the Thai government declared a war on drugs, compelling stringent changes in drug law, policy, and criminal justice practice. Today, as noted in the

Gender, Criminalization, Imprisonment and Human Rights in Southeast Asia, 93–107
doi:10.1108/978-1-80117-286-820221006

first chapter of this book, Thailand imprisons more women than any other country in Southeast Asia, there has been substantial growth in prisoner numbers, and it has the highest female incarceration rate in the region (Jeffries & Chuenurah, 2016). Within this castigating context, alongside the fact that Thailand's general population is rapidly ageing, the number of older people incarcerated has also risen from 1,785 in 2007 to 6,525 in 2020, and approximately 21% of Thailand's older prisoners are women (Chitswang, 2020; Fujioka & Thangphet, 2009).

Thailand was the driving force behind the development of the United Nations Rules for the Treatment of Women Prisoners and Non-Custodial Measures for Women Offenders (the Bangkok Rules) (United Nations General Assembly, 2010). This makes the comparatively high use of imprisonment for women in Thailand concerning. Furthermore, older women (aged 50+ years) in prison have been identified as a "minority within a minority," in that they face the intersectional disadvantages of both gender and age (Handtke, Bretschneider, Elger, & Wangmo, 2014; Leigey & Hodge, 2012; United Nations Office on Drugs & Crime, 2009). Knowing what brings older women into prison can help us to ensure that correctional systems are both gender and age responsive. However, to date, no existing studies have explored older women's incarceration pathways in Thailand or elsewhere. Utilizing a feminist pathways approach, this chapter reports findings from a qualitative life-history study of older women's journeys into the Thai prison system.

Prior Research

Beginning with Daly's (1994) seminal work, feminist pathways researchers have adopted a whole of life approach mapping the gendered experiences that lead women (and to lesser degree men) into the criminal justice system (Wattanaporn & Holtfreter, 2014). By unmasking the inimitable combination of frequently interconnected life-history factors driving women's criminalization, feminist pathways scholarship has contributed to the advancement of gender-responsive criminal justice policy, practice, and human rights standards, such as the Bangkok Rules (Owen, Wells, & Pollock, 2017; Wattanaporn & Holtfreter, 2014).

In general, feminist pathways studies demonstrate that women's imprisonment is underpinned by a grouping of interrelated life-history factors. These comprise victimization and trauma, substance abuse and other mental health problems, male influence and control, limited education, poverty, familial caretaking responsibilities, limited access to justice, and other adverse life experiences in childhood and/or adulthood. Although men's pathways are characterized by many of these same factors, women's experiences are gendered and distinct (Jeffries, Chuenurah, Rao, & Park, 2019).

Consider victimization and associated trauma. Studies of imprisoned women report higher rates of victimization (i.e., physical, sexual, and emotional abuse) and trauma exposure than in the general female population. Moreover, in contrast to male prisoners, victimization and trauma experiences are more common, start earlier, and last longer for women (Owen et al., 2017). Many criminalized women are victims of gender-based violence perpetrated against them during childhood and adulthood by predominately male family members (Artz, Hoffman-Wanderer, & Moult, 2012; Jeffries, Chuenurah, Rao, et al., 2019). Domestic violence, for example, is linked to women's criminalization in both direct and indirect ways. Directly, women may be threatened or coerced into acts defined by the state as criminal by abusive male, intimates or may come into conflict with the law because they "take the fall" for these men out of fear or love. Indirectly, domestic violence can have a negative economic impact limiting victimized women's financial means and leading them into prison for engaging in acts of economic survival (Jeffries, Chuenurah, Rao, et al., 2019).

In addition to victimization, research shows that criminalized women experience more adverse childhood (e.g., parental abandonment and loss, poverty) and adulthood events (e.g., relationship dysfunction, financial stress) than their male counterparts. Victimization, trauma, and other life adversities can spearhead mental health problems and associated substance abuse (as a form of self-medication), which then results in women coming into conflict with the law (Artz et al. 2012; Bloom, Owen, & Covington 2004; Cherukuri, Britton, & Subramaniam, 2009; Drapalski, Youman, Stuewig, & Tangney, 2009; Jeffries, Chuenurah, Rao, et al., 2019, Owen et al., 2017) .

Most imprisoned women have limited education, leading to poor employment prospects, and, in turn, economic precarity. Poverty is feminized and exacerbated by ageing. Women are more likely than men to live with financial hardship, and older women are more likely than their younger counterparts to live below the poverty line (Morris, 2014). Economic marginalization plays a key role in many women's pathways to prison and often intersects with family caregiving responsibilities. With low levels of education and limited employment prospects, women can find themselves imprisoned because of actions they have taken to support themselves and their families (Artz et al., 2012; Cherukuri et al., 2009; Jeffries & Chuenurah, 2018; 2019; Jeffries, Chuenurah, Rao, et al., 2019; Russell, Jeffries, Hayes, Thipphayamongkoludom, & Chuenurah, 2020).

Imprisoned women are commonly mothers and recurrently their family's only source of financial support. This is particularly so in non-western nations where women's familial caretaking extends beyond western ideals of the nuclear family. Women are often faced with sole responsibility for their children (children's fathers regularly abandon them), parents, grandparents, and other extended family members. In Thailand, there are cultural expectations placed on women to meet the needs of both immediate and extended family. Dutiful Thai daughters take care of their ageing parents and extended kin, including the provision of financial support (Angeles & Sunanta, 2009). In later adulthood, caring for grandchildren is a cultural expectation. A substantial proportion of older women in Thailand live with their grandchildren and commonly provide grandparental care, alongside their adult children. However, there is a growing trend, particularly in poorer rural communities, for parents to migrate to the city to find work, leaving their children behind, in the care of grandparents, in what is referred to as skipped-generation households (Ingersoll-Dayton, Punpuing, Tangchonlatip, & Yakas, 2018; Ingersoll-Dayton, Tangchonlatip, & Punpuing, 2020; Knodel & Nguyen, 2015). While adult children are expected to send financial remittances home to their parents, whether they are caring for grandchildren or not, it is noted that older Thai women are increasingly becoming "sole breadwinners" (Charoensuthipan, 2019).

Research also shows that women often come into conflict with the law because of intimate and familial relationships. Many women are in prison because they have found themselves entangled in the criminalized actions of the men in their lives (most frequently an intimate partner), and often, women's roles are secondary (Berko, Erez, & Globokar, 2010; Jeffries & Chuenurah, 2019). Finally, we know that in contrast to men, women's generally lower education levels and associated economic marginalization constrain their ability to access justice or take advantage of corrupted criminal justice systems (Cherukuri et al., 2009; Jeffries & Chuenurah, 2019; Russell et al., 2020).

Feminist pathways scholarship has, for the most part, failed to distinguish between older and younger women's criminalization. Instead, what is known about how older women come into conflict with the law derives from a handful of studies undertaken by life-course and developmental criminologists, and studies looking at the needs of older women in prison. Overall, this literature suggests that older criminalized women have either been in and out of prison throughout their lives or are convicted of an offense for the first time in later life (e.g., Block, Blokland, van der Werff, van Os, & Nieuwbeerta, 2010; Gunnison & McCartan, 2010; Moffitt, 2015; Simpson et al., 2016; United Nations Office on Drugs & Crime, 2009). In terms of the background characteristics, developmental and life-course research suggests that victimization (in childhood and adulthood), mental illness, substance misuse, and association with "deviant" peer groups are common for the former group of women but less frequent for the latter (e.g., Broidy, Payne, & Piquero, 2018; Gunnison & McCartan, 2010; Simpson et al., 2016). These findings are supported by research exploring the backgrounds of older imprisoned women, which also shows that social isolation and familial caregiving can feature in pre-prison life (Aday & Farney, 2014; Aday & Krabill, 2011; Arndt, Turvey, & Flaum, 2002; Baidawi, 2016; Davoren et al., 2015; De Smet, 2017; Greiner & Allenby, 2010; Steele, 2015).

However, the developmental and life-course research is predominantly concerned with quantitatively mapping "criminal careers" in terms of how these are shaped by the presence or absence of various "criminogenic" "risk factors." Statistically mapping the existence of certain variables fails to explain how these manifest in the lived experiences of women. Furthermore, prison research has been more concerned with the incarceration experiences of older women rather than how they came to be criminalized in the first place, and, as noted above, feminist pathways scholars have not specifically focused on this group of women. The current research provides a step toward addressing this by mapping and describing the pathways taken by a group of older women into the Thai prison system.

Methodology

We examined the narratives obtained via in-depth life-history interviews with 16 older women (aged 50 years and older) imprisoned in Thailand. The most common definition of "elderly inmate" has been those aged 50 years and over. While a 50-year-old person is not normally considered elderly, research undertaken by correctional health experts has consistently identified a 10 to 15-year differential between the overall health of prisoners and that of the general population (Grant, 1999). These studies attribute this difference to numerous life stressors (e.g., poverty, poor diet, substance abuse, other adversity) typical in the lives of criminalized people on the "outside" that negatively impact health and exacerbate ageing. Additionally, on the "inside," prisons are unhealthy environments with collateral consequences, including to life expectancy (Easton, 2018; Joynt & Bishop, 2018; Maschi & Aday, 2014; Wahidin & Aday, 2012). Every year spent in prison can decrease a person's life expectancy by two years (Patterson, 2013).

Our interview schedule was open-ended, encouraging women's responses to a broad range of discussion topics. This approach provided women with the opportunity to describe significant life events from childhood through to adulthood, and to analyze links between their varied life experiences and how they came into conflict with the law. The interviews with this group of older women were part of a more extensive program of research that involved three separate studies exploring gendered pathways into Thai prisons. These studies were undertaken between 2016 and 2019, and included interviews with women imprisoned throughout Thailand for multiple offenses.

Background Characteristics

Participants ranged from 50 to 63 years of age, with an average age of 54 years. They were generally under-educated, with 10 of the 16 women's schooling ceasing in grade 4. Close to 80% of the women identified as Buddhist.

Childhood Experiences

Most of the women had experienced some form of childhood adversity. This included severance of the parent/child relationship (through parental abandonment or death), living with poverty, and having to work from a young age to help support their families. Some recounted growing up in homes marred by family violence perpetrated by their fathers directly against them, their mothers, and/or siblings. One woman relayed, that at the age of 13 years, she had been raped and beaten by her boyfriend.

Adulthood Experiences

During adulthood, half the women experienced financial deprivation, and almost a third recounted having lived with domestic violence. Other intimate relationship challenges were also reported. Boyfriends and husbands were unfaithful, involved with illicit drugs, and many of these intimate relationships broke down. By the time they had entered adulthood, nearly half had a problem with substance misuse. Eight of the women had served previous terms of imprisonment. Most had come into conflict with the law for the first time in their 40s and 50s, and only one woman reported having been in and out of prison throughout her life, starting in her early twenties.

Criminal Justice System Experiences, Offenses, and Incarceration Terms

Three women reported that the police had asked them for bribe money, and two narrated having experienced police verbal and/or physical abuse. Three women relayed having been coerced or tricked into signing a "confession" document. When appearing before the courts, four women were without legal representation. Twelve were imprisoned for a drug offense. This included methamphetamine (Yaba[1] and Ice[2]) possession, trafficking, or distribution. Two women were incarcerated for fraud, one for murder, and one for a human trafficking offense. Imprisonment terms ranged from one year to life, with the majority sentenced to terms of between one and nine years.

Pathways to Prison

We mapped the life circumstances, experiences, and central mechanisms that constituted the women's pathways into prison. Three pathways emerged: (1) economically motivated, (2) adversity, emotional distress, and addiction, and (3) intersectional, diffuse and unique (see Table 4). The key features and common themes arising within each are described in detail below.

Table 4.   Pathways to Prison.

	$N = 16$
Economically motivated	10
Familial provisioning	7
Material desire	3
Adversity, emotional distress and addiction	3
Intersectional, diffuse and unique	3

Economically Motivated

The narratives of over half the women constituted the economically motivated pathway to prison, making it the most common trajectory. Everyone had engaged in criminal activity for monetary gain. However, there were two distinct subgroups. For seven of the women on this pathway, the central theme was one of

---

[1]Tablets containing methamphetamine and caffeine.
[2]Crystal methamphetamine.

pervasive life-long poverty and criminalization against the backdrop of economic familial provisioning. This stood in contrast to the remaining three women, who experienced relative economic privilege and offended out of an expressed desire to obtain more. Below we discuss, for each subgroup, the circumstances underpinning these women's imprisonment journeys.

Familial Provisioning. All these women were convicted and incarcerated for possessing, selling, or trafficking methamphetamine. Two of the women reported having used Yaba or Ice, and four had official criminal histories, having served previous terms of imprisonment. However, in every case, whether concerning the current criminalized event, previous entanglements with the criminal justice system, or drug use, the precursor was always financial necessity stemming from the need to provide for their families.

As children, all these women grew up in rural Thailand. They came from large families with between 4 and 10 siblings. Their parents and caregivers either worked as farmers or as low paid general laborers, and every woman described their childhood family situation as poverty-stricken. A lack of money within the familial home resulted in the women either never attending school or exiting education prematurely (between grades one and six). These penurious childhood circumstances compelled the women into different forms of adult work. The women described helping their parents undertake farm labor, working in factories as general labors, and/or undertaking domestic duties at home, such as caring for younger siblings, cooking, and cleaning.

Chantana, for example, left school in grade four. She explained that,

> [there were] nine children in the family including me, and it was tough for them [her parents] to take care of all of us... My parents told me that I should leave school and help them do farming, so I listened to them.

Suchin narrated,

> The reason why I didn't continue my study was because when my mother was working as a laborer, my father had never given us any money. My mother had more children, and we needed to help each other to take care of our family. There were grandmother and grandfather as well. I was around 11-12, I must take care of my younger siblings and grow rice. That is why I did not continue my study. [Then] when I was about 12-13 years old, I moved to Bangkok with my mother and helped her work at the construction site. We had to sleep at the construction camp.

For all these women, the poverty of childhood extended into adulthood. Here, under-education, resultant low paying employment, and intensifying pressure to provide for their families constrained the women's choices, leading them to be criminalized for actions they had taken to financially survive. Apra reflected that she would not have trafficked drugs across the Thai-Lao border if she had received a better education, because then she would have been able to get a "better job" and support her family through legitimate channels.

The women on this pathway all had children to support, and some had grandchildren, ageing parents, and other extended family members who were financially reliant on them. Most were the sole economic providers within their families because intimate partners (and the fathers of their children) were no longer around.

After Lamai's boyfriend died, she "got a job as a taxi driver" to support her three children, but could not "earn enough money." She started to use methamphetamine to stay awake so she could work longer hours, and was eventually arrested and imprisoned. Upon release, Lamai's ex-prisoner label made it even more difficult to find work. She narrated that her return to society "didn't work out as planned. I didn't have any money and couldn't find a job because I was an ex-prisoner." Lamai needed to support her "own children and nieces and nephews [because her] siblings were either in prison or had died." She decided to deliver methamphetamine for a friend because of "poverty," and was then arrested and imprisoned for a second time.

Other women found themselves solely responsible for economic familial provisioning because of intimate partner abandonment or illness. Vandia's husband had an affair and left. She started using yaba to,

> escape the sadness and give me the strength to work. When I did drugs, I had the strength to do the work and when I did work, I got money to provide to the family.

However, the money Vandia earned selling "vegetables" and "fish" at the market "was not enough, like all my life [and] so I sold drugs. I thought it would be a good way to make money. Life got easier selling drugs." When we spoke to Vandia, she was serving her third term of imprisonment. She told us, "it is like a cycle, I get released and there is not enough money, I sell drugs, get caught, released, sell drugs… I have to fight to [economically] survive."

Chariya was left as her family's only source of financial support after her boyfriend, who had a long-term addiction to methamphetamine, was imprisoned because "he got into a fight, the other person died." She worked in a restaurant "washing dishes" and used yaba "a couple of times," putting it in "energy drinks" to help her work longer hours. However, the "money [from washing dishes] was not enough." When a "friend" suggested that she go to Laos to collect drugs for "a lot of money," Chariya agreed to go. Chariya explained that "if I wasn't struggling with the financial problem, I wouldn't have gone to Laos."

Ying's 72-year-old husband was unable to work due to "heart disease." She explained that this left her as "the only one who was responsible for taking care financially of the [adult] children and grandchildren." Two of Ying's adult children were "addicted to drugs" and unable to care for their children, leaving Ying, at the age of 60 years, with the responsibility of supporting five of her grandchildren. She narrated her angst around her children's drug use, stating, "I really hate drugs, my children they use drugs, and I don't want them to." She told us that, despite her best efforts, her children "didn't quit." Ying had tried to support her family by selling "things" at the market, but "couldn't make ends meet, we had a lot of debt." She decided to sell methamphetamine because "if I hadn't of dealt drugs, we wouldn't have had enough to live because I have the grandchildren who need the milk, need food." Selling drugs enabled Ying to feed her grandchildren, send them to "pre-school," and look after her husband.

However, Ying was eventually arrested and imprisoned. Upon release from her first term of incarceration, she attempted to "sell things" at the market again, but by now she had a chronic health condition, which made this type of work particularly difficult. She explained,

> I have diabetes. Often, I feel like I don't have any strength. I have
> pain in my joints, and I feel numb every day when I wake up and
> I feel very tortured.

Additionally, Ying was suffering emotionally. She said, "if I think about life, sometimes I get teary and I cry and I think about how I have been struggling [financially] all my life." Three months after being released from prison the first time, Ying returned to "drug selling" because "I had no idea what to do for a living, I had to make ends meet for the family and I didn't know what to do." Now, back behind prison walls, Ying was worried every day "about the grandchildren, will they have food to eat, will they get to go to school?"

The remainder of the women had boyfriends or husbands who also worked, yet the money was still not enough. Chantana relayed, "our income from farming was very little. We had such a hard time living day by day." Chantana had cared for her elderly parents for many years (they eventually passed away) and decided to sell drugs because "we didn't have enough money to pay for the kids' school, water, or electricity." Apra and her husband also struggled to support their children and Apra's ageing mother. As noted previously, Apra was imprisoned for trafficking drugs because she "needed to support her family."

Suchin and her husband met working at a construction site. She explained,

> both of us were poor, we worked at the construction site. We
> stayed at the construction camp at the site. When we had children,
> we still lived there. We both had no house or our own land. We just
> moved when the camp is moved to other places.

Later in life, like Ying, Suchin found herself financially responsible for her grandchildren, due to her adult son becoming "addicted" to methamphetamine. At this time, Suchin was selling "food in front of a temple" to earn a living because, as she aged, construction work had become too physically taxing. She explained how she decided to offend as follows,

> My oldest child had his own family, and he was selling and using drugs. He told me to take care of those three kids. So, I had to take care of my three grandchildren. He did not even help me with the money. One day, [when I was selling food outside the temple] a teenager came to me and asked if I was okay with this burden. Because I had to pay for everything, such as food, clothes, everything. So, I replied to him I had no money. I knew that he had drugs. He suggested me to take the drugs, sell them, then when I got money, I had to bring it to him. And that time was the time when I got arrested. I only thought that I need money for my grandchildren. My family needed to have something to eat every meal. I was poor, and I had no choice. I did not receive good education [only attended school in grade 1] and I had to take responsibility in taking care of my family.

Material Desire. The remaining three women in the economically motivated pathway were driven by the material desire to obtain more, rather than economic familial survival. Unlike the women above, these women described being raised in economically privileged middle-class families, and had concomitantly higher levels of education. Kanda attended university, while Preeda and Sarai both graduated from high school. As adults, they described owning lucrative businesses, and Sarai also worked at a bank. None of these women was serving time for drug offending, or had prior convictions. Kanda and Sarai were imprisoned for fraud, while Preeda was convicted of human trafficking-related offenses.

When Kanda was in technical school, she "start to have an idea that I had a way to earn my own money…I start to have this little loan group at the school." After she graduated, she started working in a shop that sold electronic devices, but she wanted to make more money, so "I also sold underground lottery." She used the money she made from this to buy a car and a house. Then, she started selling land and taking out loans, but "when I did not return the money in time for these people that I got a loan from, they sue me for the cheque, and the cheque is bounce." She said her income before her arrest was,

> a lot… it's like playing gambling and you make a lot of profit. I make 800,000 THB [255,200 USD] from another land profit within a month. So, I got carried away.

Sarai owned a restaurant and worked in a bank, where she started obtaining credit cards under the names of friends and associates, drawing down the money and keeping it for herself. In total, Sarai defrauded 300,000 THB (10,000 USD) from the bank. She told us that she did not really "need it" [the money], I would still be able to survive "but this [committing fraud] was [a] quicker [way]" to renovate the restaurant.

Unlike Kanda and Sarai, Preeda was not convicted of fraud. Rather, she was imprisoned for sex trafficking. Preeda and her husband had a successful karaoke bar business, which "hired" 20 young women from Cambodia to provide sexual services to male clients. She explained that initially,

> my intention was [just to] open a karaoke bar, but the girls who work at my place, they were already working like that [sex work]. And I just thought there might be a way to attract customers... the client would pay 500 THB [16 USD]; I will take 250 THB [8 USD] and the girl will take 250 THB.

Preeda explained that she and her husband were financially well-off before starting their new business, but "got a lot more money [operating the karaoke bar] and we could buy a second house from the profits." Preeda's father was a police officer, and with these connections, she was able to pay bribe money to ensure that the authorities "turned a blind eye." The "girls stayed in one room together" on-site at the karaoke bar, but one of these young women "ran away, someone found her, then send her to the immigration office." A human trafficking organization then interviewed the young woman. This triggered police action. Preeda was arrested, charged, and imprisoned.

Adversity, Emotional Distress, and Addiction

Chailai, Busaba, and Hansa constituted this imprisonment trajectory. All had suffered through childhood adversity, including living in abusive familial environments. As teenagers and/or adults, they were intimately involved with men who mistreated them. Some had lived with domestic violence, while others endured intimate partner infidelity, abandonment, and/or were partnered with men who abused drugs. Unlike the women on the previous pathway who used methamphetamine to increase their ability to work, all these women reported substance misuse as a form of self-medication, a way to cope with the stress and trauma of their lives. While also struggling financially, none of these women's offending was directly motivated by monetary gain. Rather, childhood adversity, compounded by problems in intimate relationships, manifested in them harming themselves through substance abuse, leading to them selling drugs to support their dependence, and in the case of Hansa, harming others through interpersonal violence. Two of the women on this pathway had an official criminal history.

Chailai never went to school, she grew up in a "slum," and lived with her father perpetrating domestic violence against her mother. She narrated "they fight very often. He [father] hit my mother, he breaks her head." Chailai described her father as an "alcoholic and thug [who also] used heroin," and explained that this made her feel "sad, I hated men." Chailai's parents later abandoned her, leaving her in the care of extended family members. When she was 13 years old, Chailai moved in with her boyfriend, who sniffed glue, raped her, and "hit me every day." Chailai became pregnant and miscarried "three babies" between the ages of 15 and 17 years because of the physical assaults she endured. She started sniffing glue as a coping mechanism. As an adult, Chailai endured more domestic violence in intimate relationships with other men, who she described as "party animals" who drank too much "alcohol" and "cheated" on her. By the time Chailai was in her 30s, she was working in a "bar," and became "addicted" to methamphetamine after being introduced to it by her work colleagues. She sold drugs in partnership with another physically abusive boyfriend to support her habit. She had one prior conviction on her criminal record, and was at the time of the interview, in prison for selling drugs.

Like Chailai, Busaba was under-educated (left school in grade 4), she had lived with domestic violence as a child, and during adulthood, was the victim of intimate partner abuse. After being abandoned by her domestically violent boyfriend, Busaba started drinking alcohol "every day" because it "makes me forget things." Eventually, she described being "addicted" to methamphetamine, which she also sold to support her dependence. Busaba had also been introduced to drugs by her co-workers while working in a bar. She was eventually imprisoned for selling drugs, her second term of incarceration for this type of offending.

Hansa grew up in a family characterized by poverty and family violence. Her father would "slap mum and maybe slap her in her face or smash her head," and would "hit us [Hansa and her siblings] with a small stick that we used for fishing. It hurt." Hansa had a limited education, having left primary school in grade four because "we were really poor, life is really difficult. I took care of all [my] younger siblings." As an adult, Hansa was married to a man who was "addicted to gambling." He had an affair and left Hansa when she was eight months pregnant with their child. Her second boyfriend was also "addicted to gambling" and "just disappeared," abandoning her and the children. When her brother went to prison (for drug offending), she had to take care of his two children, as well as her daughter, and her granddaughter. Hansa began abusing alcohol, directing her harm inward at herself. She explained that she consumed alcohol "every day" because "I was stress[ed]." When she could no longer deal with the stress, she directed her harm outwards onto her nephew who stole "something from the house again but would not admit it." Hansa relayed,

> I was really drunk on that day... I ask who took the money... none of them would accept it. And the teachers at school informed me that this boy stole things at school, so I use a stick to hit the boy and hold his head in the bucket that fills with water. I was really drunk. And [then] I left.

Hansa's nephew died, and she went "on the run" for a few years, before returning and being arrested for his murder.

Intersectional, Diffuse and Unique

The pathways to prison taken by the final three women did not fit well with the trajectories previously described. Kalaya and Chalerm both had prior convictions for selling drugs, and while their past actions could be classified under the economic familial provisioning pathway, in that this had occurred against a backdrop of life-long poverty and familial economic need, they were currently imprisoned for taking "the rap" to protect their grandchildren and adult children. Thus, the pathways of both women could be classified as being intersectional and diffuse.

Chalerm narrated initially using drugs so that she could work longer hours in the rice fields to earn more money to support her three children. Eventually, she also sold drugs "occasionally" to bolster familial income. This resulted in her being imprisoned for drug dealing the first time. Upon release, Chalerm did not re-offend, but her adult son was using and selling methamphetamine out of the family home. She explained that her son had mental health issues, and to protect him, she "took the blame." Similarly, Kalaya sold drugs to support "my children and there was not enough money, [we were] poor and in debt. That was the first time I was arrested; this time is my second." After serving a seven-year prison term, Kalaya relayed that, upon release, she had "worked so hard. I did everything. I never thought I would go back to drugs again." However, having an adult son who used and sold drugs in the family home eventually resulted in Kalaya being arrested and imprisoned for a second time. To protect her grand-child's future, Kalaya decided to shoulder the responsibility, explaining,

> one person needed to go with the police. I had to be that person because my daughter in law had a baby to take care of. I told the police that those drugs were all mine.

Finally, Ubon was a first-time offender imprisoned for a drug offense, and her offending trajectory was unique because it was not economically motivated, there was no indication of adversity, trauma, or emotional distress leading to substance misuse, and she had not "taken the rap" out of care for a family member. As a child, Ubon was raised in a loving middle-class family. As an adult, she married a "good husband." This relationship broke down because Ubon "was bad…I used drugs." "Some teenagers" introduced Ubon to Ice when she was "40 something." She explained, "I just walked to them and asked if I could try [because] I was lonely and bored." Ubon started using Ice "every day," despite her now-adult children and ex-husband supporting her and begging her to stop.

Discussion and Summary

Nearly every woman in this research came into conflict with the law for the first time in her 40s and 50s. The predominant pathway was that of economic famil-ial provisioning. Many of the women were criminalized, for a drug offense, in response to life-long poverty and needing to provide for their families, includ-ing children, ageing parents, other extended family members, and, later, grand-children. Low levels of education, due to childhood poverty, had excluded these women from well-paying legitimate employment. To make "ends meet," some women started to use methamphetamine to increase work productivity. This invariably resulted in substance dependence. Some decided to sell drugs. Others took the blame for the drug offending behaviors of their adult children because they wanted to protect either them, or their grandchildren, from the negative impacts of imprisonment. For others, addiction, and, in turn, criminalization, evolved in response to adversity, including victimization, trauma, and associated psychological distress. In other words, most of the women were in prison due to the criminalization of impoverishment, or victimization associated with trauma and substance abuse. A few "more privileged" women offended out of a desire for expediential financial gain, or because using drugs made life more interesting.

The pathways to prison taken by the older women mirror those found in the previous feminist pathways literature. Poverty, familial caregiving, victimization, trauma, and substance abuse were central to many stories. There were nevertheless points of contrast between the experiences of older women in this research and those found in previous feminist pathways scholarship. We know that older people are more likely to live with poverty than their younger counterparts, and older women are at the greatest risk because poverty is both feminized and exacerbated by ageing (Morris, 2014). Economic precarity plays a key role in many women's pathways to prison and often intersects with family caregiving responsibilities, but may play out differently in the lives of older women.

The stories told above illustrate how familial caregiving and economic precarity can present differently in older women's prison trajectories, and how ageing may intensify financial hardship. As the women grew older, some faced problems with their health, and this limited their capacity to earn a legitimate living, a problem made worse for those who carried the stigma of the ex-prisoner label. For some, drug use gave them the strength to keep working as their bodies aged and health waned. Drug use to "stay strong" and continue working is not a story commonly told by younger women who have the physical advantages of youth. Furthermore, in contrast to younger women who are often criminalized for actions taken to support their growing children in the wake of intimate partner abandonment, some of the older women in this research found themselves in the role of primary familial provider due to the death or failing health of their ageing husbands. Others explained that they were imprisoned because they needed to care for grandchildren and adult children who were unable to contribute to familial income due to mental illness (including substance abuse).

Finally, and in contrast to prior studies, domestic violence as a directed pathway into prison was absent from the older women's stories. None of the women came into conflict with the law because of being threatened or coerced by intimate partners nor did they "take the fall" for husbands or boyfriends out of fear or love. None of the women was incarcerated due to entanglement in the criminalized acts of intimate partners. Instead, some "took the rap" for their adult children out of love for them and their grandchildren.

Knowing what brings older women into prison can help us to ensure that prison systems are appropriately responsive to gendered and age-related requirements. Tentatively, as is the case for younger women, this research points to the need for gender-responsive, trauma-informed care, practice, and programming, including substance misuse treatment. Given the centrality of family in the lives of women, prison systems should also encourage and support familial connectedness wherever possible. Of particular importance, given the relationship between poverty and criminalization, and what we know about the feminization of poverty, particularly for older women, is the provision of vocational training within prisons that will lead to age-appropriate adequately paying post-release employment. However, can we expect older women to indefinitely bear the burden of economic familial provisioning as they continue to age? Prison reform should only be an interim step. Ideally, the state needs to stop criminalizing and imprisoning women's survival strategies. Women must be extended the support they need to live free of poverty, heal from trauma and adversity, and achieve quality of life in older age in community, not behind prison walls.

Chapter 8

Transgender Prisoners in Thailand: Gender Identity, Vulnerabilities, Lives Behind Bars, and Prison Policies

Jutathorn Pravattiyagul

Abstract

Transgender prisoners are subject to violence of many kinds. They are tortured, beaten, sexually assaulted, raped, and denied access to qualified public health services. This is because legal and justice systems in most countries disregard the unique conditions, needs, and requirements of transgender people. Transgender prisoners around the world suffer from mental health issues and lack of continuous access to sexual health services and hormone treatment. Like most countries in Southeast Asia, and regardless of a significantly large population of transgender prisoners, Thailand still provides no standard policies on how transgender prisoners should be managed, and transgender prisoners' experiences remain under-researched. Through an anthropological and gendered lens, this chapter theoretically and practically examines transgender prisoners' gendered life experiences behind bars in Thailand, debates transgender prisoners' vulnerabilities and the myths behind them, identifies challenges around gendered-housing, analyses cultural nuances of Thai (trans) gender performativity in prisons, discusses the impact of heterosexual-binary prison management, and offers real-world policy recommendations, which are urgently needed by the Thai justice and correctional system.

Keywords: Transgender; prisoners; Thailand; human rights; gender performativity; prison policies

Gender, Criminalization, Imprisonment and Human Rights in Southeast Asia, 109–124
Copyright © 2022 by Jutathorn Pravattiyagul
Published under exclusive licence by Emerald Publishing Limited
doi:10.1108/978-1-80117-286-820221007

Introduction

As Thai law does not recognize transgender identity, a structural hierarchy of discrimination by social and legal institutions is systematically exacerbated. This discrimination impacts the rights of transgender people in Thailand to employment, education, access to welfare and healthcare, and more (Jackson, 1999; Jenkins, Pramoj na Ayutthaya, & Hunter, 2005; Mahidol University, Plan International, United Nations Educational, Scientific and Cultural Organization, 2014; Pramoj na Ayutthaya, 2003; Pravattiyagul, 2018). Stigmatization and discrimination against transgender people through social structures and policies have pushed transgender people to the margins of society (United Nations Development Programme & Ministry of Social Development & Human Security, 2018) where they are vulnerable to human trafficking, sex work, drug networks, and are at higher risk of sexually transmitted infections (STIs) (see UNAIDS, 2014). Finally, the unwillingness of many legitimate businesses and the public sector to hire them leads many transgender people to lives of transgression and crime.

This chapter offers an important corrective to scholarly literature in which the story of transgender prisoners is a story of victimhood. Evidence from around the world emphasizes that behind bars, transgender prisoners must confront increasing risks stemming from discrimination, including extreme forms of physical and sexual violence (Rodgers, Asquith, & Dwyer, 2017; Tanguay, 2019). They are habitually tortured, beaten, raped, and denied access to qualified public health services (Tanguay, 2019), and they have a higher rate of self-harm and suicide than cis-gender[1] male and female prisoners (Lynch & Bartels, 2017). I do not dispute any of this. However, findings from my anthropological research in Thai prisons indicate that the dominant narrative is certainly not the only experience and may not be the dominant experience of Thai transgender prisoners. Some prisoners I interviewed described power nuances that are absent from earlier studies or even described themselves as sexual predators in male wings. They also discussed how their transgender identity empowered them to position themselves higher in social hierarchies within Thai prison settings.

Even though more than 4,300 transgender prisoners are living in Thai prisons (Prachatai, 2018), Thailand has not drafted official national standard policies on how these prisoners should be managed. Transgender prisoners' vulnerabilities and the myths behind them, including life experiences behind bars and the impact of heterosexual-binary prison management and policies, have not received the scholarly attention they deserve. The limited evidence makes it difficult to analyze the dynamics of the Thai justice system's infrastructure, much less assess the quality of rehabilitation and prospects for social reintegration. My qualitative research data and anthropological analysis in this chapter contribute new empirical knowledge of transgender prisoners using the Thai context as the main case study. In addition to addressing the situation of trans prisoners, this

---

[1]Cis-gender describes a person whose gender identity is identical to their sex assigned at birth.

anthropological work examines their gender identity formation/reproduction behind bars and how trans prisoners use their transgender identity and vulner-abilities to strategically negotiate power and to even improve their position in the social hierarchy. An examination of the implications of this analysis facilitates the generation of policy recommendations that, when implemented, can enhance transgender prisoner safety and minimize the risk of human rights violations.

Methodology and Reflexivity

This research project used mixed qualitative methods that focused on the lived everyday practices of transgender prisoners in Thailand. The research was conducted in prisons in Bangkok and Pattaya City where large populations of Thai transgender people live within the confines of prison walls. During 2019, interviews were conducted with 18 transgender prisoners, 5 guards, 1 correc-tional officer, officers of 2 LGBTIQA+-related NGOs, 7 cis-gender male prison-ers and 6 cis-gender female prisoners.[2] Participation took the form of in-depth semi-structured interviews, focus group interviews and interactive observation. I managed to interview each participant for more than three hours (over sev-eral sessions), and each interactive observation session continued for more than five hours. I was allowed to visit both male and female wings. Narratives from transgender prisoners contained data that enabled me to grasp their reflexive meanings and to further understand the experiences and interpretations of the many gendered aspects of life in the Thai prisons.

However, limitations of this anthropological research include the small scale of the study and constraints on access to some prison areas and facilities, both of which hindered comprehensive data collection. Furthermore, guards were pre-sent for interviews in the male wings, and their presence, in my opinion, worked as a constraint on the participants to reveal information. Finally, all prisoner participants were selected by prisons' guards, who explained that the selected par-ticipants "behave better." From my observation, the guards seemed to expect the selected prisoners to respond in ways that would not damage the reputation of the establishment.[3]

When guards were listening, participants were more reluctant to describe negative experiences. On many occasions when head guards were not too close, participants revealed much more intimate information to me. In the female wings, during the first hours, the officers formally showed me around the facili-ties and explained some practicalities. Afterwards, I was allowed to perform my ethnographic study. I was allowed to hang out casually with prisoners, without officers following us. Observations noted during these hours generated insightful

---

[2]More information regarding participants and interviews cannot be revealed due to personal safety and professional security of informants.
[3]The prison guards were very attentive during the first hours of the interviews. Later, from loads of work and boredom, they became less attentive. While in the female wings, after the first hours I was left alone with the prisoners.

narratives about identity, experience and conditions that have not been presented in earlier criminological or anthropological studies. After situating trans-ness, this chapter will discuss the cultural nuances of trans identities, performativity in hetero-binary prisons, gendered experiences behind bars, as well as provide practical policy recommendations for trans prisoner management in Thailand.

Before returning directly to trans identity in Thailand, the global meaning of "hermaphroditism" and "transgenderism" as understood in the anthropological literature should be discussed. Hermaphroditism, which describes individuals who carry both male and female genitalia, has existed throughout history and across cultures. Such individuals have appeared in mythology and sacred texts.[4] These global mythologies reflect fluidity and compatibility of femininity and masculinity (Duangwises, 2014). Anthropologists see blendings of male/female gender as cultural productions (Herdt, 1987; Ramet, 1996). The idea that a person can play both male and female gender roles relates to social order and cultural construction. Anthropologists have learned that, historically, transgender individuals are both respected and responsible for special duties, such as being shamans who connect with spirits, gods, and deceased family members, or being local doctors, fortune tellers or leaders of spiritual ceremonies (Duangwises, 2012).

Note, however, that these and other characteristics of Thai trans identities are beyond the experience of Western transgender persons and therefore might be under-emphasized or even disregarded completely in studies of transgender phenomena in the West. From such starting points, scholars would be unprepared to engage with the Thai term *Kathoey*, which is used to explain the term *"Bhun-doh"* which first appears in Buddhist scriptures, in a story where it describes

> a man who gives oral sex to other men, a man who enjoys seeing other men having sex, a man with one testicle, a man who becomes *Bhun-doh* occasionally, a man with sexual flaws or sexual ambiguity.[5]

The word has been used since then to describe people who differ from sexual norms in some ways, but not all. By the 1990s, the concept came to be perceived as describing a person whose sexual ambiguity is acknowledged by Thai people as a "third sex" (เพศที่สาม), which intervenes between male and female (Jackson, 2004; Morris, 1994).

Kathoey signifies a distinct sexual axis that does not abolish the male/female binary. Dissimilar to Western interpretations of transgenderism, *Kathoey* includes both transsexuality and transgenderism (Morris, 1994) and occasionally also male homosexuality (Jackson, 1999) and for some local communities, lesbianism.

---

[4]The Ancients' engagement with transgenderism includes (but is by no means limited to) Hindu god Ardhanarishvara, Hermaphroditus in Greek mythology, Inari in Japanese culture, Sumerian goddess Inanna, and Ometotl, the source of the Aztec universe.
[5]Information from Museum of Siam (www.museumofsiam.org).

Studies of the identities of LGBTIQA+ people in the global south have challenged Foucault's post-structuralist discussion of sexuality as a Eurocentric and universalizing framework (See Jackson, 1997). In contemporary Thai culture, transwomen describe themselves as "a woman in a man's body" or "a man with a woman's heart": (i) *Kathoey* (กะเทย), (ii) "second-type women" (สาวประเภทสอง) and (iii) "transsexual women" (ผู้หญิงข้ามเพศ) (See Pravattiyagul, 2018). The transman gender identity is generally termed *Tom*, a term that originated from the English word *Tom*boy. Unlike transman identity in the Western contexts, *Tom* identity is positioned against both norm-constrained Thai femininity and masculinity. Compared with "typical" transmen in Europe, *Tom*s have very different attitudes toward romantic relationships and sex (Sinnott, 1999).

Regardless of cultural nuances of trans identities in Thailand, Thai authorities and prison management officers have explained that they categorize trans prisoners into four categories. (1) ผู้หญิงข้ามเพศ (*Phuying-Kham-Phet* or transsexual woman in English) denotes a person assigned as male at birth. Later in life, this person underwent sex-reassignment surgery. She now has female genitals and lives as a woman. (2) กะเทย (*Kathoey* or transgender woman in English) denotes a person assigned as male at birth. Later in life, this person began to live in accordance with her inherent feminine gender identity. She continues to have male genitals but might have undergone breast surgery. (3) ผู้ชายข้ามเพศ (*Phuchai-Kham-Phet* or transsexual man in English) denotes a person assigned as female at birth. Later in life, this person underwent sex-reassignment surgery. He now has male genitals and lives as a man. (4) ทอม (*Tom* or transgender man in English) denotes a person assigned as female at birth. Later in life, this person began to live in accordance with his inherent masculine gender identity. He continues to have female genitals but might have undergone breast surgery.

The Gender Equality Act B.E. 2558 (2015) is the first Thai law to "indirectly" protect hate crime toward transgender people. It also implies that it is legal to be "a person who has a sexual expression different from that person's original sex" (Kaleidoscope, 2016, p. 3). Furthermore, it makes discrimination on the basis of gender or sexuality a criminal offense punishable by imprisonment for up to six months (Kaleidoscope, 2016, p. 3). In spite of this more positive direction, legal protections against discrimination on the basis of sexual orientation and gender identity are still deficient. Under Thai law, trans people continue to have fewer rights and protections than cis-gender people have, and they continue to have limited legal recourse in response to the complications and humiliations that are a part of their daily lived experience. There are limits to their right to have official documents that reflect their sexual identity, they face employment issues, and they are subject to a range of challenges regarding social welfare, education, health and well-being, legal recognition of same-sex union, family law, rights to adoption, rights to go to gender-appropriate prisons, and so on (Pravattiyagul, 2018). Legal documentation and legal status issues of trans people have been the objects of a heated debate in Thailand for the past decade. Although the country's proportion of transwomen is well above average, the inability to change their legal status affects trans people's lives: no matter how they identify, and even if they have gone through sex-reassignment surgery, their personal documents say they are the sex assigned at birth, they are treated in the wrong section and by the wrong methods when they are hospitalized, and they are incarcerated together with people who have the same genitalia as they have.

Thai prisons are separated into male and female wings and prisoners are assigned wings on the basis of their existing genitals. *Phuying-Kham-Phet* or transsexual women with female genitalia are housed in female wings, *Phuchai-Kham-Phet* or transsexual men with male genitalia are housed in male wings. Prisoners whose genetalia are ambiguous are assigned to the wing on the basis of their sex as assigned at birth and reported on their government documents. Correctional officers and guards I interviewed informed that Thai prisons have housed large numbers of *Kathoeys* and *Toms*, smaller numbers of *Phuying-Kham-Phet*, and as yet not a single *Phuchai-Kham-Phet* (transsexual man). *Kathoeys*, with female breasts and male genitalia, are housed in male wings. During the interviews, authorities reasoned that due to long-term severe overcrowding issues in Thai prisons, in their opinions, this is the best system for overall prison safety, prison management, and prison discipline that reduces harm, sexual harassment and rape.

Guards in Bangkok[6] recalled that several years back one correctional authority, inspired by best practices as recommended by international human rights organizations and successful housing models from other countries, had organized a pilot housing project in their remand prison. Transwomen prisoners were housed separately from all cis-gender prisoners. Data from internal studies, risk assessments and evaluations were unambiguous: transwomen prisoners inflicted more harm on one another than cis-gender males and females had inflicted on them. Separation from the general prison population also seemed to exacerbate psychological issues, including depression. Many prisoners in the separated trans wing requested to be moved back to male or female wings, as they felt abused and unhappy sharing spaces with gender-equivalent people. The correctional authority, thus, withdrew the plan to have separate housing for trans people.

Cultural Nuances of Trans Identities: Performativity in Hetero-Binary Prisons

Housing of transgender prisoners is a challenging issue around the world, and one-size-fits-all regulations are often inappropriate, due to variations in cultural norms. When attempted, transgender prisoners encounter the vital ideologies that underpin the rigid binary cis-normative environment that defines the modern Western correctional system (Jenness & Fenstermaker, 2014). Remarkably, when I asked Thai trans prisoners about their perception of housing policies, they replied that they are very satisfied with the current housing regulations. Some explained that seemingly conservative, gender-binary housing policy allows space for transgender prisoners to perform and reproduce their personal gender identities and perform as themselves (see Butler, 2002). Many trans participants,

---

[6]Name of prison is protected due to informants' professional security.

especially *Tom* and *Kathoey* prisoners, informed that prison sub-cultures allow them to perform their gender identity in a more open way than they could in the outside world. They feel more social acceptance from other cis-gender prisoners, and they are given more opportunities to have serious relationships, to create their own sub-culture and customs. Participants also clarified that they feel that their masculine/feminine identity is confirmed by being in relationships and having sexual intercourse with cis-gender prisoners in both wings. As one prisoner explained,

> Nobody dreams of being jailed. But I have to say that I am more socially accepted here than I was in the outside world. As you know, general Thai society is not fond of *Tom*s. But since I got here, I am much more sexually desired in female wings. It is a totally different world in here. Usually, newcomers take some time to adjust to the ethos. Many straight women became *Dee*[7] here. It is common that *Dee* and even transsexual women fight over *Tom*s in female wings. All of us here have serious girlfriends. We get to sleep next to our girlfriends and to even have sex with them. We get to be much more macho in the female wings because there are probably no other male figures here, I guess. I very much prefer to be jailed in the female wing than male wing. I have the heart of a male person but I still have female genitalia. There are thousands of male prisoners in male wings walking freely, *Tom*s will for sure not be safe from rape or sexual assault there.
> (This prisoner self-identifies as a *Tom*, 26 years old, convicted for selling drugs and sentenced to 17 years in prison).

Transexual women or *Phuying-Kham-Phet* prisoners emphasized that they feel uncomfortable and unsafe in male wings. However, *Kathoey* groups in this study clarified to me how personally and (they claimed) all *Kathoey* prisoners prefer to be in male wings, even though some have female breast implants. *Kathoey*s seem to be the most satisfied group that live according to the sex assigned at birth on the male wings. When asked about sexual harm toward transgender people in prisons, many *Kathoey*s themselves explained to me that they think *Kathoey*s are more dangerous than men especially if they gather in groups because *Kathoey*s sexually harass men more than the reverse. As one prisoner explained:

> Imagine the lives of prisoners, especially those who have to live in confinement for many years. After a few months, life becomes meaningless and depressing. Families and friends come visit you less and less. You just have to find a way to survive. That includes integrating to the new prison society, to make friends and have relations

---

[7]*Dee* describes a more feminine lesbian and derives from the English word "Lady." The term denotes a woman who is attracted to and dates Toms.

with people here. It is your whole new world; you have to adjust a lot. For *Kathoey*s here, to have a relationship with a male prisoner gives meaning, excitement and hope in here. I feel more needed by male prisoners here. They are of course more attracted to *Kathoeys*. After some months, I accepted that this will be my life, I joined my *Kathoey* gang in here and we have quite a lot of fun together. I will never ever go to female wings. I do not want to live with females. So much drama. There would be lots of fights with them. Another thing is, we have penises. We will eventually have sexual urges and I definitely do not want to have sex with women. [...] No, we are not under risk of being harassed, at least not in my wing. We harass men for fun and we live like sisters here, helping each other.
(This prisoner self-identifies as a *Kathoey*, 37 years old, convicted of fraud and theft, and sentenced to 6 years in prison).

Participants have narrated to me intense stories of their fulfilling love and sexual life in their wings. They further explained how their constructed gender (Butler, 2002) is hyper-performed with the support of guards and prison guards. For example, in some prisons, they are allowed to wear makeup, to execute gendered social performances (such as singing, feminine Thai dancing and walking in prison fashion shows, and wearing identity-specific costumes during annual events). They are also allowed to have sex with protection in private corners, to love and be loved by cis-gender prisoners, and to be supported and protected financially and psychologically by their "sugar-daddies" (male prisoners in male wings). Transgender and cis-gender prisoners who participated in this study reported that inside the prisons, transgender prisoners occasionally receive higher positions in the social hierarchy than cis-gender prisoners, and have more social acceptance behind bars than before entering prisons. However, a minority report mistreatment in prison, and their perspectives are deliberated in the next section.

Gendered Experiences Behind Bars

We act as if that being of a man or that being of a woman, is actually an internal reality or something that is simply true about us, a fact about us, but actually it's a phenomenon that is being produced all the time and reproduced all the time. So, to say gender is performative is to say that nobody really is a gender from the start. – Judith Butler (2013)

The ongoing debates among scholars of transgenderism focus on the "hidden truth of self" hypothesis, which claims that, for example, feminine individuals in male bodies have been psychologically feminine since their birth. The body – the way one presents oneself to the world – acts as a "source of information about the self," and it indicates an individual's sexual identity as either male or female. In other words, the body acts as a signifier of identity (Bischoff, 2011, p. 118).

The body cannot specify its own identity; it is an object that subtends meanings, and is a space of constructed gender performativity (Butler, cited in Chotiwan, 2014). Thus, gender is not a role construction based on physical sex, but a practice of performativity that is controlled by heteronormative social pressures. And, heteronormativity defines how men and women should express themselves (Duangwises & Jackson, 2013). As discussed in the previous section, my research results also indicate that through romantic relationships and sexual intercourse with cis-gender prisoners, trans informants affirm their identity and conform to ideologies of femininity or masculinity, while the sexual identities of many cis-prisoners becomes more fluid behind bars. Prisoners' gender identity reproduction and affirmation processes are not limited to their sexual practices or the sexual attentions they received inside prisons. Aside from prison housing regulations, the sub-culture and general management in Thai prisons are heavily heterobinary and unaccommodating for people with non-conforming gender identities. In this section, I analyze research data gained from ethnographic fieldwork within the framework of gender studies, anthropology and human rights disciplines.

I conducted my ethnographic study in both male and female wings. The male wings are much more overcrowded and facilities are assigned on the basis of the sentence, age, health conditions and days until the release date. Hygienic conditions in the female facilities I was shown were relatively clean,[8] but overcrowding forced prisoners to share too-small spaces for all aspects of life.

*Tom*s *and Phuying-Kham-Phet* are allowed to sleep together with cis-gender female prisoners. But in the male wings, the correctional authorities arranged for *Kathoey*s to sleep in *Kathoey*s-only rooms for safety reasons and to prevent rape. More than 20 prisoners sleep in the same room on a mattress, and each person has very little space. They often have to spoon each other to sleep. The worst part is that the only available toilet at night is inside the sleeping room, with no partitions; everyone shares the experience of each person's defecation.

Heteronormativity plays a significant role in all Thai prison management policies. Prisoners in male wings, regardless of their sexual identity, are forced to wear pants and have closely cropped hair. All prisoners in female wings, including *Tom*s, are forced to wear a bobbed haircut a female uniform with a skirt. The binary gender regulations enforced by officers to exert control over their bodies, uniforms and occasionally the behaviors or speaking language of transgender prisoners, affect them deeply on a psychological level. As one *Tom* explained,

> Most *Tom*s feel ashamed with our female breasts because it makes us feel too much like women. But in prisons, we are not allowed to use breast binders to flatten our breasts. I really hate that we have to walk around with big boobs, are forced to wear skirts and to grow our hair longer, like this. I feel humiliated that I am forced to look like a woman and I start to walk with a crooked back because

---

[8]Note: The prison officers showed me around the forefront facilities. I cannot claim other toilets or bathrooms' hygiene in other buildings are good.

I don't want people to notice the curve of my boobs. One of our guards corrects our language (*Tom* prisoners) all the time. If we say *krub* [masculine particle in Thai language] he strictly orders us to say *ka* [feminine particle] instead.

(This prisoner identifies as a *Tom*, is 31 years old, was convicted of drugs and sentenced to 8 years).

Privacy is also crucial for Thai transgender prisoners. Each wing has a common shower area, where all prisoners stand around relatively unhygienic public bathtubs. Each prisoner has one water dipper bowl and is allowed to dip water from the public shower tub several times. In one of the prisons, each time guards blow a whistle, prisoners can take water in their bowls and I was informed by prisoners that sometimes the guard blew only five times and they do not feel clean enough. There are no partitions in any shower space or toilet. Trans prisoner participants complained that they feel very uncomfortable that everyone can see their genitals while using toilets and showering. However, the prisons solved this issue by arranging a special time slot for all trans people in each wing to shower together.

Several other alarming situations stem from institutionalized misunderstandings, biased sexual predispositions, heterosexual binarism and negligence in the treatment of transgender prisoners. Prison officers often use stigmatizing wording that embarrasses and demeans transgender prisoners, such as เบี่ยงเบนทางเพศ วิปริตทางเพศ (*Biang-baen-tang-phet, Viparit-tang-phet*, in English: gender deviant, abnormal sex) จิตวิปริต (*Jit-viparit*, in English: perverted), including words implying that transgender people are mentally ill, both verbally and occasionally in governmental documents. Many interviewees felt that the inability to access hormones in Thai prisons is the most crucial issue. Local NGOs and scholars have also been requesting access to hormone therapy for transgender prisoners. They have petitioned the Department of Corrections and Ministry of Justice to acknowledge that gender dysphoria is a medical condition where the sex an individual was assigned at birth does not match their gender identity. Gender dysphoria can severely harm transgender people, and hormone treatments support the enabling of transgender people to live in consonance with their self, including their gender identity. They have also begged for acknowledgement that transgender people who lack hormones, misuse them or withdraw from a treatment too quickly face a substantially increased risk of physical and psychological issues. Despite this full-throated advocacy, prison officers who participated in this study see hormone therapy as an "unnecessary beauty catalyst" that can only support a transgender prisoner's desire to act hyper-feminine or hyper-masculine, which can cause "prison anarchy" and "security issues."

Sub-culture in Thai prisons is highly patriarchical and the guards play important roles in creating prison hierarchies as they structure semi-feudalism and often articulate transprejudices. As in contemporary Thai society, prison social hierarchy is tremendously visible and respecting seniority is important. Also, macho culture dominates in the male wings, where both guards and prisoners perform their masculinity through macho language, lifestyle, activities, and relationships with others. For instance, often, when I went into a male wing guards' office, I observed three or more male prisoners massaging a guard's head, shoulders and feet. The "well-behaved" prisoners who have some computer knowledge are also permitted to work in offices instead of doing harder labor. In both men's and women's wings, prisoners call some of their male guards *Phor* (In English: Dad) and some female guards *Mae* (In English: Mom). Transgender prisoners, especially *Kathoeys*, are seen as the prison's "jokers." Even as officers who participated in this study seem to be supportive of gender identity expression, upholding paternalistic relationships between them and all prisoners, adoring *Kathoeys* and transsexual women, they habitually expressed unconsciously sexist notions to me. For example, a head guard responded as follows to questions regarding trans safety in light of escorting, body searches and sexual harassment:

> People loves *Kathoey* here [in the prison]. You asked me about the clothes-changing area without partitions? Don't you know their nature? They are laughter for us, they bring lots of joy and they love to show off! They like to be stars and be seen. Nobody bullies them from hatred here.

When international organizations and local NGOs campaign about trans access to hormones in prisons, all guards and officers who participated in my study reacted similarly. They believe that providing hormones or special facilities to trans prisoners is both unnecessary and for some, could be "unfair" to cisgender prisoners:

> Look at Thai prisons. We have too many criminals! We don't have enough money or facilities for everyone. Males and females are detained in the same facilities. Why do we have to use more tax money on them specially? Everyone should be equal [...] Hormones are unnecessary. When they take it, their bodies will become more beautiful and when they are beautiful, more issues will arise. More men will be attracted to them, and it will be very messy and hard to get them in order. Just more unsafe and unorganized. Also, we let some trans prisoners receive hormones from their family, but it turned out they smuggled drugs inside the prison. Was a total disaster. (Another head guard).

From my observation, many officers do not always find human rights doctrines suitable for the Thai prison context. Still, medical knowledge, biopower (see Foucault) and its principles are highly influential in decisions to change regulations in support of trans prisoners. One *Kathoey* prisoner reported how officers like to pillory trans prisoners. She whispered to me when the guard was not around during the interview:

Usually there is a partition fabric during body searches for us when coming back from the court. But a guard teased me by letting me get naked in front of other people for a laugh. He thought it was funny but I was so embarrassed. And when they find out that people had sex, he puts a sign saying 'we just had sex' or some terrible texts on the couple's necks and forces them to walk around the prison so people can see.
(A prisoner who self-identifies as *Kathoey*, 21, convicted of drugs and sentenced to 5 years).

Captivatingly, all trans prisoners who participated in this study informed that in general, they feel less bullied in the Thai prisons than on the outside. Cis-male prisoners also explained vividly to me how they think *Kathoey* prisoners have higher social status in the prisons than on the streets. In prison, *Kathoey*s are in a male prisoner informants' words, "adored and more forgiven," especially by officers and prisoners. They are sexually desired by many straight males, some of whom fight each other over a *Kathoey*. Marriages through cultural ceremony between cis-males and *Kathoey*s are performed with an officer as master of ceremonies. Moreover, monogamy is a strong value within the Thai prison sub-culture. When a prisoner is attracted to another who is housed in a different wing, they sometimes ask for each other's prisoner numbers and buy consumer products for one another, which they send through the prison's convenience store system. They also can send love letters to each other, but the length is limited to fifteen lines and officers read everything on all letters, to make sure they are not inducements to organized crime or otherwise inappropriate. *Kathoey*s in male wings seem to be given more freedom to gender identity expression than *Tom*s in female wings. They are allowed to wear make-ups and feminine costumes, and to conduct feminine performances during prison events. *Tom*s in this study reported that guards in female wings are very conservative and do not have a good understanding of gender variety.

During fieldwork, I always felt a big contrast walking across male and female wings. Female wings always looked much tidier, more spacious, better-organized, and less overcrowded (faint praise, but praise nonetheless). Most of the prisoners were convicted of drug-related crimes. I always felt safer in the female wings and, after a while, guards there let me walk freely and talk freely to the prisoners without them following. There is a nursery for infants of female prisoners who are under one year old. Several female prisoners work as nannies in the nursery, assistant nurses in the hospital wing, or supporters in different "feminine" prison functions. Vocational training there focuses on embroidery, sewing, Thai massage, cooking, hairdressing school, handcrafting clothes, perfume making, baking, knitting and so on. It is well-known that local business owners contact Thai prisons if they wish to have cheap labor; prisoners work many hours a day and rarely get paid for their skilled craftsmanship. Library holdings are sketchy and free distant university education is offered, but somehow rarely availed of by prisoners. The contrast of vocational training in male and female wings is stark: in the male wings, prisoners are trained for "masculine jobs" such as metalwork, furniture making and more. The government believes binary-gender-specific vocational training is beneficial for prisoners' rehabilitation and social reintegration.

As in the male wings, relationships between guards and prisoners in the female wings are paternalistic and feudalistic. The culture, approach to discipline and all activities inside the female wing are tuned to the goal of "reforming" prisoners, so that they will behave according to Thai ideology of femininity and a way of being of "good women." When I arrived the first time, the guard prepared a group of prisoners to sit on the floor with legs tucked back to one side and hands together in a *wai* (Thai greeting) gesture, saying *Sawasdee-ka* (hello in English) in unison. Every time this particular head guard walked past, many prisoners showed extreme respect and submission, like small children, to the level that I felt somewhat uncomfortable as I witnessed, even though I grew up in the same culture and understand where the submission and respect for seniority comes from. The flip side of respect is repression, and both *Phuying-Kham-Phet* (transsexual women) and *Tom*s shared vivid details about the inhumane ways they were body searched when first entering the prisons. They explained that officers in the female wings permitted "well-behaved" prisoners to work as their assistants and asked these prisoner assistants to do the body searching. These fellow prisoners put their fingers deeply into the newcomers' genitals to check for hidden drugs. Informants explained that they felt damaged and humiliated by the process, and many *Tom*s described the procedure as equivalent to rape. Heteronormative binarism in different contexts as revealed plays significant roles in current prison management and policies in Thailand, resulting in several topics to be improved as I recommend in the next section.

Policy Recommendations for Trans Prisoner Management in Thailand

At present, there is still no national standard operating procedure for transgender prisoner management in Thailand, even though the country has a large population of trans prisoners. Based on data collected from my fieldwork, I address challenges and give practical recommendations with the goals of supporting the rights of transgender prisoners, respecting prisoners' human dignity, and developing equitable and non-discriminatory policies. Policymakers are my main audience at this moment, but scholars are welcome to follow along and work through my logic.

Because transgender rights and identities are not recognized legally in Thailand, there is no official governmental record of transgender people. This has created several social and legal issues, including the housing and management of trans prisoners discussed in this chapter. I recommend that to start with, Thai prisons should systematically collect information on all transgender people in Thai prisons. Store the data in a statistically meaningful and useful way in the Department of Corrections' computer system. Secondly, Thai correctional officers must accept the principles of self-identification on sexuality and gender expression of transgender individuals. There should be no reason for a correctional officer to refer to medical documents, genital organs, appearance or sex assigned at birth. In addition, all prisoners should be addressed by using the names and pronouns they prefer. Both verbally and especially in written documents, officers must stop using stigmatizing wording that embarrasses and demeans transgender people's dignity or imply they are mentally ill. Thirdly, when transgender prisoners are transported from one place to another, requests to be accompanied by officers of trans prisoners' preferred gender identity should be accommodated. Moreover, when determining housing for each and every transgender prisoner, the prison director, wardens and relevant officers must assemble and decide together on a case-by-case basis. As a part of this process, it is important to ask all transgender prisoners about their gender identity and their wing preferences. Officers and prison social workers must provide thorough and clear safety information and describe sub-cultural and lifestyle differences in each wing before a final decision about where an individual will be housed is taken.

The safety and dignity of transgender prisoners in Thailand remains problematic, especially inappropriate intrusions on personal privacy during body searches and time spent in showers and bathrooms. I suggest that transgender prisoner requests about the gender of officers who can search particular parts of their bodies must be accommodated. Whenever possible, body searches of transgender prisoners shall be conducted by medical or public health staff, and never by fellow prisoners. Routine body searching must be conducted in a private area, with privacy partitions. Officers must respect prisoner privacy and human dignity by avoiding words, actions or demeanor that are known or expected to vilify or humiliate transgender people. In addition, all transgender prisoners must be issued sarongs, free of charge, which they can choose to use when they use toilets, to avoid humiliation from revealing parts of their bodies to other people. Transgender prisoners should also be provided with separate shower rooms; at a minimum, a specific collective time slot must be established for transgender prisoners, so they do not have to shower together with cis-gender prisoners. This is especially important for *Kathoey*s in male wings and *Tom*s in female wings. At a minimum, privacy partitions that can conceal the area between chest and genitals must be provided in shower and toilet areas. These will create a safer environment, reduce stigmatization and sexual harassment, and address some health issues that are specific to transgender prisoners.

Cis-gender and transgender informants alike reported that officers failed to respect transgender prisoners' private information. Officers were reported to intentionally shame trans prisoners by joking about them with other prisoners. Officers must never share information on transgender prisoners' gender, genitalia, gender identity, gender transition or sex-reassignment status with other prisoners. Indeed, this information should not be discussed among officers. Only medical officers, public health officers and prison directors should have access to transgender prisoners' confidential information. Furthermore, access to clothes and personal commodities of transgender prisoners must be improved. Uniforms in both male and female wings must be the same color, for gender neutrality. Transgender prisoners should be able to choose the uniform that most closely conforms with their gender identity. That is, if they wish, *Tom*s and transsexual men may choose to wear male prisoners' pants. *Kathoey*s and transsexual women may choose to wear female prisoners' skirts. One result is that a single wing might contain some prisoners who wear "male" clothes and others who wear "female" clothes. This is not a problem. Allowing transgender prisoners to live according to their gender identity will reduce the risks of gender dysphoria.

Many trans informants have requested the right to purchase commodities that conform to their mode of expressing their gender identity. These requests should be accommodated. That is, *Kathoeys* should be allowed to purchase or wear for example cosmetics, beauty products, bras, female underwear/lingerie, and all other personal commodities that other female prisoners may purchase and use. *Toms* and transsexual men should be able to purchase for example male underwear, shavers, and all other commodities that male prisoners are allowed to use. Breast binders should be provided at no charge, or at least be made available for sale, especially for *Toms* and transsexual men. Officer training must include dissemination of information about binders, which are appropriate physical and mental health equipment for *Toms* and transsexual men. These enable transgender men to express their gender identity. Transgender prisoners may choose a hairstyle that suits them; officers must stop forcing them to wear a hairstyle according to the wing they live in.

There should also be better access to specialist health services for transgender people, including gynaecological services. These services must be made available as often as needed, or at least once per month. Most importantly, trans prisoners must have access to appropriate hormone treatments. In the event of prison budgetary constraints, transgender prisoners must have the right to use their own money to purchase medical consultations and hormones while in prison. Transgender people who lack hormones, or misuse or withdraw from a hormone treatment too quickly face a substantially increased risk of prostate cancer, mood swings, depression, and other severe conditions. Transsexual women who no longer have testicles (the organ that naturally produces male hormones) and lose access to hormone therapy are likely to develop physical and psychological issues such as hair loss, weight increase and unstable emotions that could become the cause of fights and physical assaults in prison.[9]

It is also important that prisons must offer vocational training that matches transgender prisoners' gender identity and career interests, without limitation. Lastly, I highly recommend that Thai prisons provide much greater access to HIV services and psycho-social support. Every prison should establish a transgender committee and organize more, and more focused, staff training. All staff, but especially those who work directly with transgender prisoners, must be trained and regularly retrained about gender issues. These training sessions should be designed to build capacity and comprehension on SOGIE (sexual orientation, gender identity, and gender expression, an inclusiveness platform), gender diversity and other LGBTIQA+ issues, as well as provide proper guidance on the implementation of standard operating procedures for officers.

Through the ethnographic fieldwork and anthropological lens, this chapter has theoretically and empirically scrutinized different aspects of the situation, as well

---

[9]Information from Tangerine clinic, Sirisak Chaited and Dr Nitaya Phanupak, interviewed in 2020.

as challenged the regime of truth concerning gender identity, vulnerability myth, lived experiences and offered practical state policy recommendations within the context of transgender prisoners in Thailand. For future research and policies implementation for transgender human dignity, I highly recommend that organizations and researchers should focus more on transgender prisoners' marginalization and ideologies behind it in different facets such as their pathways to prisons, forbidden hormones services, rehabilitation and social (re)integration processes, post-release life, and recidivism. Furthermore, prison regulations should be further examined in parallel with critical analyses of human rights organizations' political implementations and their epistemological assumptions on gendered management policies to support transgender prisoners. To support prisoners who identify as transgender, governments worldwide still have a long way to explore and facilitate further what kind of support might be needed to face the challenges that they confront.

Chapter 9

Gendered Pathways to Prison: Women's Routes to Death Row in the Philippines

Diana Therese M. Veloso

Abstract

This chapter delves into the experiences and social worlds of women pre-viously sentenced to capital punishment and now imprisoned in the Phil-ippines. Drawing on in-depth interviews and participant observation, the pathways of 27 women previously on death row are presented. Narratives reveal multiple constraints stemming from gendered familial, relational, and economic responsibilities, vulnerability to gendered control and vio-lence, poverty or financial precarity. These gendered inequities were com-pounded by structural barriers in the context of a low-income, postcolo-nial nation with entrenched corruption. The women's stories reveal four pathways to criminalization: (1) responding to violence; (2) economic precarity; (3) drug abuse; and (4) guilt by association and corrupted jus-tice. The research reported in this chapter enriches feminist criminological knowledge on gendered pathways to criminalization by adding the voices of women in the Philippines to a now growing body of Southeast Asian scholarship. In line with previous studies, findings reveal the ways in which women come into conflict with the law because of choices made within constrained social circumstances.

Keywords: Feminist pathways; women; death penalty; Philippines; prison; life imprisonment

Introduction

Until recently, the experiences of women in conflict with the law have received little attention in academic and public discourse (Chesney-Lind, 1997; Howe, 1994; Nagel & Johnson, 1994; Schram & Koons-Witt, 2004; Thomas, 2003).

Gender, Criminalization, Imprisonment and Human Rights in Southeast Asia, 125–137
Copyright © 2022 by Diana Therese M. Veloso
Published under exclusive licence by Emerald Publishing Limited
doi:10.1108/978-1-80117-286-820221008

Feminist research in criminology asserts that women's pathways to criminalization and imprisonment deserve serious study (Britton, 2004; Chesney-Lind, 1997; Daly & Chesney-Lind, 1988; Girshick, 1999; Muraskin, 2007; Steffensmeier & Broidy, 2001). However, most research on women's journeys into and experiences of criminal justice has been undertaken in western nations. In the Philippines, despite recent rapid growth in the female prison population numbers (see Chapter 1), justice-involved women remain invisible in academic discussions and public debates.

For the most part, information about criminalized women in the Philippines consists of reports from non-government organizations and journalistic mainstream media articles (Amnesty International, 1997, 2002, 2003; Aning, 2004; Jimenez-David, 2004; Labro, 2004; Palasi, 2003). Incarcerated women previously on death row are especially invisible, given their small numbers – around 3% of the total death row prisoner population – before the suspension of capital punishment in the Philippines in June 2006 (Philippine Human Rights Information Center & Women's Education, Development Productivity and Research Organization, 2006). Women's experiences and issues have been subsumed under those of men previously on death row (Gluckman, 1999a, 1999b; Simbulan, n.d.).

Since the passage of the Republic Act 9346, titled "An Act Preventing the Imposition of the Death Penalty in the Philippines," in June 2006, the sentences of women sentenced to death have been modified to life imprisonment without parole. The only exceptions to this trend are the women who: (1) had their sentences modified to regular life imprisonment upon the review of their cases by the Court of Appeals and/or the Supreme Court prior to the suspension of capital punishment in June 2006; and (2) had benefitted from the blanket commutation of death sentences – that is, those finalized by the Supreme Court – to life imprisonment by then-President Gloria Macapagal-Arroyo (Fernandéz & Nougier, 2021; Pabico, 2000).

Only one study has been conducted about the life histories and issues of women on death row in the Philippines, and since the suspension of the death penalty, there has been limited follow-up research about this group of women who are now behind prison walls for life (Philippine Human Rights Information Center & Women's Education, Development Productivity and Research Organization, 2006; Veloso, 2016; Villero, 2006). In this chapter, I report findings from a study exploring the circumstances that led to the incarceration and sentencing of women previously on death row in the Philippines. The aim is to consider how the women framed their pathways to criminalization.

Methodological and Theoretical Approach

Over 18 months between 2008 and 2009, I undertook participant observation at the Correctional Institution for Women (CIW) in Mandaluyong City, Metro Manila, and Correctional Institution for Women-Mindanao (CIW-Mindanao) in Davao del Norte province. I also conducted in-depth interviews with 27 women previously on death row, 9 of these women's family members and 8 prison staff.

During the participant observation stage, I observed the women's routines in prison and the different activities of the penal facilities over the course of a year. I had been a volunteer prior to my research, so I was already acquainted with most of the women. There were times when I slept over at the prisons to acquire a fuller sense of the women's lives. My participant observation helped me identify interviewees. I undertook document analysis of prison and dormitory rules, regulations and, articles on capital punishment.

I drew on feminist approaches within criminology, including Daly's (1992, 1994) pathways approach and Richie's (1996) concept of gender entrapment. Both Daly (1992, 1994) and Richie (1996) have highlighted the centrality of survival, abuse, and intimate relationships to women's criminalization. However, I was not constrained by either of these approaches. Rather, employing what could loosely be defined as a grounded theory approach, I waited for key themes to emerge from the interview transcripts, starting with individual cases, progressing to abstract concepts, and identifying patterns (Charmaz, 2003). Below, I present my research findings starting with a brief overview of the women's cases before discussing the central themes that arose from the analysis. I will only be providing snippets of the lives of the women to illustrate thematic points, rather than their entire complex life histories.

A Brief Overview of the Women's Cases

Eighteen of the women that I interviewed were convicted of violent crimes, including homicide and kidnapping. The remaining nine women were imprisoned for drug-related offenses. Twenty-two of the women were criminalized alongside people with whom they had a pre-existing interpersonal relationship. This included intimate partners, family members, friends, and acquaintances. Twenty-two of the 27 women had no previous criminal convictions, 10 admitted their culpability in the events that resulted in their imprisonment, while 17 explained that they were innocent.

Central Themes in the Women's Stories and Pathways into Prison

Overall, and as evidenced in the prior research literature on pathways to prison, the women narrated having experienced multiple constraints in their lives stemming from gendered familial, relational, and economic responsibilities, vulnerability to gendered control and violence and financial precarity (Cherukuri et al., 2009; Daly, 1994; Jeffries et al., 2019, 2021; Owen, 2003; Richie, 1996; Russell et al., 2020). These gender-based vulnerabilities were compounded by structural barriers in the context of a low-income, postcolonial nation with entrenched corruption. The women's stories revealed four pathways to death row and imprisonment: (1) responding to violence (three women); (2) economic precarity and "hard living" (four women); (3) drug abuse (three women) and (4) guilt by association and corrupted justice (17 women). The women's marginalized social positioning impacted their experiences with the criminal justice system. These pathways and themes are discussed in more detail below.

Responding to Violence

Most of the women in this research relayed having endured an astounding level of victimization throughout their lives. Twenty-four narrated having lived with child abuse and as adults, 11 experienced various forms of gender-based violence and other abuses. This included but was not limited to intimate partner abuse, sexual violence, forced marriage and prostitution, labor exploitation, and abuse by in-laws. Three women, Jane, Bianca, and Abigail,[1] were imprisoned for acts of direct violence committed in response to victimization, either of themselves or their children. Their stories are outlined below.

Research shows that when women kill, it is often a defensive and victim-precipitated strategy directed against physically and sexually abusive current or former intimate partners (Daly, 1994; Ferraro, 2006; Jeffries et al., 2019; Jeffries & Chuenurah, 2018; Jones, 1996; Kaukinen, Gover, & Hays, 2006; Leonard, 2002, 2003; Owen, 2003; Radford, 1994; Watterson, 1996). Jane was imprisoned for killing her domestically violent husband. She narrated having survived incest and sexual harassment as a teenager and suffered domestic violence later in life. Her grandparents forced her to marry her husband (an acquaintance) because he kissed her against her will. When she married, Jane already had a child after being raped by her uncle. She went on to have four more children with her husband. In the beginning, Jane explained that her marriage was fine, but after the children entered their lives, her husband started coming home drunk. After the birth of their fifth child, Jane caught him having sex with his ex-girlfriend, but she decided to remain in the marriage for the sake of the children. Fifteen months after the birth of their fifth child, Jane's husband pushed her down the stairs. She was two months pregnant with her sixth child and miscarried. Jane decided not to have sex with him anymore due to heavy bleeding and in response, he beat her severely. She spotted a steel pipe, struck him and fled from the family home to seek help from the barangay (smallest administrative unit) headquarters. Jane expressed that at the time she feared that her husband would catch up with her. When the police went to Jane's house to arrest her husband for physically assaulting her, they found him dead. The police noticed that Jane was beaten, insisted that she undergo a medical examination, and then summoned her for questioning. If no complainant had come forward, she would have been released. Yet her sister-in-law pressed charges. In the Philippine justice system, when a complainant files a criminal case, it goes through the prosecutor before it is tried at the Regional Trial Court. The Philippine legal system criminalized Jane for defending herself against her own victimization.

In addition to defending themselves against domestic violence, we also know that when women kill, this can be in response to violence being perpetrated against

---

[1]All names have been changed to ensure anonymity.

those they love, including children (Gilfus, 1992; Jeffries & Chuenurah, 2018; Morris & Kingi, 1999; Owen, 2003). Bianca, a college-educated self-employed woman, murdered her ex-husband to avenge his nephew's abuse of her children.

Bianca endured verbal and emotional abuse by her in-laws when she and her husband lived with them. While her husband defended her, they had an on-and-off relationship, which eventually ended after eight years. Bianca's sister-in-law set her husband up with another woman three months after their final separation. When Bianca's now ex-husband asked to reconcile the following year, Bianca refused, as his new partner was pregnant and Bianca had formed a new intimate relationship.

Bianca and her new partner moved to his hometown in the southern Philippines. She left her three young children with her ex-husband, who agreed to support them, but left them with his sister instead. Two years later, Bianca visited her children at their school and learned that their cousins had abused them physically and sexually. She confronted her ex-husband, who denied the abuse. This disavowal triggered Bianca's plans to kill him, instead of calling the police.

The cases of Bianca and Jane show how victimization is directly related to the criminalization of women. However, there are also complex indirect relationships between abuse and women coming into conflict with the law. Victimization can lead women into situations that place them at risk of criminalization (Chesney-Lind & Rodriguez, 2013; Covington & Bloom, 2003; Gilfus, 1992; Owen, 2003; Watterson, 1996). This is demonstrated in the case of Abigail described below.

Abigail's parents had an on-and-off relationship during her childhood. This compelled Abigail and her mother to move around the northern Philippines to get away from her father. He would then track them down, there would be a reconciliation, another separation, and relocation. Eventually Abigail's mother ended the marriage leaving her daughter in the care of her father. Abigail's father raped her when she was 12 years old. She stabbed and killed him in self-defense. Victimization introduced Abigail to the criminal justice system – and ensnared her in an organized crime syndicate headed by a police officer, who assumed custody over her. She described the illegal rackets of the syndicate,

> That syndicate is involved in different kinds of work – killing people, gambling. The only exception is drugs because that's what we're mad at. As [they] say, you can cheat other people, but don't sell *shabu* (crystal methamphetamine) because it kills the youth. That's also the line of reasoning of my boss, since my boss, who raised me, is a policeman.

She attempted to escape the syndicate by working as a dancer at a "beer house" an establishment that operates as a strip club and venue where prostitution often occurs. Abigail clarified that she was not involved in prostitution but in any case, she entered another domain of the underground economy. She met her husband, a regular patron at the beer house, and married him shortly afterward. It turned out that Abigail's husband was part of the same syndicate she had attempted to leave, which led to her continued entrapment.

Abigail's husband was domestically violent. He frequently beat Abigail, burnt her with cigarettes, and relied on her to bring in money. Now living in a rural community, she ventured into farming and worked as a guest relations officer (GRO) at a club. The term GRO is used as a euphemism for dancers and entertainers at strip clubs. Sometimes, prostitution is also involved. Abigail met Jerlyn, a recruit of the syndicate, whom she helped become a GRO. When Jerlyn got pregnant, she sought help from Abigail and her husband. Abigail thought her husband's cousin, also a syndicate member, was the father. Abigail was criminalized because of her loyalty to Jerlyn. She knew that her husband and her friend Jerlyn were plotting to kill his cousin due to financial disputes but in hindsight, Abigail believed that her husband was jealous of his cousin's intimate involvement with Jerlyn. Abigail orchestrated the murder by luring the victim, her husband's cousin, to a vacant apartment, where she killed him. She, her husband, and her friend escaped to a nearby province and hid in a hotel owned by another syndicate member. Jerlyn surrendered and emphasized Abigail's role as the mastermind. Abigail was livid and puzzled when her husband sided with her friend. Only in detention did Abigail discover their long-standing affair. She stated, "maybe...the reason why it happened was because I was looking for care and nurturing." For Abigail, love and abuse were inextricably intertwined. It appears that her complex history of victimiation at the hands of those who were meant to care for her led Abigail into violence to garner the love, of which she had been deprived, from her friend and husband.

Economic Precarity

Prior research on women's pathways to prison has shown that women frequently come into conflict with the law due to economic precarity (Belknap, 2001; Cherukuri et al., 2009; Daly, 1994; Howell, 1991; Jeffries et al., 2019, 2021; Russell et al., 2020). Four of the women were in prison for either kidnapping or drug offenses committed in response to financial difficulties.

Gilda and Pops were convicted of kidnapping a five-year-old girl for ransom. Gilda was a college student, working as a secretary in exchange for tuition assistance, as her impoverished parents could not support her. Pops, Gilda's boss, had grown up poor but became a businesswoman after marrying a wealthy widower. Both women tagged each other as the masterminds behind the child's abduction. Despite their conflicting statements, both women were motivated by financial needs. Further, Gilda relayed cultural obligations pertaining to pakikisama (cooperation/compliance) and utang na loob (indebtedness) had played a role in her decision to support Pops in the kidnapping.

Rubia and Catherine were in prison for a drug offense. Both women explained that their pathway to criminalization was paved by financial hardship and economic familial provisioning, against the backdrop of intimate relationships with controlling men. Before entering the drug trade, Rubia owned a cocktail lounge, and a mahjong and card game establishment. Her husband had established a tailoring company. However, the owners reclaimed the latter business space and Rubia's husband insisted that she close her business after becoming jealous when he discovered her ex-boyfriend in the area. To support her family, Rubia culti-vated fruits and vegetables and helped her mother, who worked at a cemetery. However, the money that Rubia earned was not enough to meet the family's daily expenses. She met Chinese nationals, who enticed her to traffic shabu to and from Hong Kong, to which Rubia agreed because she needed to provide for her family.

Catherine was a stay-at-home mother before she sold shabu. Her first intimate partner was addicted to drugs and because of this, when she was six months preg-nant with her eldest son Catherine decided to leave him. A year later, Catherine met her second intimate partner, a married man. She had five children with him, although only four survived. He was involved in the drug trade and his gambling addiction led to their eviction from the house they were living in at the time, com-pelling Catherine to sell shabu. Her "business," as she put it, enabled her to send her children to school, buy them material possessions, invest in land and have a savings account. However, Catherine's intimate partner was financially control-ling and would become abusive to her and the children if she refused to give him money. She also helped her sister with financial problems. Catherine claimed the police arrested her to make her snitch on her partner, which she refused to do.

Both Rubia and Catherine received the death penalty despite their status as first-time offenders. In the Philippines, drug laws exclude the possibility of mitigating circumstances with penalties based solely on the amount of drugs possessed or sold. Prior to the suspension of capital punishment in June 2006, sentences for drug cases ranged from life imprisonment to the penalty of death (Pabico, 2000). When the death penalty was still in effect, possession of as little as 750 grams of marijuana could result in a sentence of death by lethal injec-tion. Regardless of the abolition of the death penalty, excessive sentences for drug felonies persist (Fernandéz & Nougier, 2021). For instance, to this day, selling 18 grams of marijuana or less than one gram of shabu could provide grounds for life imprisonment (Gluckman 1999a, 1999b; Pabico, 2000; Palasi, 2003). Manda-tory sentencing under drug laws has almost always resulted in disproportionate sentences for many minor or low-level drug offenders. In such a setup, a one-time courier with a marginal role in drug transactions receives the same treatment as a manager of a major drug distribution network (Pabico, 2000). In the Philippines, women are disproportionality caught up in the harsh sanctioning of illicit drugs. For example, in 2017 nearly 60% of women sentenced to prison were incarcerated for a drug offense, compared to just over 15% of men (Fernandéz & Nougier, 2021, p. 4).

Drug Abuse

Women's substance misuse is understood to be a defining factor in their path-ways into the criminal justice system (Bush-Baskette, 2000; Maher & Daly, 2011; Radosh, 2002; Sharp & Eriksen, 2003). Many of the women in this research narrated that addiction underpinned their criminalization. Here, financial moti-vation intersected with addiction ensnaring them in the drug underworld. The women in these cases were involved in the illicit drug trade for financial gain, oftentimes familial economic provisioning, but this was interwoven by the need to support their substance dependence. Buying illicit drugs is a costly exercise (Chesney-Lind & Rodriguez, 2013; Covington & Bloom, 2003). Furthermore, the women's substance misuse was often connected with their intimate partners, other family members and friends. Prior research has shown that in contrast to men, close interpersonal bonds are more likely related to women's criminalization trajectories (Belknap, 2001; Joe Laidler, 1996; McShane & Williams, 2006; Richie, 1996; Steffensmeier & Allan, 1996).

Consider Rhodvil's story. She was middle-class and college-educated but imprisoned for drug distribution. Rhodvil described her husband as an "addict" who introduced her to illicit drug use. Rhodvil narrated that over time she also developed an addiction to drugs. She expressed that her drug dependence resulted in her neglecting her sickly daughter, who subsequently passed away. Her marriage broke down and Rhodvil returned to her parents' home and raised her son on her own before landing a job in Thailand as a secretary for an airline. She supported her mother, and her younger siblings, especially after her father died. Rhodvil met a couple who invited her to distribute drugs in the Philippines. While economic responsibilities toward her family influenced Rhodvil's decision to distribute drugs, she also explained that her addiction was a key motivating factor. She said, "I was hooked on drugs at the same time, so I readily took up the offer."

In another example, Sarah's substance misuse stemmed from her close interpersonal relationships – in this case, her husband, extended family members and friends. Sarah married Shahzad when she was 17 years old. They both went to college, settled in his family's compound in the southern Philippines and had six children together (two of these children passed away). Her mother raised the three older children, whom Sarah visited sporadically. Sarah's brother-in-law and his wife Leti used shabu with their neighbors and sold the drug. Sarah revealed that some drug customers were her husband's friends, who used their home for their "sessions." This started Shahzad's drug use and eventually led to Sarah's substance abuse and involvement in the drug trade. Sarah became a "drug retailer," working with her brother-in-law, Leti and mutual friends to buy shabu in bulk and sell it in smaller quantities. She used the money earned to support family members and friends but also explained: "it was just so I could use. That's all I was after." The arrests of both Rhodvil and Sarah occurred through the palit-ulo ("switching of heads") system, wherein drug dealers are incriminated by their customers in exchange for lighter sentences or freedom.

Guilt by Association and Corrupted Justice

Being framed and "dragged into" the crimes of others was the most common pathway to prison and death row narrated by the women in this study. Seventeen women relayed that they were in prison for murder, kidnapping, and drug offenses that they did not commit. Their narratives illuminated how they were caught up in the behaviors of others including intimate partners, family members, friends, and acquaintances. Institutional corruption by government officials, who protected those involved in illegal activity, and police officers also played a key role which is unsurprising considering the well documented structural problems in the Philippine criminal justice system, such as warrantless arrests, ill-treatment, planted evidence, forced confessions, coached witnesses, and torture (Amnesty International, 2002; Joint Civil Society, 2009; Simbulan, n.d.). Notably, the problem of corrupted systems of justice is raised by the authors in other chapters of this book and in prior feminist pathways research undertaken in non-western countries (Cherukuri et al., 2009; Jeffries et al., 2019; Jeffries & Chuenurah, 2018, 2019; Russell et al., 2020).

Intimate Partners

Two women were implicated in their partners' crimes of murder and kidnapping. Their experiences illustrate gendered abuse and powerlessness in controlling, violent relationships that constrained their choices and compromised their well-being. For example, Inday met her partner while working as a waitress. He was a violent man twice her age. Inday knew he was capable of murder but decided to stay in the relationship because she feared becoming his next victim. She used shabu with her husband and his workers and made the fateful mistake of voicing to them all that the drugs they were using had been watered-down by the dealer. Inday's partner and his two workers decided to kill the drug dealer who they lured to Inday's house on the pretext of buying shabu. Inday was locked in the bedroom by her partner while the murder was taking place. Two teenagers witnessed how the men disposed of the victim's body in a gutter and called the police, who arrested them. The police alleged that Inday was also liable because she was home during the murder, she was subsequently arrested and imprisoned.

Before her incarceration, Margaret managed car dealership sales, sold clothes, and opened a video shop. Her husband was then working in Japan and sporadically sent money for their two children, as he had a mistress. Margaret had an extramarital affair with Christian, who helped her with her financial problems but after he entered an arranged marriage, Margaret attempted to avoid him, but he continued contacting her. Christian was involved in illegal logging and smuggling and invited Margaret to sell drugs, which she feared he would pressure her to do out of indebtedness for his previous kindness to her.

Margaret began a relationship with Jordan, a married man and her driver at the car dealership. She told Christian and while both men were initially civil this began to change. Before the crime, she and Jordan had gone to a restaurant, where Christian met them and offered them a ride. Both men got into a heated argument in the car. Jordan spotted his best friend Greg on the road and enlisted his assistance. Jordan ordered Christian and Margaret to move to the back of the car, while Greg took over the steering wheel and drove to a deserted location. Margaret recalled,

> They took Christian out of the car. I tried to stop them, but Jordan punched me in the stomach. I was left in the car…I wanted to get off, but Greg came back right away…[Jordan] was wondering whether I would escape or ask for help. Greg kept an eye on me…Jordan arrived later…He didn't say anything much…Then I

caught a whiff of the smell [of blood] …I became nauseous from
the smell. We went home.

The police called Margaret for questioning, and she was torn between telling
the truth and covering up for Jordan. Margaret was nearly acquitted due to lack
of evidence, but Christian's wealthy mother used her connections to have the case
reinvestigated and Jordan shifted the blame onto Margaret.

Family Members

Four women were caught up in kidnappings committed by family members. In
every case, the women's pathway to prison resulted from family members and
associates deliberately conspiring to implicate them in a crime for which they were
mere bystanders.

Melanie was convicted of kidnapping a Chinese businessman in the northern Philippines but asserted that her brother Eugene and his accomplices were
responsible. She lived with Eugene after migrating from the southern Philippines,
where she left her ex-husband and three children but insisted that she did not
support his illegal rackets. Melanie and her new intimate partner occupied a unit
attached to the main house, where Eugene hid his victims.

The last kidnapping was fraught with problems in collecting ransom and
Eugene was killed. Melanie asked Eugene's accomplices, particularly his live-in
girlfriend Nida, their cousin, and three associates, to release the victim, but they
refused. Nida continued negotiating the ransom and even approached Eugene's
other girlfriend, Denise, to borrow her cellular phone to contact the victim's family. The police raided their house. Melanie, her partner, Eugene's accomplices, and
Denise were arrested. The police did not arrest Nida despite her primary role in
the crime. Melanie voiced her misgivings about her and her boyfriend's conviction
but recognized: "We were included because we were there."

In another example, Shirley was implicated in her cousin Milo's kidnapping scheme. Her cousin ordered her to fetch Patrick, his wife's 12-year-old
nephew, from school, claiming that his grandfather had an accident. Her
partner accompanied her, and they boarded a jeep, where Milo was waiting.
Shirley was an unwitting accessory in a kidnapping that her cousin master-
minded to force the boy's grandfather to repay money borrowed from him, so
he could pay his hefty debts. Milo warned Shirley that Patrick's teacher and
the security guards at the school recognized her and threatened to kill her
partner if he reported the crime. Milo took them to the house of his mistress
and her parents and ordered Shirley and her partner to pretend they were
renting a room, along with Patrick. A man named Bruno dropped by and
negotiated the ransom.

Shirley looked after the boy. She and her partner planned to escape and
decided to take a tricycle to a nearby town, where he had relatives, so they could
borrow money for their fare and bring Patrick back to his parents. The police
arrested them before they could execute their plan. Milo and Bruno were arrested
separately. Milo's mistress and her parents were also summoned for questioning,

being the owners of the house-turned-hideout. During the investigation, Patrick's grandfather denied having a debt to pay. It also turned out that Milo's wife had supported his scheme to implicate his mistress. Shirley, her partner, and Milo were convicted of kidnapping, while Bruno was acquitted.

Friends or Acquaintances

Five informants were implicated in the kidnapping and drug-related offenses of significant interpersonal networks. These included friends and acquaintances. For instance, Babes' boss duped her into delivering ecstasy. She had migrated from the southern Philippines to try her luck as a domestic helper in Manila and a province in the north. She looked for another job to support her four children, who lived with her ex-husband. She accepted a job offer to deliver vitamins, not knowing it was ecstasy. A customer incriminated her. Her partner, who had accompanied her, was also implicated. Her boss managed to escape.

In another example, Izzy was framed for kidnapping and homicide committed by organized crime syndicate members. Her friend Antoinette had offered her a vaguely-defined job after her contract as a factory worker expired and asked her to tag along to fetch her niece. Izzy went with Antoinette to fetch the child and then on to a house which Izzy would discover belonged the syndicate. She disclosed that her attempts to escape the syndicate, along with the child, ended in failure,

> "When I tried to escape at night...I got caught...You had to remove many padlocks (from the door)...I took a stool so I could reach it. When I reached it, I got caught. There was someone behind me. They said, 'Ah, so you had plans of escaping after all...Next time, we'll double our surveillance on you. And you plan on getting us in trouble because of your escape, huh?' Of course, my purpose [for escaping] was the child. If I could take her along, we could go to the police and I would reveal everything...I could say, 'It's (the syndicate) in this place.'" She encountered more difficulties in trying to leave the syndicate afterward: "Someone always stuck close to me...I wanted to run, run, [and] leave them. But people in the syndicate kept an eye on me. If they drew their gun, they could shoot me. I was scared. I didn't want to die yet."

The organized crime syndicate then assigned Izzy the task of snatching purses and wallets for them, but the syndicate head eventually decided to get rid of her because of her blunders. Her boss ordered the killing of the child whom she had fetched with Antoinette after the plan to traffic the girl fell through. Izzy and the child were blindfolded and brought to a river, along with the two women who had lured her to the syndicate. One woman drowned the child and fled with the other woman. A passerby witnessed the crime and assumed Izzy was responsible. The real culprits remain at large.

Corrupted Justice

The remaining women narrated being in prison because of corrupted systems of justice. For example, Sheila, who belongs to the Tinggian Indigenous community, said that she was framed by police for drug trafficking. Her second husband was a lawyer and she had provided him assistance with his cases most of which were drug related. Sheila sympathized with her clients and disposed of evidence for them, rather than surrendering them to corrupt police officers, who used or re-sold confiscated drugs. She explained that she was in prison because she had been unlawfully arrested on drug possession charges because of (narco)politicking (i.e., protection of drug lords by the legitimate institutions of the state who have a stake in the illicit drug trade) in that she encountered conflicts with a general from the Philippine National Police Narcotics Group, whom she accused of coddling drug traffickers. Her husband, who was a lawyer, represented Sheila in court but was shot dead by an unknown assailant on the eve of her final hearing. Eleven days later, the court released its decision, convicting Sheila and sentencing her to death. Sheila framed the speedy trial as a conspiracy.

Mia claimed she was implicated in her driver's and his associates' law-breaking, compounded by police misconduct. Before her incarceration, Mia was a business-woman who traveled back and forth from the southern Philippines and Manila to purchase her wares wholesale. Her husband had contracted a former neighbor as Mia's driver. Mia lent a mobile phone to her driver so that she could reach him but in hindsight, it became clear that he had used this phone, registered in Mia's name for illegal rackets.

On the day of Mia's arrest, she and her driver were traveling north. Under-cover police pulled them over and arrested Mia without a warrant. Two Filipino-Chinese brothers, who lived with her driver and his wife, were with them. The police accused them of kidnapping her driver's younger ward. Understanding the problem with endemic corruption in the Philippine police, Mia and her driver pretended to be spouses, hoping to be released. Her driver's four associates were also separately arrested. Everyone remained in detention, even when no victim was identified. She claimed the police blamed them for unresolved kidnappings, coached kidnap victims to incriminate them and fabricated numerous other charges. Mia, her driver, and his associates were convicted and sentenced to death for three counts of kidnapping for ransom. Her driver died in prison.

Sapphire and Kisses, were convicted of drug trafficking, being implicated in offenses attributed to family members who sold marijuana. They explained that being connected to people in the drug trade made them easy targets. Sapphire's sister disclosed that the police offered to release them in exchange for Php 25,000, which their impoverished families could not afford.

Conclusion

Daly's (1992, 1994) feminist pathways approach and Richie's (1996) gender entrapment theory illustrates how women come into conflict with the law due to a constrained set of life circumstances. Similarly, for the women in this research, their choices and therefore agency was narrated as being significantly restricted. For many, their journeys to death row and then life imprisonment without the possibility of parole were constructed as being survival choices and coping strategies. In the first three pathways, the women narrated being both victims and agents. They were responding to the violent victimization of themselves or others by killing abusive husbands in self-defense or retaliating against those who had abused their children. Others relayed being criminalized for behaviors they had engaged in to alleviate poverty, meet family caretaking and/or other cultural obligations. These women portrayed themselves as agentic albeit within the confines of subjugation. Others were criminalized for drug addiction and the actions they had taken to support themselves and their families alongside their need for drugs. For these women, close interpersonal relationships with intimate partners and family members frequently paved their course to substance dependence and subsequent entrapment in the drug underworld.

The last pathway revealed how women can be criminalized because of their close personal ties including to intimate partners, family members and others. While Philippine society portrays interpersonal connectedness as important for support and protection, for the women in this research, these relationships resulted in them being implicated in the illegitimate actions of those closest to them. These women were imprisoned because of interpersonal association with people involved in activities deemed criminal by the state. Corrupted systems of justice were also narrated by many women as having underpinned their pathway to death row and prison. This problem presented itself in the other pathways where it influenced the women's routes to prison and death row.

Chapter 10

Expanding the Promise of the Bangkok Rules in Southeast Asia and Beyond

Chontit Chuenurah, Barbara Owen and Prarthana Rao

Abstract

The Universal Declaration of Human Rights outlines fundamental protections for all human beings. Critically, such rights and protections are particularly applicable to those imprisoned throughout all carceral spaces: the right to physical security; freedom from torture and other cruel and unusual punishments; equal protection under the law; and a right to a community standard of living, including food, clothing, medical care, and social services. The need for special vigilance in applying these principles to justice settings for children and women entwined in these spaces has been met with the development and implementation of the United Nations Rules for the Treatment of Women Prisoners and Non-Custodial Measures for Women Offenders (2010) or the Bangkok Rules. These Rules provide for a women-centered approach to human rights within correctional environments. The Bangkok Rules are based on several dominant themes relevant to women in prison and additionally emphasize the importance of alternatives to custody. Since their adoption over 10 years ago, there has been clear progress in implementing and promoting the Bangkok Rules throughout Southeast Asia, as we will describe in this chapter. While we applaud these efforts, there is still much work to do within the region. We argue that attention is needed both within and outside of women's prisons to expand the promise of the Bangkok Rules beyond current efforts. In our view, the attention inside prison walls must now turn to addressing intersections between gender and other marginalized statuses, ensuring all forms of safety, dignity, and respect. Outside prison, reform of egregious and punitive drug laws is essential. Equally important, is the critical need to develop a more robust response in terms of non-custodial measures and other non-prison-based responses to women in conflict with the law.

Gender, Criminalization, Imprisonment and Human Rights in Southeast Asia, 139–154
Copyright © 2022 by Chontit Chuenurah, Barbara Owen and Prarthana Rao
Published under exclusive licence by Emerald Publishing Limited
doi:10.1108/978-1-80117-286-820221009

Keywords: Bangkok Rules; Southeast Asia; marginality; non-custodial measures; intersectionality; gender; war on drugs

Introduction

The Universal Declaration of Human Rights outlines fundamental protections for all human beings including: the right to physical security; freedom from torture and other cruel and unusual punishments; equal protection under the law; and a right to a community standard of living, including food, clothing, medical care, and social services. Critically, such rights and protections are particularly applicable to those removed from society through imprisonment. Such rights are further emphasized in Article 10 of the International Covenant on Civil and Political Rights, which specifies that "all persons deprived of their liberty shall be treated with humanity and with respect for the inherent dignity of the human person" (United Nations, 1966).

World over, prison policies, practices and architecture have been designed with the majority male population in mind (see Chapter 1). Women have been adversely impacted by the gender blindness of carceral spaces. Recognizing the need for special vigilance in applying human rights principles to justice settings for women and their children, the historic United Nations General Assembly (2010) Rules for the Treatment of Women Prisoners and Non-Custodial Measures for Women Offenders, also known as the Bangkok Rules, were adopted on December 21st, 2010 (United Nations General Assembly, 2010). These Rules – for the first time – provide a gender-appropriate blueprint for a women-centered approach to human rights within correctional environments, in keeping with their gender-specific contexts and backgrounds. Most importantly, the Bangkok Rules emphasize the need to prioritize alternatives to imprisonment using non-custodial measures and community corrections.

The journey toward the adoption of the Bangkok Rules began in Southeast Asia as a local initiative in Thailand. In 2006, Her Royal Highness Princess Bajrakitiyabha initiated the Kamlangjai Project (the Inspire Project) to support women prisoners in Thailand, particularly pregnant women and children living with their mothers in prison. After the success of the Inspire Project, Thailand engaged in a range of international activities, playing an active role in promoting a gender-specific set of international guidelines on the treatment of women prisoners. To raise awareness about this issue, Thailand presented the Inspire Project to the 17th session of the Commission on Crime Prevention and Criminal Justice in Vienna in 2008, which was well received by the international community. These events led to a long process of negotiation, after which the Bangkok Rules was formally adopted by the United Nations General Assembly in 2010. The drafting process was a joint effort among the Member States, international and civil society organizations around the world which drafted the Rules grounded in good practices and correctional advancements in different regions. Since its adoption, the Bangkok Rules have become a point of reference for gender-responsive policy and practice in criminal justice systems around the world.

As will be discussed in detail below, in Southeast Asia, following the adoption of the Bangkok Rules, considerable headway has been made in developing human rights protections. However, despite these positive developments, significant challenges remain. Specifically, punitive war on drugs policies in some Southeast Asian countries, the overuse of detention including at pre-trial, and the under-utilization of non-custodial measures are resulting in prison over-crowding with concomitant negative impacts to criminalized women in the region. In addition, there is relative silence around intersectional disadvantage. The progress, challenges and way forward will be discussed in the latter sections of this chapter. First, it is important to understand the key principles of the Bangkok Rules and provide a snapshot of women's imprisonment in Southeast Asia.

The Bangkok Rules, Gender and Imprisonment in Southeast Asia

Since being adopted, the Bangkok Rules have led the movement to understand and provide for the distinct gendered needs of women in prison. The 70 rules are based on several dominant themes arising from the varied profiles of women who come into conflict with the law and those behind prison walls. These themes include understanding their backgrounds and histories, safety and security needs, distinct healthcare needs including for pregnant women, breastfeeding mothers and women with accompanying children, rehabilitation, and social reintegration needs. The Rules also emphasize the importance of training correctional personal on these specific issues as fundamental to increasing gender sensitivity in prisons. The rationale behind these themes stems from the principle of non-discrimination as stated in Rule 1 of the Bangkok Rules, which makes clear that providing for the distinctive needs of women prisoners is necessary to accomplish substantial gender equality and thus, "shall not be regarded as discriminatory" (United Nations General Assembly, 2010, p. 12).

As outlined in several chapters in this book, women's pathways into prison are shaped by gender and as such, their needs during incarceration will be different from those of men. For example, most women who come into conflict with the law have backgrounds of gender-based violence and resulting trauma. Research tells us that they can suffer unnecessarily in masculinist prison regimes (Owen et al., 2017). A case in point is prison operational practice which can both create and recreate the damaging experience of gendered trauma (Benedict, 2014). Loud noises and insulting words can destabilize and re-traumatize women, recreating the psychological and physical experience of harms. Elements of male-centric operational practice, such as strip searches, cell extractions, segregation and supervision by male prison staff can also threaten women's well-being as can staff violations of women's rights through disrespect, harassment, and violence (Owen et al., 2017).

In addition to the centrality of gender in women's pathways to and experiences of imprisonment, the Bangkok Rules (40–56) also highlight the importance of addressing the needs of minority groups in prison, including foreign nationals, ethnic minorities, and other marginalized peoples. The need to understand the ways in which gender intersects with other social and structural oppressions to impact experiences of imprisonment is highlighted in several chapters in this book.

Finally, it is important to note that the Bangkok Rules (Rules 57–66) emphasize the use of imprisonment as a measure of last resort, by prioritizing the use of non-custodial measures. Research shows that most women are in prison for non-violent, minor offenses related to poverty and familial caretaking responsibilities. In such cases, locking women up in prison does little to address the reasons underpinning their criminalization. In fact, in many cases, imprisonment exacerbates the conditions that brought women into contact with the criminal justice system in the first place. Yet, despite the Bangkok Rules advocating for prison as a sanction of last resort, and as noted in Chapter 1, large numbers of women are imprisoned in Southeast Asia. Furthermore, these numbers have grown in most countries in the region since the adoption of the Bangkok Rules in 2010 (see Table 5).

Table 5.   Female Prison Population Growth by Country 2010–2019 (or as Noted).

Country	Percentage Change 2010–2019
Brunei Darussalam	+18%
Cambodia	+168%
Indonesia	+83%
Laos	+49% (2015–2019)
Malaysia	+27%
Myanmar	+21%
Philippines	+117%
Singapore	-7%
Thailand	+52%
Vietnam	+5%
Timor Leste	+575%

Source: Data compiled from World Prison Brief (2021) and the Thailand Institute of Justice's database.

By all measures, women are more likely than men to be in prison for drug-related offenses. United Nations Office on Drugs and Crime (2018) (UNODC) World Drug Report estimates that 35% of women in prison globally are incarcerated for drug offenses, compared to 19% of men. In Southeast Asia, punitive drug laws and policies have disproportionately impacted women and contributed to the rise in the number and proportion of women in most prison systems many of whom are imprisoned for low-level drug crimes. For example, Alvarez (2018) found that the proportion of women imprisoned for drug offenses in the Philippines was four times that of men (60% of women compared to 15% of men. In Thailand, the ratio of women prisoners convicted of drug offenses has gradually increased since

2010, accounting for 80%, 83%, and 84% in 2010, 2015, and 2020 respectively, as compared to 55%, 70%, and 80% of men during the same period (Department of Corrections Thailand, 2020). As noted in the first chapter of this book, punitive drug policies including harsh sentencing alongside the overuse of pre-trial detention majorly contribute to overcrowding in most prisons in the region.

In Southeast Asia, following the adoption of the Bangkok Rules, there has been substantial progress in promotion and implementation, including in research, capacity building, and change in policy and practice. Much of the work has been led by human rights based NGOs and research institutes such as the Danish Institute Against Torture (DIGNITY), the International Drug Policy Consortium and the Thailand Institute of Justice (TIJ). TIJ is a research institute affiliated with the United Nations Crime Prevention and Criminal Justice Programme Network and has been at the forefront of regional change. One of the core strategic directives/plans of TIJ is to "promote and support the implementation of the [Bangkok Rules] in Thailand and at the international level as guidelines for the criminal justice system" (Thailand Institute of Justice, 2021). Below we discuss progress that has been made in the region.

Research

The Bangkok Rules 67–69 suggest that research should be undertaken to expand understanding about the profiles of women in custody, the reasons underpinning women's criminalization, their backgrounds and needs, as well as the impact of women's imprisonment on their children in and outside prisons. The Bangkok Rules emphasize the importance of data and evidence-based research, as it serves as a concrete foundation for gender-sensitive policy development and enhances a common understanding of women's pathways to prison. In recent times, as evidenced by the scholarship discussed in previous chapters of this book and the reference list that follows, there has been an increasing number of research efforts documenting the background and experiences of women prisoners before conviction, during and post-imprisonment in some countries in Southeast Asia. Research on women in conflict with law has been recently conducted in Cambodia, Indonesia, Malaysia, Singapore, Thailand, the Philippines and Myanmar (e.g., Chuenurah & Jeffries, 2019; Danish Institute Against Torture, 2014; International Drug Policy Consortium, 2021; Jeffries et al., 2019, 2020, 2021; Jeffries & Chuenurah, 2018; 2019; Mustofa et al., 2019; Ng et al., 2019; Park & Jeffries, 2018; Rahmah et al., 2014; Russell et al., 2020; Samuel & Omar, 2012; Thailand Institute of Justice, 2014; Thailand Institute of Justice & Griffith University, 2021; This Life Cambodia, 2019; Veloso, 2016). Outcomes from these studies emphasize criminalized women's social and economic marginalization, histories of victimization, and familial caring responsibilities as well as the disproportionate impact of punitive drug policies in the region.

As the United Nations Special Rapporteur on Violence against Women has stated, the continuum of violence during and after incarceration is a reality for many women globally. By every measure, women enmeshed in the criminal justice system have experienced much higher rates of childhood and adult victimization than male offenders and the general population (Owen et al., 2017). For example, a recent study undertaken in Thailand revealed that of the 75 imprisoned women interviewed, 44% had experienced child abuse, 23% had been the victim of domestic violence during adolescence, and 40% as adults (Thailand Institute of Justice & Griffith University, 2021). The findings revealed that abuse and victimization often shaped women's pathways into prison, experiences of incarceration and journeys back into the community post-release.

With the punitive drug laws in the region, women's involvement in drug offenses has become one of the important research aspects. Here, studies show that women are generally convicted of low-level drug offending such as small-scale drug trading or possession (e.g., Jeffries, et al., 2019, 2020). Research exploring more "serious" drug offenses (as defined in legislation via particularly harsh penalties) such as international drug trafficking, has revealed the women in Southeast Asia are frequently criminalized due to poverty, out of love for a romantic partner, or because they were tricked, exploited or pressured into carrying drugs across an international border (Chuenurah & Jeffries, 2019; Jeffries et al., 2021; Jeffries & Chuenurah, 2019). These issues are also highlighted by Lucy Harry in Chapter 3 of this book. Moreover, women imprisoned for drug-related offenses could face additional layers of gendered stigma and discrimination. For example, a study conducted in the Philippines found that women criminalized for drug offenses are perceived by their family, community and sometimes by service providers agencies as being especially "immoral" (Alvarez, 2018). This social attitude combined with punitive drug laws hampers access to services in prison and poses challenges to imprisoned women's community reintegration prospects.

Research in the region also highlights the ways in which familial bonds may play-out differently in women's imprisonment pathways. Here heightened cultural requirements within many Southeast Asia countries necessitate women to care and provide for extended kin. Research in the region has subsequently shown that bonds with family (as well as intimate partners) are more likely related to women's criminalization than men. Here, it is suggested that many aspects of women's pathways into the criminal justice system are best understood through the lens of relationships and women's specific familial obligations (Jeffries et al., 2019 and see Chapter 7 in this book).

More recent research undertaken in Thailand and Singapore has revealed the challenges that familial and intimate relationships, alongside poverty, gender-based violence victimization, trauma and associated mental ill-health, poverty and a lack of community acceptance may pose in the lives of women post-release. What these studies have highlighted is that prisons may not be the best solution to address the structural inequality that led women into prison in the first place. Moreover, being imprisoned exacerbates women's marginalization posing challenges as they returned to communities (Jeffries et al., 2020; Ng et al., 2019).

Another unique feature of the research undertaken in Southeast Asia is the challenges faced by women in trying to access justice when they come into conflict with the law. Criminal justice involved women in the region can face various forms of obstacles and human rights violations. This includes police intimidation and violence, corruption at every stage of the criminal justice process and procedural injustice. For example, in Cambodian research, imprisoned women have reported going to court with no or inadequate legal representation, being intimidated, threatened, or assaulted during police questioning, and being asked for or needing to pay bribes to police, judicial officers and in some cases prison staff to access justice and/or basic services, such as healthcare, within the prison (International Drug Policy Consortium, 2021; Jeffries & Chuenurah, 2018, 2019). Women are also disproportionately impacted by discriminatory practices involving contact with the outside world. As demonstrated in DIGNITY and Justice for All's research (2019) on Prisoners' Contact with the Outside World in Myanmar, women's visitation needs throughout the justice continuum were an afterthought, resulting in additional barriers to accessing time with family, other loved ones and legal representatives. Many of these issues are highlighted in numerous chapters within this book.

This growing number of studies on women's journeys to prison have provided important insights and improved overall knowledge on gendered pathways to prison in the region. However, research is not being conducted in all countries and there remains limited research on women's experiences of imprisonment and post-release. Thus, it is crucial that further work be undertaken in all these domains.

Capacity Building

Regional dialogue and training are fundamental in increasing policy makers' and practitioners' understanding of women prisoners' backgrounds and pathways, their gender-specific needs and appropriate treatment. Since 2016, TIJ has provided annual training for senior correctional staff from numerous ASEAN countries on the Bangkok Rules – *Training on the Management of Women Prisoners for Senior Correctional Staff in the ASEAN Region* (the Bangkok Rules Training). The training program aims to provide guidance on translating the Bangkok Rules into practice. Using an Action Plan format, participants work together to design a framework for implementing the Bangkok Rules in their prisons. Post-training, participants and TIJ remain connected through social media, creating regional relationships of support and knowledge sharing into the future. TIJ's training program has translated into the development of several local initiatives. One example is Indonesia's national mapping exercise on women's health and health care in prisons conducted by UNODC in collaboration with the Indonesian prison department in 2017. (United Nations Office on Drugs and Crime, 2017).

Each woman's prison in Southeast Asia will have different challenges and priority issues. During the past few years, and in addition to the annual training program, TIJ has provided tailor-made training for prison staff in various countries at the request of national authorities, prison heads, or international organizations. These specialized training programs are directed by correctional staff, designed to meet their needs, and support local women's prisons to overcome challenges specific to them. Participants learn about the guidelines provided in the Bangkok Rules and practical skills to put the rules into practice in their daily work.

In addition to TIJ's training programs, practitioners and members of civil society have also had an opportunity to meet and share their view on the treatment of women prisoners in a number of regional events such as *Women, incarceration and drug policy: Regional dialogue in Southeast Asia* (organized by the International Drug Policy Consortium and the Inspire Project), an expert group meeting to review the draft Toolkit on Gender-Responsive Non-Custodial Measures, as well as the expert group meeting on Gender-Sensitive Rehabilitation Programs held in Bangkok in 2019. These platforms allow countries to learn from each other and have created a regional network that allows participants to stay connected and support each other in the future.

Policy and Practice

The Bangkok Rules have inspired change in prison policy and practice in the region. This includes legislative change, government directives, the development of the Bangkok Rules Model Prison Project and partnerships with NGOs, the business community, and universities. Each are looked at in more detail below.

In February 2017, Thailand amended its 1936 Penitentiary Act which, for the first time, specifically refers to the Bangkok Rules and adds clauses on female prisoners with children and pregnant prisoners to be in line with the Bangkok Rules. Under Vietnam's Criminal Code 2015, a woman's sentence can be postponed if she is pregnant or has a young child (up to three years of age). If the woman is the only breadwinner in the family, and imprisonment will cause extreme hardship to the family, the sentence may be deferred for up to one year. In 2019, the Cambodian Prime Minister acknowledged the need to accelerate trial procedures, reduce sentences, and consider suspended sentencing for female prisoners who are single mothers. A legal aid team comprised of voluntary lawyers to support women prisoners who could not afford legal representation has also been established.

In 2015, TIJ in cooperation with the Department of Corrections (DoC) of Thailand established the *Model Prison Project on the implementation of the Bangkok Rules (the Model Prison Project)*. This initiative aims to develop an evaluation checklist on the Bangkok Rules implementation, enhance the understanding of prison staff about the Bangkok Rules, and encourage correctional institutions across Thailand to carry out their policies and practices in line with the Bangkok Rules.

In practice, prisons across the country are invited to join the project and are being evaluated in several aspects using indicators developed by TIJ and the DoC which is based on Penal Reform International and TIJ's (2019) Index of Implementation on the Bangkok Rules. Throughout this process, technical support is provided by TIJ to help prisons improve their compliance with the Bangkok Rules and then each prison is assessed against specific criteria in the checklist. Thus far, 15 facilities across Northern, Eastern, Central and Southern Thailand, have achieved Model Prison status in their progress in implementing the Rules. The model prison checklist has been adopted by DoC as a national tool for prison performance evaluation nationwide (Chuenurah & Sornprohm, 2020, pp. 131-139). The aim of the Model Prison project is to provide a space for regional knowledge sharing between criminal justice practitioners and policymakers, to exchange ideas and be inspired to advance human rights standards for women prisoners.

In August 2019, Thailand's Model Prison project has inspired cross-border partnerships between Thailand and Cambodia through the *"Model Prison Project: A Pilot Project on the Implementation of the Bangkok Rules in Cambodia 2019-2020."* To elevate the standards of gender-sensitive prison management, the project has been implemented at Correctional Centre 2 (CC2), the largest women's prison in Phnom Penh, Cambodia. From 2019 to 2020, TIJ provided provide training to CC2 correctional officers in prison management as per the principles of gender-sensitive prison management and the Bangkok Rules.

Successful implementation of the Bangkok Rules requires community involvement and support. In some Southeast Asian countries, NGOs play an important role in supporting prisoners during imprisonment and post-release. For example, in Cambodia, the organization *This Life Cambodia* provides holistic case management to families in conflict with the law, to support vulnerable families at risk of separation. This Life Cambodia's Life in Family project is discussed in detail in Chapter 4.

The community plays an important role in determining successful outcomes for women returning home post-imprisonment. In Thailand, efforts are being made to build community awareness, understanding, and empathy among multiple community stakeholders so that women can be supported beyond prison walls. Business owners can be utilized to offer women employment, the media to soften the stigmatizing narratives, and community members to lend a helping hand and emotional support. For example, in 2017, the Rule of Law and Development Program (RoLD) was established in Thailand by TIJ. The RoLD program brings together executives and decision-makers from sectors beyond the criminal justice system including business leaders, universities, and the media. RoLD members learn about social justice, the rule of law, and sustainable development through a series of activities including special lectures, immersive field visits and hands-on projects. Through RoLD, TIJ has created an active network of over 260 influential and passionate people from over 170 organizations who are ready to tackle a justice-related issues including gender-based violence and social reintegration.

The RoLD network has contributed to developing the Hygiene Street Food Project, an initiative aimed at enhancing reintegration support for formally incarcerated women. Thailand, like other Southeast Asian countries, is known for its street food industry, which attracts both local and foreign customers. Street food businesses are familiar to many women prisoners in Thailand. Some women will have operated a street food business prior to being imprisoned while others have received training while in prison. Using a collaborative approach, TIJ partnered with DoC, private sector business, and the King Mongkut's Institute of Technology Ladkrabang whose Food Industry Academy offers food safety and hygiene training for street food vendors in Thailand. The outcome was the establishment of an innovative eco-friendly food cart program for formally imprisoned women which began operating in 2020. The project offers women a micro-entrepreneurship opportunity, it seeks to reduce the stigma of the ex-prisoner label and provide women with meaningful well-paying employment opportunities enabling them to support themselves and their families.

In recent years, there has also been an increasing collaboration between the prison, university sector and students in Thailand. The aim is to educate and involve young people in addressing gendered human rights for criminalized women. For example, in 2020, Chiangmai Women's Correctional Institution partnered with Bangkok University on a project to improve a pre-release center for women prisoners in line with international human rights standards.

Moving Forward: The Promise of the Bangkok Rules

In this chapter we have highlighted positive developments that are taking place in Southeast Asia in terms of change-making around the Bangkok Rules while also broadly positioning women's imprisonment in the region. In the next section, we reflect on the challenges faced in implementing the Bangkok Rules in Southeast Asia. We note that to fulfill the promise of the Bangkok Rules, punitive drug policy within the region alongside the over-utilization of pre-trial detention, under-utilization of non-custodial measures and concomitant prison over-crowding must be addressed and more attention must be given to intersectional disadvantage. We reflect on the broader problem of gendered inequality inside and outside prison walls and argue that the future of the Bangkok Rules rests on a more expanded and comprehensive understanding of safety, dignity, and respect as well as gendered forms of social harm, including the harm of imprisonment.

The Drug Wars: A War against Women

Bloom, Chesney-Lind, and Owen (1994, p. 2) found that "without any fanfare, the 'war on drugs' has become a war on women, and it has contributed to the explosion in women's prison populations." Almost 30 years later, international research has shown this trend has accelerated beyond any rational explanation. As demonstrated above, women in Southeast Asian countries are getting caught up in these drug wars, even though there is substantial evidence to prove that women are being criminalized for behaviors related to poverty, familial caretaking, trauma and mental ill-health including substance abuse. The growing number of women in Southeast Asian prisons is creating major barriers in implementing the Bangkok Rules, through prison overcrowding and resulting budget deficits, resulting in inadequate supplies of basic necessity items, healthcare, programs and humane treatment (United Nations Office on Drugs and Crime & Thailand Institute of Justice, 2020).

As the International Drug Policy Consortium clearly states, the Bangkok Rules and the principles enshrined therein can be used as a basis to reform drug laws (Fernandéz & Nougier, 2012). They argue, and we agree, that prisons are not the appropriate setting to address women's pathway needs. They provide compelling detail on the systematic and sustained discrimination and bias in sentencing among marginalized and other non-majority communities. They call for a comprehensive examination of the drug laws that continue to propel so many women into unnecessary prison sentences. The International Drug Policy Consortium also asserts that the current punitive drug laws disregard women and the way their pathways are shaped by poverty, caregiving responsibilities and the violence and trauma prevalent in so many lives.

There is a need for urgent and long-term reform to existing punitive drug policies, to fulfill the promise of the Bangkok Rules. Substance misuse needs to be looked at through the lens of public health, not criminal justice, and sentencing for drug offenses needs to demarcate small-time drug sellers/mules from big-time drug traffickers (also see Chapter 3 in this book). Decongesting prisons and reducing the number of women sentenced to prison for drug use/selling is the main way to actualize the Bangkok Rules globally.

Pre-trial detention is one example of disadvantage stemming from gender. In many Southeast Asian countries, the number of women held in pre-trial detention exceeds those sentenced (see Chapter 1 in this book). Gender-based inequality finds harmful expression in that women are often too poor to afford bail and effective legal representation. This inability to pay results in confinement in under-resourced local prisons, adding to the existing struggle with providing gender-based services and human rights protections to women housed in pre-trial detention (Walmsley, 2020).

The over-reliance on pre-trial detention of women and others is a reflection of countries' prioritization of imprisonment over non-custodial measures. Although most attention in the first decade of the Bangkok Rules has been given to custodial measures, we argue that the future of the Bangkok Rules includes prioritizing non-prison options and expanding their application. While the egregious conditions in prison continue to need attention, it is time to elevate the discussion in Southeast Asia (and beyond) on non-custodial measures. There is an emerging awareness of the benefits of non-custodial measures for women, and how these community-based sanctions can both eliminate some of the gendered harms of incarceration and promote better outcomes for all (United Nations Office on Drugs & Crime, 2020).

Research and practice have consistently held that the goals of the justice system can be met without incarceration. Community-based programs and other non-custodial measures provide accountability without imprisonment. There is significant evidence that outcome efficiency (i.e., rehabilitation) is more likely to be achieved via community corrections than behind prison walls. Non-custodial measures are more successful in integrating those in conflict with the law without the deleterious gendered harms of imprisonment. We argue here that promoting the use of non-custodial measures represent an investment in the future. As stated in the UNODC-TIJ "Toolkit on Gender-Responsive Non-Custodial Measures" (United Nations Office on Drugs and Crime & Thailand Institute of Justice, 2020, p. 14):

> Effective use of non-custodial measures can reduce the substantial social and economic cost of imprisonment, in particular pretrial detention, as well as reoffending and help to reduce the prison population in the long term by providing greater opportunities for rehabilitation and social reintegration. Incarceration, in turn, can

lead to further contact by women with the criminal justice system and can impact a woman's earning abilities or housing. The community is better served by community-based interventions which address the underlying causes of women coming into contact with the law, such as drug or mental health treatment.

While more fully expanding the gendered human rights protections within prison is a critical role of the Bangkok Rules, promoting non-custodial measures and other community interventions is the next essential step.

Mandatory minimum sentencing to prison for drug crimes is but one example of the policy of imprisonment as a first resort, with alternatives to prison seen as optional. Policy language is important. Rao (2020) makes a salient point: framing non-custodial measures as an "alternative to prison" privileges prison as the policy of first resort. As she says, "when we define something as being 'alternative', there is an implicit assumption that it is not the first choice." This, in our view, is the central point of promoting non-custodial measures and the human rights approach. We propose a twin emphasis drawn from the Rules – using their guidance to improve conditions and reduce gendered harm inside prisons and promoting the priority use of non-custodial measures. Therefore, maximum effort should be made – especially in the case of drug-related offenses committed by women – to minimize the harmful effects of drug policies and to ensure gender-sensitive criminal justice systems in the region and beyond.

Intersectionality

The complexities of the women's prison population present layers of vulnerabilities to harm. While the typical operational practice may not address all women's pathway needs, there are challenges to providing for and protecting non-majority women across the dimensions of race, ethnicity, culture, gender and sexual diversity. Within the women's prison population, gendered disadvantage is replicated exponentially among those with non-majority identity.

Those with non-majority status confront varying forms of discrimination inside prison. Racial discrimination in the outside world is often echoed by continuing oppression in prison communities. In most countries around the world, women from ethnic minority and Indigenous communities are disproportionally represented in detention populations. The intersectional disadvantages faced by women from ethnic minority groups is highlighted in Chapter 6 of this book and in the research of Park and Jeffries (2018) which explored the experiences of ethnic minority Vietnamese women categorized as foreign and imprisoned in Cambodia. Both studies elucidate the intersectional disadvantages faced by certain groups of women incarcerated in the region. More research is needed in this area and we call for urgent measures to counter racial and ethnic discrimination of all kinds.

Similarly, gender diversity and sexual orientation, especially for those who are outside conventional identity and sexuality, is rarely incorporated in standard policy and practice. Barberet and Jackson (2017) argue that the Bangkok Rules are built on a cis-gender approach and inflexible normative definitions of women and femininity. This disadvantage is dangerous as prisoners who present outside of cisnormativity and heteronormativity will face additional challenges. Trans and gender non-binary people are often harmed by such practices through classification systems, housing assignments, requirements for traditional-gendered clothing, makeup or grooming items, and lack of appropriate treatment and services. The lack of medical and mental health services designed for this population contributes to their vulnerabilities. Here, too, we find few systems embracing these principles to counter this discrimination of those who present outside of the cisgender norm.

While there is emerging evidence from Southeast Asia showing discriminatory treatment within the criminal justice system toward sexual and gender minorities (see Chapters 2 and 8), data are scarce and the research limited. As highlighted in a recent report (United Nations Development Programme & United Nations Office on Drugs and Crime, 2020, p. 9) on protection against violence and discrimination based on sexual orientation and gender identity

> information about the lived realities of lesbian, gay, bisexual, trans and gender-diverse persons around the world is, at best, incomplete and fragmented; in some areas it is non-existent. It means that in most contexts policymakers are making decisions in the dark, left only with personal preconceptions and prejudices or the prejudices of the people around them.

Thus, and as also argued in Chapter 8, data must be collected and research undertaken using tools and approaches that remain sensitive to the pervasive stigma and discrimination faced by LGBTIQA+ communities, in compliance with fundamental human rights obligations. Further implementation of the Bangkok Rules must ensure that marginalized societal groups are accorded full human rights protections and equal access to all prison programs, services, and opportunities.

Inequality Inside and Out

We make the argument here that gender inequality and discrimination lead to vulnerabilities in the risk of harm within all justice processes. As the most pervasive form of social inequality, gender inequality overlaps with other forms of inequality such as class, caste, race and ethnicity, leading to forms of intersectional harm. While such gender-based inequality is based on women's status in any given society, we also know that women from minority communities can be further disadvantaged by additional forms of inequality beyond gender.

Before prison, issues surrounding gender inequality are clear. In almost every society, women tend to be less educated, earn less income, have more negative health outcomes, and possess a lower social standing in their communities. Gender inequality is intersectional: ethnic minority women, those without free world capital, non-normative sexual and gender identities, and other non-majority characteristics are often the most marginalized members of society and the most imprisoned. Throughout the world, violence against women is another measure of these intersectional inequalities: emotional, sexual, and physical violence and the resulting trauma shape women's pathways to prison and often continue to undermine safety when imprisoned.

All elements of the carceral complex fail to serve the interests of women: they are fewer in number, often located far from home, designed to manage and rehabilitate men, staffed by those who are trained to work with men and often unfocused on the specific pathway needs of women. These specific needs are rarely considered in the prison design or the development of prison regimes and programs. Chief among the disadvantages created by gender inequality within the criminal justice system is the "discrimination of the economies of scale" (Barberet & Jackson, 2017, p. 17). In aggravating these discriminations of scale, the prison reproduces many of the inequalities found in free society.

After prison, women face continued gender-based discrimination upon their return home. While if fit for purpose, prisons would help women prepare to return to their communities with additional skills, education and treatment, this is typically not the case. In addition to the structural and intersectional gender-based discrimination, women leaving prison face additional stigmas when they return to their communities, related to their familial responsibilities, securing housing, a livelihood, the label of "formerly incarcerated" compounded with their histories of victimization and abuse which results in lack of community acceptance and barriers to successful re-integration (Thailand Institute of Justice & Griffith University, 2021). Without holistic and comprehensive programs to improve their overall life chances through real investment, women's situations are unlikely to improve. Combining these constraints with the stigma of imprisonment, women released from prison and other forms of detention have little support or resources. While the Bangkok Rules emphasize reintegration through rehabilitative programs, the need to support women at release requires collaboration and coordination with outside criminal justice and welfare authorities as well as community agencies and other non-governmental organizations.

Promoting Safety, Respect, and Dignity

In addition to developing formal measures that protect women from the damage of harsh prison regimes, the future of the Bangkok Rules must focus on a more expanded and comprehensive understanding of safety, respect, and dignity. While the Rules do provide specific guidance on creating a more safe and secure prison regime through gender-sensitive prison management they need to go even further to include moral, emotional, and psychological safety along with greater protection from physical and sexual harm. We suggest prison systems make all forms of safety the highest priority in protecting women across multiple dimensions.

Prioritizing respect and dignity is an additional need to ensure all forms of safety. We use the concept of respect to emphasize the importance of language. Given their trauma backgrounds, verbal interactions can create gendered harm. Staff behavior creates and magnifies these harms, further injuring women through disrespect. While both the Bangkok and Nelson Mandela Rules (see United Nations

General Assembly, 2016) underline the importance of respect, few prison systems have created formal policies that monitor and, where necessary, find staff accountable when they engage in disrespectful language with women in their care.

We similarly use the notion of dignity to frame needs related to the protection of women's bodies and material needs relating to maintaining their integrity. In addition to providing gender-informed health care, practice must ensure privacy, protection from the "male gaze," proper clothing, hygiene and other supplies needed to live with dignity. Search practices, as one example, can be a significant threat to women's dignity. Gender-sensitive operational practice begins with an emphasis on gender-responsive dignity.

Final Thoughts

While progress has been made in implementing the Bangkok Rules through research, capacity building and policy advocacy, significant challenges remain. This includes continuing problems related to the ever-increasing number of women in prison, punitive drug wars, over-reliance on pre-trial detention, imprisonment as the primary method of punishment, under-utilization of non-custodial measures as well as the needs of the invisible minority populations within prisons. The first decade of the Bangkok Rules brought international attention to the gendered situation of women in the criminal justice system and the critical need for human rights reform. The work of the Non-Government Organization, Member States, non-governmental organizations, and others have amplified this message of gendered human rights reform throughout the world. Research, training, and planning activities have also revealed several shortcomings in the implementation of the Bangkok Rules. We know that gender-based inequalities and inequities that pave women's pathways to prison continue to undercut women's well-being once sentenced to prison. This global discrimination has perpetuated existing disadvantages and vulnerabilities by inadequate application of the full range of human rights protections within the Bangkok Rules. More broadly, we assert that the Rules can counter gender inequality through incorporating human rights protections into the criminal justice system. They provide a gender-based framework for reforming prisons and eliminating the personal harm done to women and the collateral damage of prisons as a first resort.

The realities of the women's prison population and the negative impact of gender inequality raise a fundamental question: how can the Bangkok Rules be utilized to address overall gender inequality? The Bangkok Rules provide a foundation for this dialogue.

We continue to believe that implementing the Bangkok Rules, with renewed attention to safety, respect, and dignity, can reduce some of the gendered harm imbedded in contemporary correctional practice. Improving conditions for women confined to prison and other forms of detention must be accomplished through a human rights framework outlined in the 70 Rules. With much of the efforts surrounding the Rules focusing on in-custody implementation, the next step requires attention to expansion of non-custodial measures.

We call for using public monies to fund the expansion of non-custodial measures in place of investing in the prison system that has failed women and the community repeatedly. Eleven years after the adoption of the Bangkok Rules, it is time to shift additional investment into non-custodial and diversionary measures for women who come into conflict with the law. By re-directing investment from prisons, community-based sanctions could tackle the material needs of women like housing, education and childcare, as well as promote internal change through treatment and therapy. Sentencing policy, particularly in the context of drug and other survival crimes, requires re-examination and reform. When courts fail to have gender-responsive investigative procedures and sentencing guidelines, the decisions made can result in unnecessary punitive outcomes for women. We recognize that our proposal is ambitious. We remain committed to gender-based prison reform and remain equally vigilant in protecting women imprisoned as directed by the Bangkok Rules. This work is not complete, however, without a concentrated effort to both developing more effective non-custodial measures, reforming sentencing, harsh and punitive drug laws.

True human rights reform must begin by declaring imprisonment as the policy of last resort and privileging non-custodial measures as the policy of first resort. Eliminating the gendered harm of imprisonment requires a global recognition of the counterproductive effects of irrational drug laws and reduced sentencing options. Protecting women, their children and their communities requires high-level collaboration from multiple stakeholders in and outside the system. As we reimagine the definition of "punishment," we must shift away from punitive and damaging regimes toward a community-based, rehabilitative framework that is grounded in the principles of human rights, safety, dignity, and respect. We call for immediate and urgent action on the critical need for prison and drug law reform with collaborative efforts across all spheres. It is the right thing to do to expand the promise of the Bangkok Rules in Southeast Asia and beyond.

Chapter 11

Conclusion: Decentering Research and Practice Through Mutual Participation

Andrew M. Jefferson and Samantha Jeffries

Abstract

The chapters in this book show that it is possible to conduct studies on the intersections between gender, criminalization, imprisonment, and human rights in Southeast Asia. In this conclusion, we draw out the implications of this emerging scholarship. More specifically, we critically examine how common talk about "individual needs" risks blinding criminal justice reformers to the structural, gendered dynamics that render people criminalizable and imprisonable. We explore the potential of the concept of participation to strengthen understandings and activism around gendered harms, and grapple with the thorny issue of for whom we speak. We advocate for cross-cultural understandings, developed in collaboration and through partnership, to productively challenge the ethnocentrism of criminology and propel truly transformative agendas. Three steps are identified to decenter research and activism: Scholars and activists must acknowledge the risks of attending to need while not attending to the drivers of need; resist the temptation to operate only within the limits defined by the authorities, the state, the academy, or agencies set up to protect; and generate "home grown," counter-hegemonic solutions that push back against the tendency to universalize, colonize and deny difference.

Keywords: Participation; ethnocentrism; collaboration; mutuality; activism; research

Gender, Criminalization, Imprisonment and Human Rights in Southeast Asia, 155–172
doi:10.1108/978-1-80117-286-820221010

Introduction

This book began with a call for papers that we put out for a panel at the *Sixth International Conference on Human Rights and Peace & Conflict in Southeast Asia* originally scheduled for October 2020 but postponed because of COVID-19.[1] The call was rooted in a desire to collaborate, to connect with other scholar-activists, and to disseminate new knowledge that we were in the process of generating. The conference was put on hold, but we forged ahead nevertheless as we realized the abstracts we received had the potential to make a meaningful contribution. This book is the result.

In our introduction, we laid out our point of departure situating the contributions within pathways and feminist scholarship and stating that our objective was

> to capture and collate the emerging work of activist scholars and grassroots advocates grappling to understand the lived experiences of cisgender women, transgender persons, and other gender, and sexual minorities, as they encounter criminal justice systems in Southeast Asia.

In this conclusion, we want to push further to reflect and think with and beyond the contributions and even beyond our own initial point of departure to illustrate the value of a kind of criminology – if we must call it that – emerging from Southeast Asia which is not right realist or administrative, but critical and transformative.

In this book, we have filled some empirical gaps in the research field, by further illuminating experiences of imprisonment and entanglements with criminal justice systems in Cambodia, Indonesia, Malaysia, Myanmar, the Philippines and Thailand, and posted some way-markers that might guide future studies. Collectively, we have looked inside and outside of prisons across several sites in Southeast Asia and considered the relationship between gender, other intersectional subjugations and criminalization, as they frame and impact people's lives while examining the potential and limitations of normative human rights frameworks.

This conclusion is structured as follows: we begin by critically examining how talk about individual needs and immediate concerns risks blinding well-intentioned criminal justice reformers to the structural gendered dynamics that render people imprisonable. Then we explore the potential of the concept of participation to illuminate, deepen and strengthen understandings and activism around such issues. From participation, we move to the thorny issue of for whom we speak and to criminology's ethnocentrism (raised in the introduction), and the necessity of developing and propagating cross-cultural understandings – in collaboration and through partnership. In a penultimate section, we point to some of the implications of a scholarship about and emerging from Southeast Asia for notions of gender, criminalization, imprisonment and human rights. We end by looking ahead and asking: is there any scope for hope?

---

[1] Our thanks go to the Southeast Asian Human Rights Network for accepting our panel proposal and by doing so pushing these issues forward.

De-Individualizing Rights and Harms

In the face of immense suffering, blatant examples of injustice or inequality and obvious examples of violations, it can be tempting to talk about how to meet gender-specific needs or how to ensure people know and are granted their rights without delving much deeper into the backstories around why needs are not met in the first place and why rights are not enjoyed and respected. Faced by human suffering it is natural to turn to the tools that are at one's disposal and to articulate social, societal, even global challenges in terms of the dominant languages available.

Sometimes these are languages of the powerful global agencies – the World Bank, the United Nations. Sometimes these are languages of the historically powerful disciplines – law or medicine. Sometimes these are languages of vested interest – of corporations, of patriarchy or those otherwise interested in the maintenance and reproduction of the status quo. Sometimes these are the languages of the academy, often the northern/western academy with its concomitant condescension, arrogance and monopolization.

In this book, we have sought to visibilize and analyze the languages – that is the voices and words – of women, sexual and gender minorities, those at the margins of other intersectional oppressions and members of organizations and actors situated at the frontline of struggles on behalf of and with people caught up in structures that render them vulnerable to violation, victimization, and criminalization.

One of the tasks of an emancipatory interpretive social science (which is what feminist scholarship is) is to wisely discern the character of situations, events, and dynamics that render particular groups of people in specific situations violable, torturable, imprisonable, and killable.

To do this, it is vital to avoid defining the problem or the goal in terms of the apparent solutions currently at hand. The ends should not be formulated in terms of the means immediately at one's disposal. A particularly blatant example of this in development and human rights work is the way in which global challenges pertaining to injustice and inequality are reframed in terms of lack of knowledge or lack of morality for which the solution is the provision of new knowledge (in the form of training) and new rules. If the conceptual tools – our understandings – that inform our interventionist practice are simply those we pull off the shelf or borrow from the arsenals (and standing languages) of the powerful we run the risk of reproducing the dynamics we desire to transform.

Another example pertinent to the field of criminal justice is the manner statist language infiltrates the way reforms are talked about and issues are defined. Criminalized populations are referred to unthinkingly as offenders; the real-life situation of life after prison is reduced to the idea of "reintegration into society"; at-risk populations are identified as inherently vulnerable or as trouble-makers or threats to good order and community decency.

Both these examples involve not only the embrace of statist language but also the acceptance of a language that personalizes the issue, leaving the individual responsible both for their situation and for their own rescue. That is the "growth conditions" for violence and vulnerability are conflated under the rubric of needs implying some kind of lack in the individual.

The tendency to individualize issues – which at heart are relational or inter-subjective – has deep roots when it comes to matters of criminal justice, as Craig Haney (2006) has powerfully argued. Haney (2006) unpacks the fundamental way in which dominant contemporary models of punishment and criminal justice are based on the transformation of social conflicts (where lines of causation might be blurred) into matters of individual behavior for which a single person can be blamed and held responsible. The person standing in the dock becomes the criminal, legally and morally responsible for their behavior and its consequences, with society's only responsibility being to punish properly and ensure needs are met and procedures adhered to. The idea that people are constituted, and behavior partially determined through relations, through the opportunities at their disposal, through their position vis-à-vis others in society, through the transactions and dependencies within which they are caught up carries little weight in such settings (except in the almost tokenistic idea of mitigating circumstances).

Human rights and development discourse and practice – within which most of the contributors to this book are one way or the other situated – is not immune to the tendency to individualize either and when it does so it too runs the risk of exacerbating problems rather than addressing them. The human rights-based approach to development (HRBA) is one example of a line of thinking that exemplifies this. HRBA, at its most basic level, figures people as either rights holders or duty bearers (echoing a crude distinction resisted by many scholars and practitioners today between victims and perpetrators). By doing so it individualizes rights discourse and practice unnecessarily.

Iris Marion Young's (1990) powerful argument about social justice not being a possession of individuals but something attached to relationships is pertinent here. While the idea of me or you or the next person "having" rights is seductive, in practice it can be a blind alley if the conditions in society are such that you or I cannot enjoy those rights because for example, society is based on patriarchal and authoritarian histories that exhibit intolerance for non-conformity, valuing instead uniformity and obedience and the perpetuation of the "natural" order of things. According to Young (1990), social justice, is not about what people have but about what they can do, what opportunities are available to them, the extent to which they have the conditions of life at their own disposal. She proposes a process-oriented, relational approach to social justice that focuses on the "social structures and processes that produce distributions rather than on the distributions" (Young, 1990, p. 18). From her perspective, and echoing the final paragraphs of this book's introduction,

> Rights are not fruitfully conceived as possessions. Rights are relationships, not things; they are institutionally defined rules specifying what people can do in relation to one another. Rights refer to doing more than having, to social relationships that enable or constrain action. (Young, 1990, p. 25)

Pursuing this line of thought, instead of individualizing collective issues attention should be directed toward the unequal distribution of possibilities to participate meaningfully in social life without risk of victimization and violation. Thus, it is important to examine the gendered distribution/patterning of harms and rights but also how possibilities to be harmed and to enjoy rights are distributed. This is ultimately about drawing attention to hierarchies of worth and the idea that some lives are more grieveable than others (Butler, 2004; Segal, 2016; Stevenson, 2014).

A focus on distribution rather than possession redirects attention toward the way rights are conditioned by relations and positionalities. Rights thus need to be understood as distributed and diffused through populations (often unequally), translated into everyday practices, and embedded in societies rather than possessed by rights holders and applied in situations of individual need, lack or inherent vulnerability.

Proponents of the HRBA would, for sure, recognize this. They are not blind to the structural dynamics and inequalities that pervade societies and subordinate some groups at the cost of others. Nevertheless, the commitment to an individualized notion of rights evident in the notions of rights holders and duty bearers does set a limit on ways of conceptualizing the issues at stake that lead practitioners more easily toward needs-based approaches than to approaches that highlight the necessity of more radical structural and societal change, to once again pick up a thread from our introduction. Of course, one kind of response is easier to offer than the other – and often more immediate – which adds to its seductive power.

But ensuring rights are accessible without addressing the reasons rights are sometimes curtailed for some members of societies is not enough. And as Upendra Baxi (1998) and others note sometimes rights are in the interests of the powerful not the powerless. So, redistributing rights as if rights were possessions is insufficient. And identifying harms[2] as if they were the property, responsibility or fault of those subject to them is unproductive.

These reflections represent a subtle rethinking of how we might think about rights less instrumentally that draws on the scholarship of the last couple of decades about human rights in practice (Cowan, 2006; Cowan, Dembour, & Wilson, 2001; Dembour, 2006; Goodale & Merry, 2007; Jefferson & Jensen, 2009). During these times of rising authoritarianism (as we have seen recently in Myanmar, the Philippines and Thailand) and the questioning of the mechanisms and systems designed to manage the protection of rights as defined in United Nations conventions and charters, it is even more important to reanimate and give renewed impetus to rights discourse and practice. One way of doing this is to think of rights as relational.

Another way to express this is to say we need to put the human back into human rights or to rediscover rights in the service of those who suffer as Baxi (1998) (might) put it. Baxi (1998, p. 128) decries the corporatization of rights

---

[2]For deeper insights into the notion of social harm see the work of the zemiologists (Canning & Tombs, 2021; Hillyard & Tombs, 2007).

discourse stating that "recovery of the sense and experience of human anguish provides the only hope that there is for the future of human rights." And further, "to give language to pain, to experience the pain of the Other inside you, remains the task, always, of human rights narrative and discourse" (Baxi, 1998, p. 149). This profoundly visceral evocation of a rights-oriented relation would seem to sit quite well with the sensory turn in criminology (Herrity, Warr, & Schmidt, 2021). It also resonates with the contributions to this book that echo the voices of women, sexual and gender minorities as they have spoken about the way their lives are rendered deserving of violence.

Pathways of Participation

We turn now to the concept of participation. In this book, authors have focused quite regularly on feminist "pathways" building on Daly's (1994) approach and emphasizing the way routes into, through and out of prison are profoundly gendered. Another critical strand running through these pages strongly implies that many of the inhabitants of prisons would not be there were it not for the forces of law, society, culture and history that thrust women, sexual and gender minorities into situations (not of their own choosing) where they are subordinated, unable to provide for themselves or their families and consequently rendered vulnerable and violable and criminalized, and incarcerated. Within such conditions, they have expressed agency within the confines of their oppression and taken action, through what the state defines as criminal, to free themselves, if only for a while, from their oppressive circumstances. As mentioned, the feminist pathways scholarship, that explicitly or implicitly informs the contributions to this book, has focused on the way (mostly) women's routes and journeys into, through and out of prison are gendered, thus casting light on the structured and structuring situations that women find themselves in at various points on that journey – be it the home, the search for livelihood opportunities, the police station, the courtroom, or the prison. The pathways approach makes explicit the fact that lives are not static but fluid and subject to change, that people are, so to speak, on life trajectories.

All the contributors to this book are concerned with people in everyday life, that is with the way people inhabit and occupy social and institutional worlds. At stake within each of the chapters – though mostly unacknowledged – are ideas about how people engage in the world, that is how they participate. The pathways approach implies that people are participants in social life, that is in the world even before they present as people with needs to be excluded or included in criminal justice systems.

Inclusion and participation have been buzzwords in the development and human rights world for decades sometimes burning hotter than others (Chambers, 1997; Cornwall, 2006, 2011; Holland & Blackburn, 1998). The concept of participation is a way of thinking about humans' deep embeddedness in social practice, the inescapability of our "thrownness" into the world. While it has become a popular mantra that context should be taken seriously when designing any form of intervention or launching any new policy, mantras are no guarantee of context-informed practice. Approaching people as situated participants in populated practices rather than history-less automatons in black boxes is an important way of inserting context more deeply into interventionist thinking and practice.

From this point of view, it is a problem when accounts of "individual needs" are insufficiently anchored in a thorough understanding of the way people are inherently embedded in social worlds. Participation is a deeper, stronger, more useful concept than often realized (perhaps even stronger than "agency"). A body of work that might help us in that regard is that of the critical psychologist Ole Dreier (2003, 2008) and his long-term collaborator anthropologist Jean Lave (2011). Lave has innovatively reframed theories of learning (and indirectly change) as less about knowledge transfer between "lollipop men" [i.e., (male) minds on sticks] and more about "changed participation in changing practice." And with Dorothy Holland, she has helpfully recast structure-agency debates in terms of "enduring struggles and intimate identities" catalyzed through "contentious local practice" (Holland & Lave, 2001). Dreier theorizes from the point of view of a "science of the subject" aimed at making sense of what we might call persons-in-practice (Jefferson & Huniche, 2009). Of particular use is his concept of "trajectories of participation" which combines an orientation to lives on the move with an understanding of participation as more than just "taking part in" a particular activity that might or might not be appropriately attuned to one's needs. To participate is to belong to the social world, to be embedded in history, and anchored in the world through embodied relationships. This embeddedness can be compromised by the structures and dynamics of any given situation leaving people unhinged and limited in their ability to exhibit agency and navigate their conditions of possibility. Critical psychologists, like Dreier (2003), direct attention to conditions, meanings and reasons for action recognizing the links between these features of everyday life (See, for example, Dreier, 2003, 2008; Motzkau & Schraube, 2015; Mørck, 1995; Nissen, 2000, 2012; Schraube & Højholt, 2016) .

With these insights in mind, it is possible to think more critically and more deeply about the gendered "exercise of existence" (to borrow Achille Mbembe's (2001) evocative phrase) of women and gender and sexual minorities as they encounter criminal justice systems and the way that exercise of existence is curtailed in harm-filled, harmful ways.

Speaking *with* and the Potential of Cross-Cultural Understandings to Decenter and Deprivilege Dominant Knowledge through Partnerships

Through this book, we have made visible some key aspects of research, advocacy, policy, and program development taking place in Southeast Asia, while also giving voice to those criminalized and imprisoned in this part of the world. Cross-cultural understandings are important. They challenge the ethnocentrism of criminology (and other disciplines), create a space from which we can listen and learn, and in turn, more accurately respond to the gendered needs of those in conflict with the law – but also the causes and drivers of those needs.

Cross-cultural understandings enable us to confront the hegemony of western rationality and the dominance of western academic institutions in determining the form and criteria for valid knowledge generation. But cross-cultural understandings do not come about without hard work and they do not come about simply by attending more to the countries of the global south or juxtaposing findings from one culture with findings from another. Cross-cultural understandings require cross-fertilization in the form of coming together in a genuine multi-directional dialogue of exchange. This we aspire to, as this book bears witness, but it is something that will always be experimental and provisional calling for a constant interrogation of position and privilege and the grounds from which "we" speak.

The chapters in this book are the product of a range of different types of collaboration many of which predated the project of bringing this book together and go back several years. Common to the different collaborations is an attempt to bridge the divide between the academy and practice. A reflexive and critical concern with practice and with enabling action draws attention to the radically situated nature of any practice of knowledge production, that is to the theme of positionality.

Positionality is a core theme of feminist (and critical race) scholarship linked to reflexivity, criticality and intersectionality as explored in a range of important foundational writings (Haraway, 1988; Harding, 2004; Hill Collins, 1990). The contributors to this book are positioned quite differently across a range of dimensions. We are an eclectic bunch involved in varying ways at different times in knowledge generation, policy work, advocacy, activism, and hands-on development projects. We often have a range of overlapping roles – serving as designers of research and interventions, advisors to civil society, governments and other agencies, mentors of students or early career researchers and so on. In our experience, the ability to occupy multiple roles and take on and off different hats has proved fruitful for research and activism.

As already mentioned, our purpose with this book was to visibilize and make available to a wider audience work being done in and on Southeast Asia. In some ways, this can be thought of as a practice of giving voice. During the process of drafting this conclusion, however, this has brought to our attention the tricky question of for whom we, as contributors and editors, speak? And, by extension for whom and to whom does research speak? The significant work of Linda Alcoff (1991) has been instructive in this regard.

Writing in 1991, and revised and republished several times since, Alcoff[3] draws attention to the epistemic salience of a speaker's location and reflects on important questions about the "discursively dangerous" authority of scholars located

---

[3]See also a highly accessible interview covering some of the same issues published in *Stance* (Alcoff, 2019).

in situations of privilege, especially when that privilege is taken for granted. She locates her main argument as being about "that small space of discursive agency we all [academic writers that is] experience however multi-layered, fictional and constrained it in fact is" (1991, p. 6). What she is pointing to here are the elements of doubt, hesitancy and caution (or, on the other hand, certainty, speed, and daring) that inform acts of writing or speaking from a position of authority.

In her attempt to unpack the "problem" of speaking for others Alcoff (1991, p. 9) examines two premises, one pertaining to the fact "that there is no possibility of rendering positionality, location, or context irrelevant to content," the second to the fact that "discursive context is a political arena." Expanding on this latter point she writes,

> rituals of speaking are politically constituted by power relations of domination, exploitation and subordination. Who is speaking, who is spoken of, and who listens is a result, as well as an act, of political struggle. (Alcoff, 1991, p. 9)

This is crucial to our developing understanding of our own reflexive position as writers, speakers, and editors working collaboratively with differentially positioned others jointly engaged in a practice of visibilizing other subjugated voices from a part of the world rendered peripheral by the standards of western-inflected academic study. We are not outside of the contestations that our differentially located positions animate. Rather, we are quite radically, and unavoidably, implicated in the practices and effects of struggle – both substantive and discursive – that our book is about. Our point here is that consciousness of this fact is vital. And the "emotionally troublesome endeavour" associated with "constant interrogation and critical reflection" (Alcoff, 1991, p. 15) on one's own position and privilege is necessary As Alcoff (1991, p. 12) puts it,

> (T)here is no neutral place to stand free and clear in which one's words do not prescriptively affect or mediate the experience of others, nor is there a way to demarcate decisively a boundary between one's location and all others.

From this perspective, it is simply not possible to only speak for oneself; one always speaks for or about or in relation to others. Recognizing this is an important political gesture and offers a provisional platform from which to speak.

In a discussion of Gayatri Spivak's (1998) "Can the Subaltern Speak?," Alcoff (1991) notes the naivety of one position that could be adopted about the concerns we are addressing here. This would be the position that says we chose not to speak for or to but only to listen and re-present, for example, the voices of the oppressed or the voices of scholars from the south. The naivety of such a position lies in the fact that it "essentializes the oppressed as non-ideologically constructed subjects"

(Alcoff, 1991, p. 16) and undermines the potential added value of research.[4] Just because people are oppressed does not make them analytically authoritative or value-free. Ironically what we sometimes find is that so much effort has been put into spreading western academic norms and rationalities that one finds southern partners so heavily invested in these norms that they find our critical self-reflexive critiques about representation and politics of knowledge puzzling. Having said this and, as Alcoff (1991, p. 16) acknowledges, "listening" is one obvious way of "giving voice" and opening space for subjugated actors to perform as "knowing agents" and not merely "objects of knowledge."

We agree with Alcoff (1991) that speaking for others is risky but sometimes necessary, though the impetus to *always* speak should be resisted. Choosing when not to speak can of course be a tricky endeavor and also rests on dynamics of privilege. Ceding position, granting the other space, choosing not to speak up or out is also a political act.

The position toward which we aspire is one that avoids the false dichotomy between either speaking for or listening to but rather cherishes dialogue and the pursuit of opportunities to speak with, to and through others mutually.[5] Ironically, many of the contributors to this book have never met each other in person. We have gotten to know each other through the exchange of textual material in the form of drafts and redrafts of chapters. It is quite possible, even quite likely, that in the editorial process we editors have engaged in clumsy acts of erasure as we sought to make this book a viable enterprise given the terms and conditions associated with contemporary academic publishing. We never set out to challenge the constraints that these conditions impose. Rather, reluctantly accepting them, we have sought to shape and reshape the chapters so that arguments were clear, voices decipherable, and analysis persuasive. In so doing, we contend that this book is a dialogical enterprise. As such it also serves as an invitation to differentially positioned readers to contest our positions and make their own sense of the arguments.

The question of for whom and about whom we speak lies at the heart of moves over the last couple of decades to decenter western taken for granted knowledges and to take seriously the colonial and imperial inflections of much knowledge production. We welcome moves within criminology and other disciplines to question epistemological foundations and presumed norms and canons more

---

[4]In an earlier piece of work reflecting on the work of anti-torture organizations the first author proposed that research in such settings might be conceived of as bringing "convergent and divergent perspectives into conversation with one another adding a meta-reflexive layer which strives to be not just one more situated voice but an analytic voice juxtaposing and questioning, hesitating and puzzling and seeking new questions and points of curiosity" (Jefferson, 2016). Through activist scholarship we strive to do more than simply echo oppressed voices and subjugated knowledge. We strive to add analytic value.

[5]As Alcoff (1991, p. 16) puts it "we should strive to create wherever possible the conditions for dialogue and the practice of speaking with and to rather than speaking for others."

fundamentally as evidenced by the emergence of decolonizing and southernizing efforts, however, splintered these may be (Aliverti, Carvalho, Chamberlen, & Sozzo, 2021; Carrington, Hogg, & Sozzo, 2016, Carrington, Hogg, Scott, & Sozzo, 2018; Cunneen, 2011; Dimou, 2021; Moosavi, 2019a, 2019b, 2020). Exposing and correcting traditions and structures that exclude certain voices and perpetuate the status quo is necessary. There may be a risk, nevertheless, that disciplines turn inwards rather than outwards during this necessary process of conscientization, even that peripheral or hitherto excluded voices are effectively and counter-productively drowned out as privileged voices continue a long tradition of speaking more to themselves than listening to the voice of the other [cf. Juan Tauri's (2021) Indigenous criminology and the counter-colonial criminology of Biko Agozino (2004)]. Neither the contestation around curricula, nor discipline-based in-fighting or drives to establish new strands or "traditions" must be allowed to distract from the practice of generating knowledge and enabling action collaboratively across cultures. It seems incumbent on scholars engaged in debates about the historical and current context of knowledge production to ensure that critical reflexivity does not slip into self-indulgence and become once again centered around the questions of who we are as "as criminologists" or what the "nature" of criminology actually is.

This book is published in the activist criminology series but most of the contributors are not strictly speaking criminologists or adherents to a discipline-oriented form of knowledge generation. Our approach is more expansive, our positionalities, as mentioned, quite varied. Where academic disciplines set boundaries, circumscribe fields, and police methods and forms of distribution in the interests of order and the production of certain types of professionals and certain forms of knowledge, our critical, feminist, practice-oriented approach allows us to transgress some of these boundaries.

But we are also captive to tradition even as we seek to transgress certain norms in the interests of inclusivity and the development of more comprehensive understandings. The most obvious of these is the choice to publish in English, not the first language of many of the contributors. Similarly, editorial work is by nature a craft form that involves a push toward conformity and uniformity in the service of the gods of cogency and coherence. As such, the task of editors or drafters of a conclusion like this might be seen as identifying common threads and imposing unity on a disparate set of chapters in the interests of clarity and on behalf of an imagined reader unable to discern for themselves. But why imagine the reader as in need of such help, as unable to hold disparate threads in mind, as only being able to decipher a linear, uniform narrative airbrushed clean of discrepancies, discolorations and wrinkles? Our imagined readers are smarter than this.

The stakes here are not issues of truth or method[6] as much as concrete constitutive matters about relations between people differently positioned across a

---

[6]For more on the issue of truth and method versus justice, power and politics see the quite hefty debate between Susan Hekman, Nancy Hartsock, Sandra Harding, Patricia Hill Collins and Dorothy Smith (in Harding, 2004).

variety of dimensions (gender, race, generation, geography, etc.) with different academic backgrounds and levels of perceived authority and different life histories and contemporary life contexts. And this is just the writers of this book. If we look beyond the writers to the others implicated in the shared production of this book – to the imprisoned women, for example – we see even deeper degrees of variation and distinction. Feminist standpoint theory/ies and the epistemological commitments associated with the recognition that knowledge is situated and some forms of knowledge more subjugated or more privileged than others remind us of the way human experience is mediated by the differential distribution of resources, perceived worth or value, and suffering (in the form of poverty, violence, domination and the ability (or not) to transgress the conditions of possibility of specific forms of life) (Das, 2007, 2020). Recognizing the legitimacy and necessity of different standpoints and experiences and deliberately choosing to listen and engage with their perspectives is one marker of this book.

This book has not explicitly sought to decolonize knowledge but if it does so we are more than happy. Our target is not western scholarship except in the sense that we wish to decenter the point of orientation or the axes around which understandings of gender, imprisonment, human rights and criminalization revolve. Our desire has been to illuminate a non-western context attentive to its own terms and conditions. By doing so, we indirectly undermine or push back at dominant circulating images of the intersection between gender, imprisonment, rights, and criminalization that are limited by their peculiar context of production being mainly in the west.

Our desire to conduct research in southern contexts and to generate knowledge in order to push back against dominant and hegemonic understandings goes back at least two decades and predates recent moves toward decolonization and southernization.[7] In some respects, our previous research demonstrates more the doing of (post)colonial scholarship than the thinking about the state of the colonial epistemological foundations of criminology. We have sought to put our privilege – our know-how, know-who as well as our access to resources – to work, together with scholars and activists the concerns of whom have been neglected in the past.

As Alverti et al. (2021) argue, it is necessary to do more than just broaden the scope of scholarship to incorporate the global south as a field for "northerners" to study. This must be accompanied by a ceding of space to enable the growth of hitherto peripheral scholarship that is not stifled by the dictates of western

---

[7]The initiation of the Global Prisons Research Network in 2009 by the first author of this piece and colleagues from Denmark, India and Ghana with its avowed purpose "to fill the empirical gap created by the hegemony of the Anglo-American axis of comparison in prison studies by promoting and supporting in-depth studies of prison practices in Africa, Asia, the Middle East, Latin America and the former Soviet States" testifies to this.

rationality or methodological dogma.[8] The normative power of research produced in Anglo-American contexts to define and police the legitimacy and credibility of research must be challenged. One way to do this of course is through doing research *other*wise and with others and yet this is not without obstacles, be these related to bureaucracies, funding possibilities, pandemics or other dangers and risks. However, we suspect that the conditions that 'militate against the production of research in Southern contexts' (Aliverti et al., 2021, p. 304) are actually over-estimated and we concur with Luisa Schneider that there needs to be a "right to risk" (Schneider, 2020).[9] In our experience field research conducted with an ethnographic sensibility (Schatz, 2009), a feminist epistemology (Harding, 2004), or an action research angle offers rich possibilities in the global south, especially when conducted through partnerships. We therefore agree that the challenges of researching in the south can also be conceived of as "a driving force for methodological and theoretical innovation to expand criminological imaginations" (Alverti et al., 2021, p. 304). Similarly, we concur with Katja Franko Aas (2012, p. 16) that "developing more democratic epistemologies is not only a question of epistemological justice, but increasingly also an analytical imperative and an opportunity for theoretical innovation." But paying heed to Cunneen and Tauri (2016, 2019), it is also incumbent on researchers from the north to acknowledge and recognize (in the deepest sense of these words) pre-existing, but hitherto ignored and peripheralized, scholarship.

In this penultimate section of this chapter, we briefly consider some ways in which research in and about Southeast Asia pushes back against hegemonic understandings and practices pertaining to gender, criminalization, imprisonment and human rights.

Revisiting Gender, Criminalization, Imprisonment, and Human Rights

In this book, we have not compared systems or institutions but engaged in an illumination of experiences and conditions of possibility, as well as responses designed to mitigate harms and ameliorate sub-standard conditions. The approach we seek to model is person-centered without being individualizing. Our focus is not essentialized gender but the effects of gender; not crime but criminalization; not the prison but the practice of imprisonment; not human rights as such but the translation and practice of human rights.

---

[8]Dimou (2021) and Moosavi (2020) both warn candidly of the risks that the current "craze" to intellectually decolonize might perversely end up reinscribing coloniality. Moosavi (2020) has helpfully drawn attention to the thought of scholars such as S. H. Alatas, S. F. Alatas, C. Ake, N. Thiong'o, W. Mignolo, A. Quijano, K.-H. Chen as well as members of the Subaltern School (not forgetting F. Fanon and E. Said) to mitigate against this risk.

[9]Schneider (2020) is not arguing that researchers should put themselves in unnecessary danger but exposing the absurdity of mollycoddling, bureaucratic, risk averse procedures that are rooted in universities' desire to protect themselves from liability.

The chapters in this book testify to the fact that it is possible to conduct studies on these topics in Southeast Asia, if that was ever in doubt. Practical challenges and bureaucratic hurdles to one side it is not impossible to study or to engage as decades of side-lined scholarship bear witness. There are opportunities for dialogue with authorities and for programming. There are opportunities for regional policy pushes, for example, the United Nations Rules for the Treatment of Women Prisoners and Non-Custodial Measures for Women Offenders (the Bangkok Rules) (United Nations General Assembly, 2010). And there are opportunities for collaborative research. So, what does our collective research and reflection from and about Southeast Asia teach us about gender, criminalization, imprisonment and human rights? Here we simply draw out a few illustrative points.

Gender is a condition or quality that is difficult to pin down but has real effects. Scholars have come to understand gender as fluid not fixed. In Southeast Asia, it is fluid in different ways to those commonly recognized in western discourses and by international actors. This point is clearly made by Pravattiyagul as she explores the struggles of trans prisoners in Thailand and by the Myanmar-based research team in their discussion of *apwints* in conflict with the law in Myanmar (both in this volume). The slipperiness of terms and the difficulty translating practices and orientations into concepts that remain meaningful across languages has been articulated very clearly by Lynette Chua and David Gilbert writing about gender identity and sexual orientation in Myanmar (Chua & Gilbert, 2015; Gilbert, 2013). Presuming that vocabularies match is a temptation that must be avoided.[10] Additionally, observable variations in ways of talking about issues and forms of life remind us that in-country, on-the-ground research is indispensable.

The launch and naming of the Bangkok Rules in Thailand suggest an attentiveness to issues pertaining to gender and imprisonment in the region and we do see evidence of considerably more policy-related efforts around these matters in Southeast Asia than elsewhere with significantly more attention here than in many western jurisdictions.[11] However, it must be noted that the push in this direction was hardly bottom up. On the contrary, it was propelled by Thai royalty with substantial input from the western-influenced research community and policy bodies. Despite this, the Bangkok Rules do serve as a kind of "lightening rod" around which to galvanize support for more gender-sensitive penal policies in the region as described by Owen (this volume).

Criminalization is a process of designation and othering that targets the poor and the disenfranchised disproportionately and enables the powerful to benefit. In Southeast Asia, a prominent trend is the imprisonment of women for their first offense and often for trivial offenses that would not bring a person near a prison in other parts of the world. This is partly the result of unscrupulous policing practices (including corruption and other barriers to impartial justice provision) and partly

---

[10]"Prisoners of freedom" by Harri Englund (2006) is instructive in this regard in relation to the untranslatability of the concept of "human rights" in Malawi.

[11]Perhaps this is another example of rights-informed policy frameworks that serve more to civilize abroad than civilize at home.

related to the relative absence of non-custodial measures in the region. The production and marketing of illicit drugs as well as the war on drugs also have particularly powerful effects in the region (especially of late in the Philippines and Thailand) but also the war on terror and the brutal crackdown on dissent by authoritarian/military regimes where opposition itself is criminalized (see Chapter 2, this volume). Of additional significance in relation to criminalization are issues pertaining to migration and cross-border labor practices as reflected in work on foreign nationals in prisons across the region (Yamada-Park & Jeffries, 2018; Chapter 3, this volume). As in other parts of the world, ethnicity is yet another marker that renders some people more subject to criminalization than others as reflected in Chapter 6 on ethnic minority women in Thai prisons (this volume).

Imprisonment is a practice that produces harm and has negative effects on imprisoned persons and their families. It rarely lives up to stated aims and is not fit for purpose. But contrary to popular imaginaries the prisons of Southeast Asia, while definitely overused, do not quite live up to their representation in the west as feral pits of inhumanity. Often their scale and the degree to which prisoners are involved in prison governance gives prisons the appearance of walled, securitized towns with economies, transactions and dependencies, businesses, entertainment facilities, churches, mosques, shrines, events, and contested political terrains, making the adage that prisons are microcosms of society more literally true than often imagined.[12] Poor conditions and scarce resources lead to situations where staff and prisoners share similar environments and staff are often heard to express considerable sympathy rather than antipathy for prisoners[13] (see Chapter 6). In our experience, prisons in Southeast Asia also exhibit considerable openness to partnerships with non-governmental organizations and other external actors compared with their western counterparts, as highlighted in Chapter 10 and Chapter 6.

Human rights are one commonly invoked solution to wrongs in the world but as already mentioned they must be "translated" to acquire meaning and not simply applied, technically implemented, or imperially imposed. In many jurisdictions in Southeast Asia, rights-oriented norms and standards feature at the level of official discourse and policy but lack bite at the level of everyday practice. The Philippines, for example, is lauded as a country with quite progressive rights-promoting legislation, including an anti-torture law, but implementation and enforcement mechanisms are lacking and the effects are thus limited. Similarly, the aforementioned Bangkok Rules are highly visible in the region but there is still a long way to go with their effective implementation. At the same time, there is

---

[12]See Jefferson, Jensen, and Turner's (2019) characterization of the New Bilibid Prison in the Philippines as reminiscent of a Bruegel painting (p. 10). And also Narag and Jones (2016) for a similar characterization of a Philippine prison as a village.

[13]See Jefferson and Gaborit (2015) for comparative analysis of similar situations in Sierra Leone (West Africa) and the Philippines.

always the risk that norm-orientated policies can be taken hostage by regressive forces resulting in imaginary rather than real reform (Jefferson, 2008).

Marie Benedict Dembour (2010) has identified four distinct but overlapping schools of rights scholarship and practice – the natural, deliberative, protest, and discourse schools. Her work helpfully reminds us of the huge range of positions that it is possible to adopt with regard to rights. For example, she elucidates the four schools along two key dimensions: more or less foundational and more or less liberal, examining how rights are perceived differently in terms of whether they are given in advance or there to be claimed, and whether they are perceived as "essential" or constructed.[14] Like Baxi's (1998) invocation of rights in the service of those who suffer (rather than to ease the conscience or marketability of profit-making corporations) Dembour's (2010) work reminds us that rights can have both conserving and liberating orientations and effects.

It is clear from the chapters of this book that in Southeast Asia, as in other parts of the world, human rights are differentially distributed, and that the differential distribution of rights corresponds to the differential distribution of opportunities and reflects positions and dynamics of privilege and power that are assumed to be natural and cry out for demystification. In this light, it may be pointless to promote rights or address needs without addressing the factors that inhibit their progressive implementation or sustain their violation in the first place.[15] For example, policies that focus on needs are typically oriented toward the individual implying that the criminal justice system is somehow in the interests of the individual rather than the state. Under such circumstances, a needs-oriented focus can have adverse effects. Prisoners can be obliged or compelled to participate in programs "for their own good" to enable them to "reintegrate" into society even while the possibilities available to them in society remain severely curtailed.

To polemically (and perhaps perversely) counter this position, one might call for *less* inclusion of women, sexual and gender minorities in prison and for *less* participation of women, gender and sexual minorities in programs designed ostensibly to meet their needs. Such a call would illustrate the absurdity of calling for needs to be met while ignoring underlying causes and drivers of inequality and criminalization. A more radical position would be to call for women (and men) to be kept out of penal systems, as called for by numerous authors in this book. If that could be achieved many of the dilemmas and quandaries that some prison authorities battle with could be avoided. For example, instead of struggling to defend themselves against the accusation of not providing the same kind of meaningful activities as those available to men authorities could channel their energies into offering

---

[14]For the natural school rights are given and for everybody; for the protest school rights are fought for and primarily for the suffering; for the deliberative school rights are agreed upon and for organizing society; and for the discourse school rights are talked about and ought to be for those who suffer (though in fact often are not).
[15]Celermajer's (2018) argument for an ecological model of torture prevention is seminal in this regard, reviewed by Cakal, Jefferson, and Martin (2021).

a decent standard of care to those who cannot be diverted from prison or helped to evade the clutches of the criminal justice system in the first place.

Another example of the tension between addressing acute need and dealing with states of chronic crisis is the much talked about issue of prison overcrowding or overpopulation (see Chapter 1). The problem is not that there are too many people *in* prison but that too many people are *put* in prison. Or put differently, there are in fact two problems but the former tends to crowd out the latter and energies are expended on acute situations at the expense of examining and changing the chronic practices and political motivations that lead to the acute situations. We know that the number of people put in prison is a political choice not a given reflection of crime statistics. But what are the concrete implications of recognizing the "chronicity of crisis" (Vigh, 2008) and the intersectionality of oppressions when it comes to concretely transforming the situations of people rendered vulnerable and violable? And from where might we identify sources of hope? In our conclusion below we briefly entertain these questions.

Conclusion: Some Hope-Filled Steps

We have argued that it is not enough to give or guarantee or distribute rights (or needs-oriented provision) if one does not address the structures that perpetuate the need or the violation. Scholar-activists who insist, as we do, on attending to structural factors as well as immediate needs face a dilemma: how exactly to do both? How concretely, in project or research terms can we address what makes populations violable, disposable, and torturable, (or some more torturable than others) and how can we begin to deconstruct the embedded habits and structures that perpetuate this at the same time as ameliorating specific harms? A first step must be to acknowledge the potential unintended consequences of attending to need while not attending to the drivers of need, rather than either denying or remaining structurally blind to this, or papering it over with band-aid solutions.

A second step is to more accurately define the problem – using collaborative, mutual research – and resisting strongly the instinct to define the problem in terms of the solutions at hand. Activists, practitioners, and researchers must beware the temptation to operate only within the limits defined by the authorities, the state, or the existing bodies ostensibly set up to protect, or by hegemonic academic norms. Hegemonic interests have a tendency of infiltrating even the most progressive and well-intended mechanisms resulting ultimately in the maintenance of the entrenched status quo.

In this light, a third step is to advocate for more "home grown," mutually co-produced, and counter-hegemonic solutions that push back against the presumption to universalize, colonize and deny difference. This is likely to involve a combination of modesty and ambition as well as pragmatism and risk. Which brings us to hope. Philosopher John Caputo (2020, p. 198) writes,

> Hope is not caused by being, être, but elicited by a may-being, a peut-être (perhaps). Hope is not caused, it is called up, called for, in the face of the cool course that being runs, affirmed in the face

of the groundlessness of being. Hope is not the effect of a cause; it is a response to a call. Hope is not sustained by a cause; the cause is sustained by hope.

Confronted by the suffering that gendered, criminalized, and other subjugated populations are subject to and the disinclination of powerful bodies or agencies to really act in the interests of all humans and of the planet, it can be difficult to identify sources of hope. Despair and cynicism knock regularly at the door. Caputo's deconstructionist, Derrida-inspired angle resists the idea of an eternal *source* of hope, a well-spring from which we might be filled up and instead alludes to the hope that is elicited by the possibilities that our living and acting in the world makes available, the maybes, the perhapses. It is our conviction that together, mutually and in collaboration, research and activism can go hand in hand to further social justice and ameliorate social harm. This book is our provisional, partial, and positioned response – our hope – to practices of violation, victimization, and vulnerability facing criminalized and imprisoned populations in Southeast Asia. We submit that together the empirically grounded chapters gathered here make a worthwhile contribution toward the development of perspectives and actions that will help in the ongoing pursuit of a more just and fairer world.

References

Aas, K. F. (2012). The Earth is one but the world is not: Criminological theory and its geopolitical divisions. *Theoretical Criminology, 16*(1), 5–20.

Aday, R. H., & Farney, L. (2014). Malign neglect: Assessing older women's health care experiences in prison. *Journal of Bioethical Inquiry, 11*(3), 359–372.

Aday, R. H., & Krabill, J. J. (2011). *Women aging in prison: A neglected population in the correctional system*. Boulder: Lynne Reinner Publishers.

Agozino, B. (2003). *Counter-colonial criminology: A critique of imperialist reason*. London: Pluto Press.

Agozino, B. (2004). Imperialism, crime and criminology: Towards the decolonisation of criminology. *Crime, Law and Social Change, 41*(4), 343–58.

Agustin, L. (2003). Sex, gender and migrations: Facing up to ambiguous realities. *Soundings, 23*, 99–102

Alcoff, L. M. (1991). The problem of speaking for others. *Cultural Critique, 20*, 5–32.

Alcoff, L. M. (2019). Feminism, speaking for others, and the role of the philosopher: An interview with Linda Martin Alcoff. *Stance: An International Undergraduate Philosophy Journal, 9*(1), 85–105.

Aliverti, A., Carvalho, H., Chamberlen, A., & Sozzo, M. (2021). Decolonizing the criminal question. *Punishment & Society, 23*(3), 297–316.

Alós, R., Esteban, F., Jódar, P., & Miguélez, F. (2015). Effects of prison work programmes on the employability of ex-prisoners. *European Journal of Criminology, 12*(1), 35–50.

Alvarez, M. (2018). *Women, incarceration and drug policies in South East Asia: Promoting humane and effective responses – A policy guide for Thailand*. Bangkok: International Drug Policy Consortium.

Ameeriar, L. (2012). The gendered suspect: Women at the Canada-U.S. border after September 11. *Journal of Asian American Studies, 15*(2), 171–195.

Amnesty International. (1997). *Philippines: The death penalty: Criminality, justice, and human rights*. Quezon City: Amnesty International.

Amnesty International. (2002). *Philippines: Death penalty Briefing*. Quezon City: Amnesty International.

Amnesty International. (2003). *Philippines: A different childhood: The apprehension and detention of child suspects and offenders*. Quezon City: Amnesty International.

Amnesty International. (2019). Fatally Flawed: Why Malaysia must abolish the death penalty. Retrieved from https://www.amnesty.org/en/documents/act50/1078/2019/en/

Amnesty International. (2020a). *Cambodia: Substance abuses: The Human Cost of Cambodia's Anti-Drug Campaign: Executive Summary [Khmer]*. London: Amnesty International.

Amnesty International. (2020b). *Cambodia: Exclusive Footage Reveals Deplorable Conditions*. The Amnesty International website. Retrieved from https://www.amnesty.org/en/latest/news/2020/04/cambodia-exclusive-footage-reveals-deplorable-prison-conditions/

Angeles, L. C., & Sunanta, S. (2009). Demanding daughter duty: Gender, community, village transformation, and transnational marriages in northeast Thailand. *Critical Asian Studies, 41*(1), 549–574.

Aning, J. (2004, January 24). "Abused wife saved from death row." *Philippine Daily Inquirer*. Retrieved from http://www.inq7.net/nat/2004/jan/24/text/nat_7-1-p.htm.

Antolak-Saper, N., Kowal, S., Lindsey, S., Ngeow, C. Y., & Kananatu, T. (2020). *Drug offences and the death penalty in Malaysia: Fair trial rights and ramifications.* Melbourne: Monash University.

Apidechkul, T., Chomchoei, C., Wongnuch, P., Tamornpark, R., Upala, P., Yeemard, F., … Sunsern, R. (2020). Associations of childhood experiences and methamphetamine use among akha and lahu hill tribe youths in northern Thailand: A cross-sectional study. *PloS One, 15*(6), e0234923–e0234923.

Arndt, S., Turvey, C. L., & Flaum, M. (2002). Older offenders, substance use, and treatment. *The American Journal of Geriatric Psychiatry, 10*(6), 733–739.

Arrigo, B. A. (2016). Critical criminology: On praxis and pedagogy, resistance and revolution. *Critical Criminology, 24*(4), 469–471.

Artz, L., Hoffman-Wanderer, Y., & Moult, K. (2012). *Hard time(s): Women's pathways to crime and incarceration.* Cape Town: University of Cape Town.

Asavasaetakul, C. (2019). *Determinants of expenditure in the Hill Tribes of Thailand.* MPRA Paper No. 93918. Retrieved from https://mpra.ub.uni-muenchen.de/93918/

Asia One News. (2008, May 4). *Malaysia's women face travel curbs over drug trafficking fears.* Retrieved from https://www.asiaone.com/News/AsiaOne%2BNews/Malaysia/Story/A1Story20080504-63260.html

Assistance Association for Political Prisoners. (2021). *AAPP Daily Briefing in Relation to the Military Coup.* Retrieved from aappb.org

Bachelet, M. (2020, September). *Death penalty and gender dimension – Exploring disadvantage and systemic barriers affecting death sentences.* Keynote Address 75th Session of the United Nations General Assembly Virtual High-Level Side Event. Retrieved from https://www.ohchr.org/EN/NewsEvents/Pages/DisplayNews.aspx?NewsID=26292&LangID=E

Baidawi, S. (2016). Older prisoners: Psychological distress and associations with mental health history, cognitive functioning, socio-demographic, and criminal justice factors. *International Psychogeriatrics, 28*(3), 385–395.

Bailey, C. (2013). Exploring female motivations for drug smuggling on the Island of Barbados: Evidence from Her Majesty's Prison, Barbados. *Feminist Criminology, 8*(2), 117–141.

Ball, M. (2014). What's queer about queer criminology? In D. Peterson & V. R. Panfil (Eds.), *Handbook of LGBT communities, crime, and justice* (pp. 531–555). New York, NY: Springer.

Ball, M. (2016). Queer criminology as activism. *Critical Criminology, 24*(4), 473–487.

Ballesteros-Pena, A. (2020). The prison trajectories of foreign national women in Spain: Intersections of citizenship, gender, race, and social class. *Critical Criminology, 28*(2), 243–258.

Banks, N., Lombard, M., & Mitlin, D. (2020). Urban informality as a site of critical analysis. *The Journal of Development Studies, 56*(2), 223–238.

Barberet, R. (2014). *Women, crime and criminal justice: A global inquiry.* New York, NY: Routledge.

Barberet, R., & Jackson, C. (2017). UN rules for the treatment of women prisoners and non-custodial sanctions for women offenders (the Bangkok Rules): A gendered critique. *Papers: Revista De Sociología, 102*(2), 215–230.

Barma, N. H. (2012). Peace-building and the predatory political economy of insecurity: Evidence from Cambodia, East Timor and Afghanistan. *Conflict, Security & Development, 12*(3), 273–298.

Baxi, U. (1998). Voices of suffering and the future of human rights. *Transnational Law Contemporary Problems, 8*(2), 125–169.

Becker, E. (1998). *When the war was over: Cambodia and the Khmer Rouge Revolution.* Hachette: Public Affairs.

Beech, H. (2021, March). *She is a Hero: In Myanmar's Protests, women are on the front lines.* Retrieved from https://www.nytimes.com/2021/03/04/world/asia/myanmar-protests-women.html

Belknap, J. (2001). *The invisible woman: Gender, crime and justice.* Belmont: Wadsworth.

Belknap, J. (2016). Asian Criminology's expansion and advancement of research and crime control practices. *Asian Journal of Criminology, 11*(4), 249–264.

Benedict, A. (2014). *Using trauma informed practice to enhance safety and security in women's correctional facilities.* Washington: National Resource Center on Justice Involved Women.

Berko, A., Erez, E., & Globokar, J. L. (2010). Gender, crime and terrorism. *British Journal of Criminology, 50*(4), 670–689.

Bermingham, V. (1996). National Vocations Qualifications (NVQs) in Prisons: A reflection of effort and achievement or the perpetuation of existing patterns of discrimination? *International Journal of Discrimination and the Law, 1*(4), 353–368.

Berrih, C., & Ying, N. C. (2020). Isolation and Desolation: Conditions of Detention of People Sentenced to Death, Malaysia. Paris: Together Against the Death Penalty (Ensemble contre la peine de mort).

Bischoff, A. (2011). *Passing the test: The transgender self, society and femininity.* Independent Study Project (ISP) Collection Paper. 1155. Retrieved from https://digitalcollections.sit.edu/isp_collection/1155/

Bissen, T. (2020). Trauma, healing, and Justice: Native Hawaiian women in Hawaii's criminal justice system. In L. George, A. N. Norris, A. Deckert, & J. Tauri (Eds.), *Neo-colonial injustice and the mass imprisonment of indigenous women. Palgrave studies in race, ethnicity, indigeneity and criminal justice* (pp. 193–222). London: Palgrave Macmillan.

Block, C. R., Blokland, A. A. J., van der Werff, C., van Os, R., & Nieuwbeerta, P. (2010). Long-term patterns of offending in women. *Feminist Criminology, 5*(1), 73–107.

Bloom, B., Chesney-Lind, M., & Owen, B. (1994). *Women in California Prisons: Hidden victims of the war on drugs.* San Francisco, CA: Center for Juvenile and Criminal Justice.

Bloom, B., Owen, B., & Covington, S. (2003). *Gender-responsive strategies: Research, practice and guiding principles for women offenders.* Washington: National Institute of Corrections.

Bloom, B., Owen, B., & Covington, S. (2004). Women offenders and the gendered effects of public policy. *Review of Policy Research, 21*(1), 31–48.

Bosworth, M., & Carrabine, E. (2001). Reassessing resistance: Race, gender and sexuality in prison. *Punishment & Society, 3*(4), 501–515.

Britton, D. M. (2000). Feminism in criminology: Engendering the outlaw. *The Annals of the American Academy of Political and Social Science, 571*(1), 57–76.

Britton, D. (2003). *At work in the Iron Cage.* New York, NY: New York University Press.

Britton, D. M. (2004). Feminism in criminology: Engendering the outlaw. In P. J. Schram & B. Koons-Witt (Eds.), *Gendered (in)justice: Theory and practice in feminist criminology* (pp. 49–67). Long Grove: Waveland.

Broidy, L., Payne, J., & Piquero, A. R. (2018). Making sense of heterogeneity in the influence of childhood abuse, mental health, and drug use on women's offending pathways. *Criminal Justice and Behaviour, 45*(10), 1565–1587.

Buan, L. (2020, January 30). *Mary Jane Veloso's Recruiters Found Guilty of Illegal Recruitment in Separate Case.* Retrieved from https://www.rappler.com/nation/mary-jane-veloso-recruiters-guilty-illegal-recruitment-separate-case

Buckland, B. S. (2008). More than just victims: The truth about human trafficking. *Public Policy Research, 15*(1), 42–47.

Buist, C., & Lenning, E. (2015). *Queer criminology.* Abingdon, OX: Routledge.

Buist, C. L., Lenning, E., & Ball, M. (2018). Queer criminology. In W. S. DeKeseredy & M. Dragiewicz (Eds.), *Routledge handbook of critical criminology* (pp. 96–106). Abingdon, OX: Routledge.

Buist, C. L., & Stone, C. (2014). Transgender victims and offenders: Failures of the United States criminal justice system and the necessity of queer criminology. *Critical Criminology*, *22*(1), 35–47.

Burgess-Proctor, A. (2006). Intersections of race, class, gender, and crime: Future directions for feminist criminology. *Feminist Criminology*, *1*(1), 24–47.

Bush-Baskette, S. (2000). The war on drugs and the incarceration of mothers. *Journal of Drug Issues*, *30*(4), 919–928.

Bushway, S. (2003). *Employment dimensions of reentry: Understanding the Nexus between Prisoner Reentry and Work*. New York, NY: Urban Institute Re-entry Roundtable, New York University.

Butler, J. (2013). *Your Behavior Creates Your Gender [Video file]*. Retrieved from http://bigthink.com/videos/your-behavior-creates-your-gender

Butler, J. (2002). *Gender trouble: Feminism and the subversion of identity*. New York, NY: Routledge.

Butler, J. (2004). *Precarious life: The powers of mourning and violence*. London: Verso.

Bylander, M. (2017). Poor and on the move: South-South migration and poverty in Cambodia. *Migration Studies*, *5*(2), 237–266.

Cakal, E, Jefferson, A. M., & Martin, T. M. (2021). Review of Celermajer's the prevention of torture. *Punishment and Society*. doi:10.1177/1462474520941938

Callamard, A. (2018). Women and Girls on Death Row Require Specific Gender-Based Responses and Policies. Paper presented at United Nations World Day Against the Death Penalty 2018, Geneva. Retrieved from https://www.ohchr.org/EN/NewsEvents/Pages/DisplayNews.aspx?NewsID=23705&LangID=E

Cambodian League for the Promotion and Defense of Human Rights. (2015). *Mothers behind bars: The impact of detention on women and their children*. Phnom Penh: Cambodian League for the Promotion and Defense of Human Rights.

Cambodian League for the Promotion and Defense of Human Rights. (2021). Voices from Inside: Women and Girls in Cambodian Prisons. Retrieved from https://www.licadho-cambodia.org/articles/20210308/170/index.html

Canning, V., & Tombs, S. (2021). *From social harm to zemiology*. A Critical Introduction. Abingdon: Routledge.

Caputo, J. D. (2020). *In search of radical theology. Expositions, explorations, exhortations*. New York, NY: Fordham University Press.

Carlen, P. (1985). *Criminal woman*. Cambridge: Polity.

Carlen, P. (1998). *Sledgehammer: Women's Imprisonment at the Millennium*. London: Palgrave Macmillan.

Carlen, P. (2012). Women's imprisonment: An introduction to the Bangkok Rules. *Crítica Penal y Poder*, 3, 148–157.

Carlton, B. (2018). Penal reform, anti-carceral feminist campaigns and the politics of change in women's prisons, Victoria, Australia. *Punishment & Society*, *20*(3), 283–307.

Carrington, K., Hogg, R., & Sozzo, M. (2016). Southern criminology. *British Journal of Criminology*, *56*(1), 1–20.

Carrington, K., Hogg, R., Scott, J., & Sozzo, M. (2018). *The Palgrave handbook of criminology and the global south*. London: Palgrave Macmillan.

Cassidy, J., Ziv, Y., Stupica, B., Sherman, L. J., Butler, H., Karfgin, A., & Powell, B. (2010). Enhancing attachment security in the infants of women in a jail-diversion program. *Attachment & Human Development*, *12*(4), 333–353.

Celermajer, D. (2018). *The prevention of torture. An ecological approach*. Cambridge: Cambridge University Press.

Chambers, R. (1997). *Whose reality counts? Putting the first last*. Bradford: Intermediate Technology.

CESP. (2019). *Cambodian Education Strategic Plan 2019–2023*. Retrieved from https://www. moeys.gov.kh/index.php/en/policies-and-strategies/3206.html#.YZ8O39AzaHt. Accessed on March 28, 2021.

Charmaz, K. (2003). Qualitative interviewing and grounded theory analysis. In J. A. Holstein & J. F. Gubrium (Eds.), *Inside interviewing: new lenses, new concerns* (pp. 675–692). Thousand Oaks, CA: Sage.

Charoensuthipan, P. (2019, June). *Elderly face increasing burden*. Retrieved from https:// www.bangkokpost.com/thailand/special-reports/1689648/elderly-face-increasing-burden

Cherukuri, S., Britton, D. M., & Subramaniam, M. (2009). Between life and death: Women in an Indian state prison. *Feminist Criminology, 4*(3), 252–274.

Chesney-Lind, M. (1991). Patriarchy, prisons, and jails: A critical look at trends in women's incarceration. *The Prison Journal, 71*(1), 51–67.

Chesney-Lind, M. (1997). *The female offender: Girls, women and crime*. Thousand Oaks, CA: Sage.

Chesney-Lind, M. (1998). Women in prison: From partial justice to vengeful equity. *Corrections Today, 60*(7), 66–73.

Chesney-Lind, M. (2006). Patriarchy, crime, and justice: Feminist criminology in an era of backlash. *Feminist Criminology, 1*(1), 6–26.

Chesney-Lind, M., & Rodriguez, N. (2013). Women under lock and key: A view from the inside. In M. Chesney-Lind & L. Pasko (Eds.), *Girls, women and crime: Selected readings* (pp. 187–198). Thousand Oaks, CA: Sage.

Chitswang, N. (2020). *The crimes committed by Thai Elderly Female Prisoners*. Retrieved from http://thaicriminology.com/the-crime-committed-by-thai-elderly-female-prisoners.html

Chomchoei, C., Apidechkul, T., Keawdounglek, V., Wongfu, C., Khunthason, S., Kullawong, N., … Yeemard, F. (2020). Prevalence of and factors associated with depression among hill tribe individuals aged 30 years and over in Thailand. *Heliyon, 6*(6), e04273–e04273.

Chotiwan, P. (2014). *"Factory Kathoey": Transgender lives and selves of migrants labors from the northeastern region*. Master Thesis, Chiang Mai University, Chiang Mai, Thailand. Retrieved from http://library.cmu.ac.th/digital_collection

Chua, L. J. & Gilbert, D (2015). Sexual orientation and gender identity minorities in transition: LGBT rights and activism in Myanmar. *Human Rights Quarterly, 37*(1), 1–28.

Chuenurah, C., & Jeffries, S. (2019). An analysis of Thai women's roles and involvement in cross-border international drug trafficking. *Social Science Asia: Official Journal of National Research Council of Thailand in conjunction with Journal of Thai Justice System, 5*, 45–55.

Chuenurah, C., & Sornprohm, U. (2020). Drug policy and women prisoners in Southeast Asia. In J. Buxton, G. Margo, & L. Burger (Eds.), *The impact of global drug policy on women: Shifting the needle* (pp. 131–139). Bingley: Emerald Publishing.

Collins, P. H. (2000). *Black feminist thought: Knowledge, consciousness and the politics of empowerment*. New York, NY: Routledge.

Colors Rainbow. (2013). *Facing 377: Discrimination and human rights abuses against transgender, gay and bisexual men in Myanmar*. Yangon: Colors Rainbow.

Constable, N. (1997). Sexuality and discipline among Filipina domestic workers in Hong Kong. *American Ethnologist, 24*(3), 539–558.

Constable, N. (2007). *Maid to order in Hong Kong: Stories of migrant workers*. Ithaca, NY: Cornell University Press.

Cornell Center on the Death Penalty Worldwide. (2013). Malaysia. Retrieved from https:// deathpenaltyworldwide.org/database/

Cornell Center on the Death Penalty Worldwide. (2018). *Judged for more than her crime: A global overview of women facing the death penalty.* New York, NY: Cornell Center on the Death Penalty.

Cornell, S. E. (2009). The interaction of drug smuggling, human trafficking, and terrorism. In A. Jonsson (Ed.), *Human trafficking and human security* (pp. 60–78). London: Routledge.

Cornwall, A. (2006). Historical perspectives on participation in development. *Commonwealth & Comparative Politics, 44*(1), 62–83.

Cornwall, A. (2011). *The participation reader.* London: Zed Books.

Couloute, L., & Kopf, D. (2018). *Out of prison & out of work: Unemployment among formerly incarcerated people.* Northampton: Prison Policy Initiative.

Covington, S., & Bloom, B. E. (2003). Gendered justice: Women in the criminal justice system. In B. Bloom (Ed.), *Gendered justice: Addressing female offenders* (pp. 3–24). Durham: Carolina Academic Press.

Cowan, J. (2006). Culture and rights after culture and rights. *American Anthropologist, 108*(1), 9–24.

Cowan, J., Dembour, M. B., & Wilson, R. (2001). *Culture and rights: Anthropological perspectives.* Cambridge: Cambridge University Press.

Cox, J., & Sacks-Jones, K. (2017). Double disadvantage: The experiences of black, Asian and minority ethnic women in the criminal justice system. *Probation Journal, 64*(3), 293–294.

Crittenden, C. A., Koons-Witt, B. A., & Kaminski, R. J. (2018). Being assigned work in prison: Do gender and race matter? *Feminist Criminology, 13*(4), 359–381.

Cunneen, C. (2011). Postcolonial perspectives for criminology. In M. Bosworth & C. Hoyle (Eds.), *What is criminology?* (pp. 249–266). Oxford: Oxford University Press.

Cunneen, C., & Tauri, J. (2016). *Indigenous criminology.* Bristol: Policy Press.

Cunneen, C., & Tauri, J. (2019). Indigenous peoples, criminology, and criminal justice. *Annual Review of Criminology, 2*, 359–381.

Daily, I. (2013, June 16). Malaysia Asked not to execute two Iranians. *Iran Cultural & Press Institute.* Retrieved from Lexis Nexis database.

Daly, K. (1994). *Gender, crime, and punishment.* New Haven, CT: Yale University Press.

Daly, K., & Chesney-Lind, M. (1988). Feminism and criminology. *Justice Quarterly, 5*(4), 497–453.

Damazo-Santos, J. (2015, April 29). Migrante: Let's bring Mary Jane Veloso home. *Rappler.* Retrieved from https://www.rappler.com/world/asia-pacific/migrante-bring-mary-jane-home

Danish Institute Against Torture. (2014). *Conditions for women in detention in The Philippines: Needs, vulnerabilities and good practices.* København: Danish Institute Against Torture.

Das, V. (2007). *Life and words: Violence and the descent into the ordinary.* Los Angeles, CA: University of California Press.

Das, V. (2020). *Textures of the ordinary.* New York, NY: Fordham University Press.

Davis, A. Y., & Rodriguez, D. (2000). The challenge of prison abolition: A conversation. *Social Justice, 3*(81), 212–218.

Davoren, M., Fitzpatrick, M., Caddow, F., Caddow, M., O'Neill, C., O'Neill, H., & Kennedy, H. G. (2015). Older men and older women remand prisoners: Mental illness, physical illness, offending patterns and needs. *International Psychogeriatrics, 27*(5), 747–755.

De Smet, S. (2017). Study into the characteristics and quality of life of older offenders. *Quality of Life Research, 26*, 1571–1585.

DeKeseredy, W. S., & Dragiewicz, M. (2018). *Routledge handbook of critical criminology.* Abingdon, OX: Routledge.

del Olmo, R. (1986). Female criminality and drug trafficking in Latin America: Preliminary findings. In E. Morales (Ed.), *Drugs in Latin America* (pp. 163–178). Williamsburg: Department of Anthropology, College of William and Mary.

Delano, D. L., & Knottnerus, J. D. (2018). The Khmer Rouge, ritual and control. *Asian Journal of Social Science, 46*(1–2), 79–110.

Dembour, M. B. (2006). *Who believes in human rights? Reflections on the European Convention.* Cambridge: Cambridge University Press.

Dembour, M. B. (2010, February). What are human rights? Four schools of thought. *Human Rights Quarterly, 32*(1), pp. 1–20.

Department of Corrections of Thailand. (2020). *National prison statistics.* Bangkok: Department of Corrections of Thailand.

Dhongchai, P., Verawongse, B., Jotiroseranee, B., Trong-ngam, S., Sivarasksa, S., Tantiwittayapitak, W., & Tang, P. (2005). *Submission to the 83rd Session of the United Nations Human Rights Committee International Covenant on Civil and Political Rights.* Retrieved from http://hrp.law.harvard.edu/wp-content/uploads/2013/08/Thai-Shadow-Report-Final.pdf

Diamond, M. (2011). *Ethnic minorities and food security in Northern Thailand.* Master's Thesis, School for International Training Graduate Institute, Vermont, United States. Retrieved from https://digitalcollections.sit.edu/capstones/2500

Dimou, E. (2021). Decolonizing Southern criminology: What can the "decolonial option" tell us about challenging the modern/colonial foundations of criminology? *Critical Criminology.* doi:10.1007/s10612-021-09579-9

Drapalski, A. L., Youman, K., Stuewig, J., & Tangney, J. (2009). Gender differences in jail inmates' symptoms of mental illness, treatment history and treatment seeking. *Criminal Behaviour and Mental Health, 19*(3), 193–206.

Draper, J., Sobieszczyk, T., Crumpton, C. D., Lefferts, H. L., & Chachavalpongpun, P. (2019). Racial "othering" in Thailand: Quantitative evidence, causes, and consequences. *Nationalism & Ethnic Politics, 25*(3), 251–272.

Dreier, O. (2003). *Subjectivity and social practice.* Aarhus: Center for Health, Humanity, and Culture. Department of Philosophy: University of Aarhus.

Dreier, O. (2008). *Psychotherapy in everyday life.* Cambridge: Cambridge University Press.

Duangwises, N. (2012). *Cultural space of transgenders and homosexuals in Southeast Asia.* Retrieved from http://www.sac.or.th/main/content_detail.php?content_id=227

Duangwises, N. (2014). *Vipak 'Kwam Pen Ying' Kong Ying Nai Rang Chai. [Criticizing 'femininity' of women in men's bodies].* Bangkok: Princess Maha Chakri Sirindhorn Anthropology Press.

Duangwises, N., & Jackson, P. A. (2013). *Cultural pluralism and sex/gender diversity in Thailand.* Bangkok: Princess Maha Chakri Sirindhorn Anthropology Press.

Easton, S. (2018). Older prisoners, gender, and family life. In B. Clough & J. Herring (Eds.), *Age, gender and family law* (pp. 142–158). Milton Park: Routledge.

Englund, H. (2006). *Prisoners of freedom. Human rights and the African Poor.* Berkeley, CA: University of California Press.

Evans, K. (2018). *Gender responsive justice: A critical appraisal.* Milton Park: Routledge.

Farrington, D. P., & Welsh, B. C. (2005). Randomized experiments in criminology: What have we learned in the last two decades? *Journal of Experimental Criminology, 1*(1), 9–38.

Fennessy, M. (2016). *Marriage, modernity and "manner": A Burmese-Buddhist woman's agency in contemporary Yangon, Myanmar. An ethnographic portrait.* GISCA Occasional Papers, No. 8, Institute for Social and Cultural Anthropology, Göttingen.

Fernandéz, A., & Nougier, M. (2021). *Punitive drug law: 10 years undermining the Bangkok Rules.* London: International Drug Policy Consortium.

Ferraro, K. J. (2006). *Neither angels nor demons: Women, crime, and victimization.* Boston, MA: Northeastern University Press.

Finlay, J., & Bates, J. (2018). What is the role of the prison library? The development of a theoretical foundation. *Journal of Prison Education and Reentry, 5*(2), 120–139.

Fleetwood, J. (2014). *Drug mules: Women in the international cocaine trade.* Basingstoke: Palgrave Macmillan.

Freedom House. (2017). *Freedom of the Press, 2017.* Washington: Freedom House.

Fujioka, R., & Thangphet, S. (2009). *Decent work for older persons in Thailand.* Bangkok: International Labour Organization.

Gainsborough, J. (2008). Women in prison: International problems and human rights based approaches to reform. *William & Mary Journal of Women and the Law, 14*(2), 271.

Garside, H. (2021, May). Less children and young people in youth custody than ever before. Retrieved from https://www.swlondoner.co.uk/news/27052021-less-children-and-young-people-in-youth-custody-than-ever-before/

Gender Equality Network. (2015). *Raising the curtain: Cultural norms, social practices and gender equality in Myanmar.* Yangon: Gender Equality Network.

George, L., & Ngamu, E. (2020). Te Piringa Poho: Healing, potential and transformation for Māori women. In L. George, A. N. Norris, A. Deckert, & J. Tauri (Eds.), *Neo-colonial injustice and the mass imprisonment of indigenous women. Palgrave studies in race, ethnicity, indigeneity and criminal justice* (pp. 239–268). London: Palgrave Macmillan.

Gerry, F. (2020). Transnational feminisms: Trafficked women, death row, autonomy and systemic reform. *ANZIL Perspective, 19*, 12–19.

Gerry, F., Harré, T., Naibaho, N., & Muraszkiewicz, J. (2018). Is the law an ass when it comes to mules? How Indonesia can lead a new global approach to treating drug traffickers as human trafficked victims. *Asian Journal of International Law, 8*(1), 166–188.

Gilbert, D. (2013). Categorizing gender queer in Yangon. *Sojourn: Journal of Social Issues in Southeast Asia, 28*(2), 241–271.

Gilfus, M. E. (1992). From victims to survivors to offenders: Women's routes of entry and immersion into street crime. *Women and Criminal Justice, 4*(1), 63–89.

Girshick, L. B. (1999). *No safe haven: Stories of women in prison.* Boston, MA: Northeastern University Press.

Global Alliance Against Traffic in Women. (2007). *Collateral damage: The impact of anti-trafficking measures on human rights around the world.* Bangkok: Global Alliance Against Traffic in Women.

Global Network of Sex Work Project. (2011). *Sex work is not trafficking.* Edinburgh: Global Network of Sex Work Project.

Gluckman, R. (1999a, July 23). "Divided by Death." *Asiaweek.* Retrieved from http://www.gluckman.com/Death'Penalty2.htm

Gluckman, R. (1999b, July 23). "Waiting to Go." *Asiaweek.* Retrieved from http://www.gluckman.com/Death'Penalty.htm

Goffman, E. (1961). *Asylums: Essays on the social situation of mental patients and other inmates.* Piscataway, NJ: Aldine Transaction.

Goodale, M., & Merry, S. E. (2007). *The practice of human rights: Tracking law between the global and the local. Cambridge studies in law and society.* Cambridge: Cambridge University Press.

Goshin, L. S., Byrne, M. W., & Blanchard-Lewis, B. (2014). Preschool outcomes of children who lived as infants in a prison nursery. *The Prison Journal, 94*(2), 139–158.

Gover, P. J., & Aalders, G. D. (2014). *Does prevention have anything to do with it? Cambodian Communication Review, 2014.* Phnom Penh: Department of Media and Communication.

Gover, P. J., & Aalders, G. D. (2016). *Beyond curiosity: A re-examination of positive preventative messages within the Cambodian Press.* Phnom Penh: Department of Media and Communication.

Grant, A. (1999). *Elderly Inmates: Issues for Australia*. Canberra: Australian Institute of Criminology.

Green, P. (1996). Drug couriers: The construction of a public enemy. In P. Green (Ed.), *Drug couriers: A new perspective* (pp. 3–20). London: Quartet Books.

Greiner, L., & Allenby, K. (2010). *A descriptive profile of older women offenders. Correctional Service Canada*. Ottawa: Correctional Service Canada.

Gueta, K. (2020). Exploring the promise of intersectionality for promoting justice-involved women's health research and policy. *Health & Justice, 8*(1), 1–10.

Gundy, A. V., & Baumann-Grau, A. (2013). *Women, incarceration, and human rights violations: Feminist criminology and corrections*. Milton Park: Taylor & Francis Group.

Gunnison, E., & McCartan, L. M. (2010). Persistent versus late onset among female offenders: A test of state dependent and population heterogeneity interpretations. *Western Criminology Review, 11*(3), 45–62.

Hales, L., & Gelsthorpe, L. (2012). *The criminalisation of migrant women*. Cambridge: University of Cambridge.

Hamid, H. A. (2019). A qualitative research report on the experiences of trafficked women in Malaysia. *Women's Studies Journal, 33*(12), 33–47.

Handtke, V., Bretschneider, W., Elger, B., & Wangmo, T. (2014). Easily forgotten: Elderly female prisoners. *Journal of Aging Studies, 32*(1), 1–11.

Haney, C. (2006). *Reforming punishment: Psychological limits to the pains of imprisonment*. Washington: APA Books.

Haney, L. A. (2010). Working through mass incarceration: Gender and the politics of prison labor from east to west. *Signs: Journal of Women in Culture and Society, 36*(1), 73–97.

Hannah-Moffat, K. (2010). Sacrosanct or flawed: Risk, accountability and gender-responsive penal politics. *Current Issues in Criminal Justice, 22*(2), 193–215.

Haraway, D. (1988). Situated knowledges: The science question in feminism and the privilege of partial perspective. *Feminist Studies 14*(3), 575–599.

Harding, S. (2004). *The feminist standpoint theory reader: Intellectual and political controversies*. Abingdon: Routledge.

Hedström, J. (2015). We did not realize about the gender issues. So, we thought it was a good Idea. *International Feminist Journal of Politics, 18*(1), 61–79.

Hedström, J. (2016). The political economy of the Kachin revolutionary household. *The Pacific Review, 30*(4), 581–595.

Herdt, G. (1987). *The Sambia: Ritual and gender in New Guinea*. New York, NY: Holt, Rinehart and Winston.

Herrity, K., Warr, J., & Schmidt, B. (2021). *Sensory penalities: Exploring the senses in spaces of punishment and social control*. Bingley: Emerald Publishing.

Hill Collins, P. (1990). *Black feminist thought: Knowledge, consciousness and the politics of empowerment*. Abingdon: Routledge.

Hillyard, P., & Tombs, S. (2007). From 'crime' to social harm? *Crime Law and Social Change, 48*, 9–25.

Hinton, A. L. (2005). *Why did they kill: Cambodia in the shadow of genocide*. Oakland, CA: University of California Press.

Holland, J., & Blackburn, J. (1998). *Whose voice? Participatory research and policy change*. London: Intermediate Technology Publications.

Holland, D., & Lave, J. (2001). *History in person. Enduring struggles, contentious practice, intimate identities*. Santa Fe, Oxford: SAR Press.

Holmes, O. (2016, April 28). *Mary Jane Veloso: What happened to the woman who escaped execution in Indonesia?* Retrieved from https://www.theguardian.com/world/2016/apr/28/mary-jane-veloso-indonesia-execution-reprieve

Hongladarom. K. (1999, July). Competing discourses on hill tribes: Media representation of ethnic minorities in Thailand. Paper presented at the 7th International Conference on Thai Studies, Amsterdam.

Hood, R. (2013). *The death penalty in Malaysia: Public opinion on the mandatory death penalty for drug trafficking, murder and firearms offences*. London: The Death Penalty Project.

Howe, A. (1994). *Punish and critique: Towards a feminist analysis of penalty*. New York, NY: Routledge.

Howell, J. T. (1991). *Hard living on Clay Street: Portraits of blue-collar families*. Prospect Heights: Waveland.

Hoyle, C. (2019). Capital punishment at the intersections of discrimination and disadvantage: The plight of foreign nationals. In C. S. Steiker & J. M. Steiker (Eds.), *Comparative capital punishment* (pp. 176–199). Cheltenham: Edward Elgar Publishing.

Hoyle, C., Bosworth, M., & Dempsey, M. (2011). Labelling the victims of sex trafficking: Exploring the borderland between rhetoric and reality. *Social & Legal Studies, 20*(3), 313–329.

Huling, T. (1995). Women drug couriers – Sentencing reform needed for prisoners of war. *Criminal Justice, 9*(4), 15–62.

Hunter, G., & Boyce, I. (2009). Preparing for employment: prisoners' experience of participating in a prison training programme. *The Howard Journal of Criminal Justice, 48*(2), 117–131.

Ikeya, C. (2011). The 'traditional' high status of women in Burma: A historical reconsideration *Journal of Burma Studies, 10*(1), 51–81.

Ingersoll-Dayton, B., Punpuing, S., Tangchonlatip, K., & Yakas, L. (2018). Pathways to grandparents' provision of care in skipped-generation households in Thailand. *Ageing and Society, 38*(7), 1429–1452.

Ingersoll-Dayton, B., Tangchonlatip, K., & Punpuing, S. (2020). A confluence of worries: Grandparents in skipped-generation households in Thailand. *Journal of Family Issues, 41*(2), 135–157.

International Drug Policy Consortium. (2021). *Briefing paper on Cambodia: Over-incarceration, drug policy and its specific harms to women and children*. London: International Drug Policy Consortium.

Irianto, S., Meij, L. S., Purwanti, F., & Widiastuti, L. (2005). *Perdagangan Perempuan Dalam Jaringan Pengedaran Narkotika*. Jakarta: Yayasan Pustaka Obor Indonesia.

Jackson, P. A. (1997). Thai research on male homosexuality and transgenderism and the cultural limits of Foucaultian analysis. *Journal of the History of Sexuality, 8*(1), 52–85.

Jackson, P. A. (1999). Tolerant but unaccepting: The myth of a Thai 'gay' paradise. In P. A. Jackson & N. Cook (Eds.), *Gender and sexualities in modern Thailand* (pp. 226–246). Chiang Mai: Silkworm Books.

Jackson, P. A. (2004). Gay adaptation: Tom-Dee resistance, and Kathoey indifference: Thailand's gender/sex minorities and the episodic allure of Queer English. In W. L. Leap & T. Boellstorff (Eds.), *Speaking in queer tongues – Globalization and gay language* (pp. 202–230). Chicago, IL: University of Illinois Press.

Jefferson, A. M. (2008). Imaginary reform: Changing the postcolonial prison. In P. Carlen (Ed.), *Imaginary penalities* (pp. 157–171). Cullompton: Willan Publishing.

Jefferson, A. M. (2016). Situated perspectives on the global fight against torture. In S. Armstrong, J. Blaustein, & A. Henry (Eds.), *Reflexivity and criminal justice: Intersections of policy, practice and research* (pp. 335–356). Basingstoke: Palgrave Macmillan.

Jefferson, A. (2019). *Prisoners' contact with the outside world in Myanmar.* Copenhagen: DIGNITY.

Jefferson, A. M. (2020). Time changing hands in Myanmar: On former prisoners' journeys into politics. In J. Chambers, C. Galloway, & J. Liljeblad (Eds.), *Living with Myanmar* (pp. 75–98). Singapore: ISEAS Publishing.

Jefferson, A. M., Caracciolo, G., Kørner, J., & Nordberg, N. (2021). Amplified vulnerabilities and reconfigured relations: Covid-19, torture prevention and human rights in the global South 1. *State Crime Journal, 10*(1), 147–192.

Jefferson, A. M., & Gaborit, L. S. (2015). *Human rights in prisons: Comparing institutional encounters in Kosovo, Sierra Leone and the Philippines.* Basingstoke: Palgrave Macmillan.

Jefferson, A. M., & Huniche, L. (2009). (Re)Searching for persons in practice: Field-based methods for critical psychological practice research. *Qualitative Research in Psychology, 6*(1–2), 12–27.

Jefferson, A. M., & Jensen, S. (2009). *State violence and human rights: State officials in the south.* Abingdon: Routledge.

Jefferson, A. M., Turner, S., & Jensen, S. (2019). Introduction: On stuckness and sites of confinement. *Ethnos, 84*(1), 1–13.

Jeffrey, L. A. (2005). Canada and migrant sex-work: Challenging the "foreign" in foreign policy. *Canadian Foreign Policy Journal, 12*(1), 33–48.

Jeffries, S. (2014). The imprisonment of women in Southeast Asia: trends, patterns, comparisons and the need for further research. *Asian Journal of Criminology, 9*(4), 253–269.

Jeffries, S., & Chuenurah, C. (2016). Gender and imprisonment in Thailand: exploring the trends and understanding the drivers. *International Journal of Law, Crime and Justice, 45*, 75–102.

Jeffries, S., & Chuenurah, C. (2018). Pathways to prison in Cambodia for homicide offending: Exploring women's life history narratives. *South East Asia Research, 26*(2), 109–132.

Jeffries, S., & Chuenurah, C. (2019). Vulnerabilities, victimisation, romance and indulgence: Thai women's pathways to prison in Cambodia for international cross border drug trafficking. *International Journal of Law, Crime and Justice, 56*, 39–52.

Jeffries, S., Chuenurah, C., & Russell, T. (2020). Expectations and experiences of women imprisoned for drug offending and returning to communities in Thailand: understanding women's pathways into, through and post-imprisonment. *LAWS, 9*(2). doi:10.3390/laws9020015

Jeffries, S., Chuenurah, C., & Wallis, R. (2019). Gendered pathways to prison in Thailand for drug offending? Exploring women's and men's narratives of offending and criminalisation. *Contemporary Drug Problems, 46*(1), 78–104.

Jeffries, S., Rao, P., Chuenurah, C., & Fitz-Gerald, M. (2021). Extending borders of knowledge: Gendered pathways to prison in Thailand for international cross border drug trafficking. *Psychiatry, Psychology and Law.* doi:10.1080/13218719.2021.1894263

Jenkins, C., Pramoj na Ayutthaya, P., & Hunter, A. (2005). *Kathoey in Thailand: HIV/AIDS and life opportunities.* Washington, DC: USAID.

Jenness, V., & Fenstermaker, S. (2014). Agnes goes to prison: Gender authenticity, transgender inmates in prisons for men, and pursuit of "The Real Deal." *Gender & Society, 28*(1), 5–31.

Jimenez-David, R. (2004, January 25). "Battered Wife Syndrome Defense a First in RP Courts." *Philippine Daily Inquirer.* Retrieved from http://www.onlinewomeninpolitics.org/archives/04_0125_ph_vaw.htm

Joe Laidler, K. A. (1996). The lives and times of Asian-Pacific American women drug users: An ethnographic study of their methamphetamine use. *Journal of Drug Issues, 26*(2), 199–218.

Joint Civil Society. (2009). *Joint Civil Society Report on torture and other cruel, inhuman, or degrading treatment or punishment in the Philippines*. Retrieved from http://www2. ohchr.org/english/bodies/cat/docs/ngos/JCS_Philippines42.pdf

Jones, A. (1996). *Women who kill*. Boston, MA: Beacon Press.

Joseph, J. (2006). Drug offenses, gender, ethnicity, and nationality: Women in prison in England and Wales. *The Prison Journal, 86*(1), 140–157.

Joynt, M. E., & Bishop, A. J. (2018). Aging behind bars: Assessing the health care needs of graying prisoners. In K. D. Dodson (Ed.), *Handbook on offenders with special needs* (pp. 342–357). Routledge.

Kaleidoscope Human Rights Foundation. (2016). *Report on Thailand regarding the Human Rights of LGBTI Persons 25th Session of the Universal Periodic Review April – May 2016*. Retrieved from https://www.upr-info.org/sites/default/files/document/thailand/session_25_-_may_2016/js6_upr25_tha_e_main.pdf. Accessed on November 20, 2021.

Kapur, R. (2002). The tragedy of victimization rhetoric: Resurrecting the native subject in international/postcolonial feminist legal politics. *Harvard Human Rights Law Journal, 15*(1), 1–37.

Kaukinen, C., Gover, A. R., & Hays, S. A. (2006). Age-graded pathways to victimization and offending among women and girls. In C. M. Renzetti, L. Goodstein, & S. L. Miller (Eds.), *Rethinking gender, crime, and justice* (pp. 57–75). Los Angeles, CA: Roxbury.

Kaur, A. (2008). International migration and governance in Malaysia: Policy and performance. *UNEAC Asia Paper, 22*, 4–18.

Kemasingki, P. (2016). *Born a threat: Highlanders with no citizenship. Citylife Chiang Mai*. Retrieved from https://www.chiangmaicitylife.com/clg/our-city/city-issues/highlanders-with-no-citizenship/

Kempadoo, K. (1998). Introducing: Globalizing sex workers rights. In K. Kempadoo & J. Doezema (Eds.), *Global sex workers: Rights, resistance, and redefinition* (pp. 1–28). London: Routledge.

Kendall, S., Lighton, S., Sherwood, J., Baldry, E., & Sullivan, E. A. (2020). Incarcerated Aboriginal women's experiences of accessing healthcare and the limitations of the 'equal treatment' principle. *International Journal for Equity in Health, 19*(1), 48–48.

Khaing, M. M. (1984). *The world of Burmese women*. London: Zed Books.

Khalid, A., & Khan, N. (2013). Pathways of women prisoners to jail in Pakistan. *Health Promotion Perspectives, 3*(1), 31–35.

Khin Mra, K. (2018). Gender. In A. Simpson, N. Farrelly, & I. Holliday (Eds.), *Routledge handbook of contemporary Myanmar* (pp. 381–392). Abingdon: Routledge.

Khin Mra, K. (2021). Women fight the dual evils of dictatorship and patriarchal norms in Myanmar. Retrieved from httpos://www.newmandala.org

Khin Mra, K., & Livingstone, D. (2020). The winding path to gender equality in Myanmar. In J. Chambers, C. Galloway, & J. Liljeblad (Eds.), *Living with Myanmar* (pp. 243–264). Singapore: ISEAS Publishing.

Kim, B., Gerber, J., & Kim, Y. (2007). Characteristics of incarcerated women in South Korea who killed their spouses: A feminist and age-graded theory of informal social control analysis. *The Southwest Journal of Criminal Justice, 4*(1), 39–57.

Kingdom of Cambodia. (2003). *Cambodian prison procedures guidance – Proclamation on the administration of civilian prisons – No 217, 31st March 1998*. Phnom Penh: Ministry of Interior.

Kingdom of Cambodia. (2010). *The constitution of Cambodia*. Phnom Penh: Kingdom of Cambodia.

Kingdom of Cambodia. (2011). *Cambodian law on prisons English translation*. Retrieved from https://cambodia.ohchr.org/~cambodiaohchr/sites/default/files/Prison%20law%202011%20-%20ENG%20%28unofficial%20translation%29.pdf

Kingdom of Cambodia. (2021). *Code of criminal procedure of the Kingdom of Cambodia. English Translation.* Phnom Penh: Kingdom of Cambodia.

Knodel, J., & Nguyen, M. D. (2015). Grandparents and grandchildren: Care and support in Myanmar, Thailand and Vietnam. *Ageing and Society, 35*(9), 1960–1988.

Krisberg, B., & Engel-Temin, C. (2007). The plight of children whose parents are in prison. Continuing the struggle for justice. In B. Krisberg, S. Marchionna, & C. Baird (Eds.), *Continuing the struggle for justice: 100 years of the National Council on Crime and Delinquency* (pp. 185–190). Thousand Oaks, CA: Sage.

Kruttschnitt, C., & Hussemann, J. (2008). Micropolitics of race and ethnicity in women's prisons in two political contexts. *The British Journal of Sociology, 59*(4), 709–728.

Kury, H. (2021). Prisoners and their families: The effects of imprisonment on the family. In H. Kury & S. Redo (Eds.), *Crime prevention and justice in 2030: the UN and the Universal Declaration of Human Rights* (pp. 125–153). Basingstoke: Springer Nature.

Labro, V. S. (2004, February 22). Blessings after the bruises. *Sunday Inquirer Magazine.* Retrieved from http://www.inq7.net/mag/2004/feb/22/mag_3-1.htm

Laidler, K., & Lee, M. (2014). Border trading and policing of everyday life in Hong Kong. In S. Pickering & J. Ham (Eds.), *The Routledge handbook on crime and international migration* (pp. 316–328). Abingdon, OX: Routledge.

Lamb, M. E., & Kelly, J. B. (2009). Improving the quality of parent-child contact in separating families with infants and young children: Empirical research foundations. *The Scientific Basis of Child Custody Decisions, 2*, 187–214.

Latouche, S. (1993). *In the wake of the affluent society: An exploration of post-development.* London: Zed Books.

Laungaramsri, P. (2003). Ethnicity and the politics of ethnic classification in Thailand. In C. Mackerras (Ed.), *Ethnicity in Asia* (pp. 157–173). Hove: Psychology Press.

Lave, J. (2011). *Apprenticeship in critical ethnographic practice.* Chicago, IL: University of Chicago Press.

Lawston, J. M., & Meiners, E. R. (2014). Ending our expertise: Feminists, scholarship, and prison abolition. *Feminist Formations, 26*(2), 1–25.

Ledgerwood, J., & Vijghen, J. (2002). Decision-making in rural Khmer villages. In J. Ledgerwood (Ed.), *Cambodia emerges from the past: Eight essays* (pp. 109–150). Illinois: Southeast Asia Publications, Center for Southeast Asian Studies, Northern Illinois University.

Lee, M., Johnson, M., & McCahill, M. (2018). Race, gender and surveillance of migrant domestic workers in Asia. In M. Bosworth, A. Parmar, & Y. Vasquez (Eds.), *Race, gender and surveillance of migrant domestic workers in Asia* (pp. 13–28). Oxford: Oxford University Press.

Lee, M., & Laidler, K. J. (2013). Doing criminology from the periphery: Crime and punishment in Asia. *Theoretical Criminology, 17*(2), 141–157.

Leigey, M. E., & Hodge, J. P. (2012). Gray matters: Gender differences in the physical and mental health of older inmates. *Women & Criminal Justice, 22*(4), 289–308.

Leonard, E. (2002). *Convicted survivors: The imprisonment of battered women who kill.* Albany, NY: State University of New York Press.

Leonard, E. (2003). Stages of gendered injustice in the lives of convicted battered women. In B. Bloom (Ed.), *Gendered justice: Addressing female offenders* (pp. 97–140). Durham: Carolina Academic Press.

Lepp, A. (2002). Trafficking in women and the Canadian feminization of migration context. *Canadian Woman Studies/Les Cahiers De La Femme, 21/22*(4/1), 90–99.

Lopez, A. (2008, September 17). 7 Filipino "drug mules" arrested in Malaysia. *Philippine Daily Inquirer.* Retrieved from Factiva database.

Lynch, S., & Bartels, L. (2017). Transgender prisoners in Australia: An examination of the issues, law and policy. *Flinders Law Journal, 19*(2), 185–232.

MacDonald, M. (2018). Overcrowding and its impact on prison conditions and health. *International journal of Prisoner Health, 14*(2), 65–68.

Maher, L., & Daly, K. (2011). Women in the street-level drug economy: Continuity or change?" In M. Chesney-Lind & M. Morash (Eds.), *Feminist theories of crime* (pp. 69–90). London: Ashgate.

Mahidol University, Plan International, United Nations Educational, Scientific and Cultural Organization. (2014). *Bullying targeting secondary school students who are or are perceived to be transgender or same-sex attracted: Types, prevalence, impact, motivation and preventive measures in 5 provinces of Thailand.* Bangkok: Mahidol University, Plan International, United Nations Educational, Scientific and Cultural Organization.

Malaysia General News. (2010, June 16). South Indian Women Fall Prey to Drug Cartels. *Malaysia General News.* Retrieved from Lexis Nexis database.

Marks, S. P. (1994). The new Cambodian constitution: From civil war to a fragile democracy. *Columbia Human Rights Law Review, 26*, 45–50.

Martin, R. E., Buxton, J. A., & Smith, M. (2012). The scope of the problem: The health of incarcerated women in BC. *BC Medical Journal, 54*(10), 502–508.

Maschi, T., & Aday, R. (2014). The social determinants of health and justice and the aging in prison crisis: A call for human rights action. *International Journal of Social Work, 1*(1), 15–33.

Matos, R. (2016). Trajectories and identities of foreign national women: Rethinking prison through the lens of gender and citizenship. *Criminology and Criminal Justice, 16*(3), 350–365.

Mbembe, A. (2001). *On the postcolony.* Berkeley, CA: University of California Press.

McCarthy, P., Schiraldi, V. N., & Shark, M. (2016). *The future of youth justice: A community based alternative to the youth prison model.* Washington: U.S. Department of Justice.

McCarthy, S., & Un, K. (2017). The evolution of rule of law in Cambodia. *Democratization, 24*(1), 100–118.

McCulloch, H. (2018). *Migrant workers, the death penalty and human trafficking.* Retrieved from https://reprieve.org/uk/2018/07/24/migrant-workers-the-death-penalty-and-human-trafficking/

McShane, M. D., & Williams, F. P. (2006). Women drug offenders. In A. V. Merlo & J. M. Pollock (Eds.), *Women, law, and social control* (pp. 211–226). Boston, MA: Pearson.

Mehta, R. (2016). Borders: A view from "nowhere." *Criminology and Criminal Justice, 16*(3), 286–300.

Mekong Club. (2019). *How technology fuels trafficking and exploitation in Asia and the Pacific.* Hong Kong: The Mekong Club.

Miller, J., & Mullins, C. W. (2008). The status of feminist theories in criminology. In F. T. Cullen, J. P. Wright, & K. R. Blevins (Eds.), *Taking stock: The status of criminological theory* (pp. 217–249). New Brunswick: Transaction Publishers.

Minority Rights Group International. (2009). *State of the world's minorities and indigenous peoples, 2009.* London: European Union and UNICEF.

Moffitt, T. E. (2015). Life-course persistent versus adolescence-limited antisocial behaviour. In T. R. McGee & P. Mazerolle (Eds.), *Developmental and life-course criminological theories* (pp. 38–74). Farnham: Ashgate.

Moon, L. (2018, April 26). Chinese drug mule facing death penalty in Malaysia trial could be latest victim of trafficking ring. *South China Morning Post.* Retrieved from https://www.scmp.com/news/china/article/2143536/chinese-drug-mule-facing-death-penalty-malaysia-trial-could-be-latest

Moosavi, L. (2019a). A friendly critique of 'Asian criminology' and 'Southern criminology'. *British Journal of Criminology*, *59*(2), 257–275.

Moosavi, L. (2019b). Decolonising criminology. Syed Hussein Alatas on crimes of the powerful. *Critical Criminology*, *27*(2), 229–242.

Moosavi, L. (2020). The decolonial bandwagon and the dangers of intellectual decolonization. *International Review of Sociology*, *30*(2), 332–354.

Morash, M., Haarr, R. N., & Rucker, L. (1994). A comparison of programming for women and men in U.S. prisons in the 1980s. *Crime & Delinquency*, *40*(2), 197–221.

Mørck, L. L. (1995). Praksisforskning som metode, teori og praksis. Refleksion over praksisforskerens positionering i og mellem handlesammenhænge. *Udkast: dansk tidsskrift for kritisk samfundsvidenskab*, *23*(1), 34–78.

Morris, R. C. (1994). Three sexes and four sexualities redressing the discourses on gender and sexuality in contemporary Thailand. *Positions*, *2*(1), 15–43.

Morris, J. L. (2014). Explaining the elderly feminization of poverty: An analysis of retirement benefits, health care benefits, and elder care-giving. *Notre Dame Journal of Law, Ethics & Public Policy*, *21*(2), 571–607.

Morris, A., & Kingi, V. (1999). Addressing women's needs or empty rhetoric? An examination of New Zealand's policy for women in prison. In S. Cook & D. Davies (Eds.), *Harsh punishment: International experiences of women's imprisonment* (pp. 142–159). Boston, MA: Northeastern University Press.

Morton, M. F., & Baird, I. G. (2019). From hill tribes to indigenous peoples: The localisation of a global movement in Thailand. *Journal of Southeast Asian Studies*, *50*(1), 7–31.

Moses, M. C., & Smith, C. J. (2007). Factories behind Fences: Do prison 'real work' programs work? *National Institute of Justice Journal*, *257*, 32–35.

Motzkau, J., & Schraube, E. (2015). Kritische Psychologie: Psychology from the standpoint of the subject. In I. Parker (Ed.), *Handbook of critical psychology* (pp. 280–289). London: Routledge.

Muraskin, R. (Ed.) (2007). *It's a crime: Women and justice*. Englewood Cliffs, NJ: Prentice-Hall.

Mustofa, M., West, B. S., Supadmi, M. S., & Sari, H. (2019). Challenges to mothering while incarcerated: Preliminary study of two women's prisons in Java, Indonesia. *International Journal of Prisoner Health*, *15*(1), 37–45.

Myanmar Prison Department. (2020). Vocational training. Retrieved from https://www.facebook.com/myanmarprisonsdepartment/photos/a.1786917894652814/3360824347262153/

Nagel, I. H., & Johnson, B. L. (1994). The role of gender in a structured sentencing system: Equal treatment, policy choices, and the sentencing of female offenders under the United States Sentencing Guidelines. *The Journal of Criminal Law and Criminology*, *85*(1), 181–221.

Narag, R., & Jones, C. (2016). Understanding prison management in the Philippines: A case for shared governance. *The Prison Journal*, *97*(1), 3–26.

Nasr, F. (2017). *Institutional maintenance in private prisons: A case of labor exploitation*. Rockville: O.L. Pathy Family Foundation.

Newsome, Y. D. (2003). Border Patrol: The U.S. Customs Service and the racial profiling of African American Women. *Journal of African American Studies*, *7*(3), 31–57.

Ng, V., Tang, A., & Ang, J. Y. Z. (2019). Challenges faced by women offenders after incarceration. *Women & Criminal Justice*. doi: 10.1080/08974454.2019.1697791

Nissen, M. (2000). Practice research: Critical psychology in and through practices. *Annual Review of Critical Psychology*, *2*, 145–179.

Nissen, M. (2012). *The subjectivity of participation: Articulating social work with youth in Copenhagen*. Basingstoke: Palgrave/Macmillan.

O'Brien, P., Kim, M., Beck, E., & Bhuyan, R. (2020). Introduction to special topic on Anticarceral feminisms: Imagining a world without prisons. *Affilia: Journal of Women and Social Work*, *35*(1), 5–11.

Office of the United Kingdom Sentencing Council. (2011). *Drug "Mules": Twelve case studies*. London: Office of the United Kingdom Sentencing Council.

Ogden, S. (2020). What was my crime? Being an American Indian Woman. In L. George, A. N. Norris, A. Deckert, J. Tauri (Eds.), *Neo-colonial injustice and the mass imprisonment of indigenous women. Palgrave studies in race, ethnicity, indigeneity and criminal justice* (pp. 173–191). London: Palgrave Macmillan.

Owen, B. (1998). *In the mix: Struggle and survival in a women's prison*. Albany: Suny Press.

Owen, B. (2003). Differences with a distinction: Women offenders and criminal justice practice. In B. Bloom (Ed.), *Gendered justice: Addressing female offenders* (pp. 25–44). Durham: Carolina Academic Press. University of California Press.

Owen, B., Wells, J., & Pollock, J. (2017). *In search of safety: Confronting inequality in women's imprisonment*. Oakland: University of California Press.

Pabico, A. P. (2000, January 10). Harsh jail terms make no dent on the drug trade. Retrieved from https://www.philstar.com/headlines/2000/01/10/86738/harsh-jail-terms-make-no-dent-drug-trade

Palasi, K. (2003). Portraits of sadness and survival: Women in prison. *Women in Action*, *6*(3). Retrieved from http://www.isiswomen.org/index.php?option=com_content&task=view&id=732&Itemid=200

Panjaphothiwat, N., Tamornpark, R., Apidechkul, T., Seeprasert, P., Singkhorn, O., Upala, P., … Sunsern, R. (2021). Factors associated with domestic violence in the Lahu hill tribe of northern Thailand: A cross-sectional study. *PloS One*, *16*(3), e0248587–e0248587.

Park, M. J., & Jeffries, S. (2018). Prisoners of identity: The experiences of ethnic minority Vietnamese women categorised as 'foreign' in Cambodian prisons. *Women's Studies International Forum*, *69*, 56–66.

Park, J. K., Tanagho, J. E., & Weicher, M. E. (2009). A global crisis writ large: The effects of being "stateless in Thailand" on hill-tribe children. *San Diego International Law Journal*, *10*(2), 495–553.

Patterson, E. J. (2013). The dose–response of time served in prison on mortality: New York State, 1989–2003. *American Journal of Public Health*, *103*(3), 523–528.

Penal Reform International. (2013). *Guidance document: United Nations Rules on the treatment of women prisoners and non-custodial measures for women offenders (The Bangkok Rules)*. London: Penal Reform International.

Penal Reform International. (2020). *Global prison trends*. London: Penal Reform International.

Penal Reform International & Thailand Institute of Justice. (2019). *Guide to the rehabilitation and social reintegration of women prisoners*. Bangkok: Penal Reform International & Thailand Institute of Justice.

Penal Reform International & Thailand Institute of Justice. (2021). *Global prison trends, 2021*. Bangkok: Penal Reform International & Thailand Institute of Justice.

Perempuan, L. (2018). *Laporan Pemantauan: Kekerasan Terhadap Perempuan dalam Pusaran Migrasi, Perdagangan Manusia dan Narkoba: Interseksi dan Penghukuman*. Jakarta: Komnas Perempuan.

Philippine Human Rights Information Center & Women's Education, Development Productivity and Research Organization. (2006). *Invisible realities, forgotten voices: The women on death row from a gender and rights-based perspective*. Quezon City: Philippine Human Rights Information Center.

Phnom Penh Post. (2019, March). Kids don't belong in Prison. Retrieved from https://www.phnompenhpost.com/opinion/kids-dont-belong-prison

Physicians for Human Rights. (2004). *No status: Migration, trafficking and exploitation of women in Thailand: Health and HIV/AIDS Risk for Burmese and Hill Tribe Women and Girls*. Boston, MA: Physicians for Human Rights.

Phyu Oo, P. (2021, February). *The importance of Myanmar's Pots and Pans Protests*. Retrieved from https://www.lowyinstitute.org/the-interpreter/importance-myanmars-pots-and-pans-protests

Pickering, S., & Ham, J. (2014). Hot Pants at the border: Sorting sex work from trafficking. *The British Journal of Criminology, 54*(1), 2–19.

Piper, N. (2008). Feminisation of migration and the social dimensions of development: The Asian case. *Third World Quarterly, 29*(7), 1287–1303.

Pollock-Byrne, J. M. (1990). *Women, prison, and crime*. Pacific Grove: Brooks/Cole Publishing.

Potter, H. (2006). An argument for Black feminist criminology: Understanding African American women's experiences with intimate partner abuse using an integrated approach. *Feminist Criminology, 1*(2), 106–124.

Potter, H. (2013). Intersectional criminology: Interrogating identity and power in criminological research and theory. *Critical Criminology, 21*(3), 305–318.

Prachatai. (2018, October). *Kook-Thai-mai-dai-mee-khae-chai-ying 'LGBT' Akati-lae-karn-luek-pa-ti-but-lung-look-krong* [Thai Prisons Do Not Only Have Cisgender Prisoners, 'LGBT', Prison's Prejudices and Discrimination]. Retrieved from https://prachatai.com/journal/2018/10/78971

Pramoj na Ayutthaya, P. (2003). *Contesting identities of "Kathoei" in Cabaret Show*. Chiang Mai: Chiang Mai University Press.

Pravattiyagul, J. (2018). *Street and state discrimination: Thai transgender women in Europe*. Utrecht: Utrecht University Press.

Puthy, P. A. T., Richter-Sundberg, L., Jegannathan, B., Edin, K., & San Sebastian, M. (2020). *Prevalence and risk factors for mental health problems and suicidal expressions among young male prisoners in Cambodia: A cross-sectional study*. Durham: Research Square.

Radford, L. (1994). Pleading for time: Justice for battered women who kill. In H. Birch (Ed.), *Moving targets: Women, murder, and representation* (pp. 172–197). Berkeley, CA: University of California Press.

Radosh, P. F. (2002). Reflections on women's crime and mothers in prison: A peacemaking approach. *Crime and Delinquency, 48*(2), 300–315.

Rahmah, A., Blogg, J., Silitonga, N., Aman, M., & Power, R. M. (2014). The health of female prisoners in Indonesia. *International Journal of Prisoner Health, 10*(4), 252–261.

Ramet, S. P. (1996). Gender reversals and gender cultures. In S. P. Ramet (Ed.), *Gender reversals and gender cultures* (pp. 1–21). London: Routledge.

Rao, P. (2020). *Making Prison the 'Alternative' for Women Offenders*. Retrieved from https://knowledge.tijthailand.org/en/article/detail/making-prison-the-alternative-for-women-offenders

Ratner, S. R. (1993). The Cambodia settlement agreements. *The American Journal of International Law, 87*(1), 1–41.

Renzetti, C. M. (2018). Feminist perspectives. In W. S. DeKeseredy & M. Dragiewicz (Eds.), *Routledge handbook of critical criminology* (pp. 74–82). Milton Park: Routledge.

Rhodes, L. A. (2018). 'This can't be real': Continuity at HMP Grendon. In R. Shuker & E. Sullivan (Eds.), *Grendon and the emergence of forensic therapeutic communities: Developments in research and practice* (pp. 203–216). Chichester: Wiley-Blackwell.

Richie, B. E. (1996). *Compelled to crime: The gender entrapment of battered black women.* New York, NY: Routledge.

Rodgers, J., Asquith, N. L., & Dwyer, A. (2017). Cisnormativity, criminalisation, vulnerability: Transgender people in prisons. *Tasmanian Institute of Law Enforcement Studies Briefing Paper, 12,* 1–13.

Rodriguez. (2018). Cambodia's juvenile justice system: Overcoming challenges to protect the rights of Cambodian Youth. *Children's Legal Rights Journal, 38,* 97–110.

Routray, B. P. (2019). *Onwards Malaysia: Rohingya focused human trafficking networks.* Global: Mantraya.

Royal Government of Cambodia. (2016). *National Population Policy, 2016-2030.* Phnom Penh: Royal Government of Cambodia.

Ruiz-García, M., & Castillo-Algarra, J. (2014). Experiences of foreign women in Spanish prisons. *Journal of Offender Rehabilitation, 53*(8), 587–599.

Russell, E., & Carlton, B. (2013). Pathways, race and gender responsive reform: Through an abolitionist lens. *Theoretical Criminology, 17*(4), 474–492.

Russell, T., Jeffries, S., Hayes, H., Thipphayamongkoludom, Y., & Chuenurah, C. (2020). A gender comparative exploration of women's and men's pathways to prison in Thailand. *Australian & New Zealand Journal of Criminology, 53*(4), 536–562.

Russell, H., & Martin, T. M. (2021). *Burmese women show a new way out of the military darkness.* København: Danish Institute Against Torture & Legacies of Detention Myanmar.

Saat, G. (2009). Human trafficking from the Philippines to Malaysia: The impact of urbanism. *South Asian Survey, 16*(1), 137–148.

Samuel, R., & Omar, R. (2012). Female prisoners in Malaysia: An examination of socio demographic characteristics. *Procedia-Social and Behavioral Sciences, 65,* 505–510.

Sassen, S. (2000). Women's burden: Counter-geographies of globalization and the feminization of survival. *Journal of International Affairs, 53*(2), 503–524.

Scharff-Smith, P. (2016). Prisons and human rights-past, present and future challenges. In L. Weber, E. Fishwick, & M. Marmo (Eds.), *The Routledge international handbook of criminology and human rights* (pp. 525–535). London: Routledge.

Schatz, E. (2009). *Political ethnography: What immersion contributes to the study of power.* Chicago, IL: University of Chicago Press.

Schemenauer, E. (2012). Victims and Vamps, Madonnas and Whores: The construction of female drug couriers and the practices of the US security state. *International Feminist Journal of Politics, 14*(1), 83–102.

Schlesinger, T. (2018). Decriminalizing racialized youth through juvenile diversion. *The Future of Children, 28*(1), 59–82.

Schmidt, B. E., & Jefferson, A. M. (2021). Sensing transition: Exploring prison life in post-revolution Tunisia. In K. Herrity, B. E. Schmidt, & J. Warr, J. (Eds.), *Sensory penalties: Exploring the senses in spaces of punishment and social control* (pp. 71–88). Bingley: Emerald Publishing.

Schneider, L. (2020). Sexual violence during research: How the unpredictability of fieldwork and the right to risk collide with academic bureaucracy and expectations. *Critique of Anthropology, 40*(2), 173–193.

Schram, P. J. (1998). Stereotypes about vocational programming for female inmates. *The Prison Journal, 78*(3), 244–270.

Schram, P. J. & Koons-Witt, B. (Eds.) (2004). *Gendered (in)justice: Theory and practice in feminist criminology.* Long Grove: Waveland Press.

Schraube, E., & Højholt, C. (2016). *Psychology and the conduct of everyday life.* London: Routledge.

Segal, L. (2016). *No place for grief: Martyrs, prisoners and mourning in contemporary palestine*. Philadelphia: University of Pennsylvania Press.

Sen, V. (2008). Cambodia's untreated wound. Retrieved from https://www.ideasforpeace. org/content/cambodias-untreated-wound/

Sharp, S. F., & Eriksen, M. E. (2003). Imprisoned mothers and their children. In B. H. Zaitzow & J. Thomas (Eds.), *Women in prison: Gender and social control* (pp. 119–136). Boulder: Lynne Rienner.

Shelley, L. (2012). The relationship of drug and human trafficking: A global perspective. *European Journal on Criminal Policy and Research, 18*, 241–253.

Shen, A. (2015). *Offending women in Contemporary China: Gender and pathways to crime*. London: Palgrave.

Simbulan, N. P. (n.d.). *The Philippine Human Rights situation: Threats and challenges*. Retrieved from http://www.asienhaus.de/public/archiv/simbulan-hrsituation-complete.pdf

Simpson, S. S., Alper, M., Dugan, L., Horney, J., Kruttschnitt, C., & Gartner, R. (2016). Age-graded pathways into crime: Evidence from a multi-site retrospective study of incarcerated women. *Journal of Developmental and Life-Course Criminology, 2*(3), 296–320.

Sinnott, M. (1999). Masculinity and Tom identity in Thailand. *Journal of Gay & Lesbian Social Services, 9*(2–3), 97–119.

Smoyer, A. B., & Lopes, G. (2017). Hungry on the inside: Prison food as concrete and symbolic punishment in a women's prison. *Punishment & Society, 19*(2), 240–255.

Soh, E., & Yuen, C. T. (2011, March 29). S'poreans wise up to "drug mule" trap; Not even one woman nabbed in 2010; spotlight still on issue as S'porean faces death in Malaysia. *The Straits Times*. Retrieved from Lexis Nexis database.

Spivak, G. C. (1998). Can the subaltern speak? In P. Williams & L. Chrisman (Eds.), *Colonial discourse and postcolonial theory* (pp. 66–111). London: Harvester Wheatsheaf.

Stark, L., Rubenstein, B. L., Pak, K., & Kosal, S. (2017). National estimation of children in residential care institutions in Cambodia: A modelling study. *BMJ open, 7*(1), e013888. doi:10.1136/bmjopen-2016-013888

Steele, S. (2015). Elderly offenders in Japan and the saiban'in seido (lay judge system): Reflections through a visit to the Tokyo district court. *Japanese Studies, 35*(2), 223–243.

Steffensmeier, D., & Allan, M. (1996). Gender and crime: Toward a gendered theory of female offending. *Annual Review of Sociology, 22*, 459–487.

Steffensmeier, D., & Broidy, L. (2001). Explaining female offending. In C. M. Renzetti & L. Goodstein (Eds.), *Women, crime, and criminal justice: Original feminist readings* (pp. 111–132). Los Angeles, CA: Roxbury.

Stevenson, L. (2014). *Life beside itself: Imagining Care in the Canadian Arctic*. Berkeley, CA: University of California Press.

Stürup-Toft, S., O'Moore, E. J., & Plugge, E. H. (2018). Looking behind the bars: Emerging health issues for people in prison. *British Medical Bulletin, 125*(1), 15–23.

Sudbury, J. (2005). Mules, Yardies and other folk devils: Mapping cross border imprisonment in Britain. In J. Sudbury (Ed.), *Global lockdown: Race, gender, and the prison-industrial complex* (pp. 167–184). New York, NY: Routledge.

Sulaksono, E. (2018). The patterns of Human Trafficking on Indonesian Migrant Workers: Case Study of Riau Islands and Johor Border Crossing. *Masyarakat: Jurnal Sosiologi, 23*(2), 167–186.

Swe Win (2016, September 1). *Exclusive: Abuse and corruption exposed in Myanmar's prison labor camps*. Retrieved from https://www.reuters.com/article/us-myanmar-prisons-idUSKCN11758R

Swe Win (2018, November 8). *Skeletons covered in skin: Inside Myanmar's labour camps.* Retrieved from www.myanmar-now.org/en/news/skeletons-covered-in-skin-inside-myanmars-labour-camps

Sykes, G. M. (1958). *The society of captives.* Princeton, NJ: Princeton University Press.

Tanguay, P. (2019). *Mapping of good practices for the management of transgender inmates.* Bangkok: United Nations Development Programme.

Tauri, J. (2021). *The Evangelism of indigenous criminology.* Retrieved from http://juantauri. blogspot.com/2021/02/the-evangelism-of-indigenous-criminology.html

Terwiel, A. (2020). What is carceral feminism? *Political Theory, 48*(4), 421–442.

Thailand Institute of Justice. (2014). *Women prisoners and the implementation of the Bangkok Rules in Thailand.* Bangkok: Thailand Institute of Justice.

Thailand Institute of Justice. (2021). Overview. Retrieved from https://www.tijthailand.org/ overview

Thailand Institute of Justice & Griffith University. (2021). *Women's pathways into, through and out of prison understanding the needs, challenges and successes of women imprisoned for drug offending and returning to communities in Thailand.* Bangkok: Thailand Institute of Justice & Griffith University.

The Indigenous Women Network of Thailand. (2011). *Report on the situation on the rights of ethnic minority women in Thailand.* Chiang Mai: The Indigenous Women Network of Thailand.

The Monitor. (2011, October 13). Uganda; Local Women Being Sold for Sex in Malaysia. *Africa News.* Retrieved from Lexis Nexis database.

Thiri Kyaw, A. (2021a). Retrieved from https://twitter.com/Aye_Thiri_kyaw/status/1367789967162937347

Thiri Kyaw, A. (2021b). Retrieved from https://twitter.com/Aye_Thiri_kyaw/status/1367410629515051010

Thiri Kyaw, A., & Miedema, S. (2020). Women's movements in Myanmar and the era of #Me Too. In J. Chambers, C. Galloway, & J. Liljeblad (Eds.), *Living with Myanmar* (pp. 265–285). Singapore: ISEAS Publishing.

This Life Cambodia. (2019). *Small children in prison – Cambodia's secret problem.* Siem Reap: This Life Cambodia.

This Life Cambodia. (2021a). *No place for a child: Alternatives to imprisoning children in Cambodia.* Siem Reap: This Life Cambodia.

This Life Cambodia. (2021b). *Understanding microfinance debt.* Siem Reap: This Life Cambodia.

Thomas, J. (2003). Gendered control in prisons: The difference difference makes. In B. H. Zaitzow & J. Thomas (Eds.), *Women in prison: Gender and social control* (pp. 1–20). Boulder: Lynne Rienner.

Time. (2019, January 7). 40 Years After the Fall of the Khmer Rouge, Cambodia Still Grapples with Pol Pot's Brutal Legacy. Retrieved from https://time.com/5486460/ pol-pot-cambodia-1979/

Truong, V. D. (2018). Tourism, poverty alleviation, and the informal economy: The street vendors of Hanoi, Vietnam. *Tourism Recreation Research, 43*(1), 52–67.

Trzcinski, L. M., & Upham, F. K. (2014). Creating law from the ground up: Land law in post-conflict Cambodia. *Asian Journal of Law and Society, 1,* 55–78.

Ulysse, G. A. (2007). *Downtown ladies: Informal commercial importers, a Haitian anthropologist, and self-making in Jamaica.* Chicago, IL: University of Chicago Press.

UNAIDS. (2014). *Transgender people. In the GAP Report.* Geneva: Joint United Nations Program on HIV/AIDS.

United Nations. (1966). *International covenant on civil and political rights.* Geneva: United Nations.

United Nations. (2000). *Protocol to prevent, suppress and punish trafficking in persons, especially women and children, supplementing the United Nations convention against transnational organized crime.* Geneva: United Nations.

United Nations Development Programme & Ministry of Social Development & Human Security. (2018). *Legal gender recognition in Thailand: A legal and policy review.* Bangkok: United Nations Development Programme & Ministry of Social Development and Human Security.

United Nations Development Programme & United Nations Office on Drugs and Crime. (2020). *Mapping of good practices for the management of transgender prisoners.* Vienna: United Nations Development Programme & United Nations Office on Drugs and Crime.

United Nations General Assembly. (1981). *Convention on the elimination of all forms of discrimination against women.* Geneva: United Nations.

United Nations General Assembly. (1984). *Convention against torture and other cruel, inhuman or degrading treatment or punishment.* Geneva: United Nations.

United Nations General Assembly. (2010). *United Nations Rules for the treatment of women prisoners and non-custodial measures for women offenders (the Bangkok Rules).* Geneva: United Nations.

United Nations General Assembly. (2016). *United Nations standard minimum rules for the treatment of prisoners (the Nelson Mandela Rules).* Geneva: United Nations.

United Nations Office on Drugs and Crime. (2000). *Palermo protocols.* Vienna: United Nations Office on Drugs and Crime.

United Nations Office on Drugs and Crime. (2009). *Handbook on prisoners with special needs.* New York, NY: United Nations.

United Nations Office on Drugs and Crime. (2017). *Women's rights and health in Indonesia's Prisons: A review of current practices.* Vienna: United Nations Office on Drugs and Crime.

United Nations Office on Drugs and Crime. (2018). *World drug report.* Vienna: United Nations Office on Drugs and Crime.

United Nations Office on Drugs and Crime & Thailand Institute of Justice. (2020). *Toolkit on gender-responsive non-custodial measures.* Vienna: United Nations Office on Drugs and Crime.

Veloso, D. T. M. (2016). Of culpability and blamelessness: The narratives of women formerly on death row in the Philippines. *Asia-Pacific Social Science Review, 16*(1), 1.

Vigh, H. (2008). Crisis and chronicity: Anthropological perspectives on continuous conflict and decline. *Ethnos,* 73(1), 5–24.

Villero, J. M. (2006). Mothering in the shadow of death. *Human Rights Forum* 3(1&2), 27–30.

Visher, C., Debus, S., & Yahner, J. (2008). *Employment after prison: A longitudinal study of releasees in three states.* Washington: Urban Institute.

Wahidin, A., & Aday, R. (2012). Older female prisoners in the UK and US: Finding justice in the criminal justice system. In M. Malloch & G. Mcivor (Eds.), *Women, punishment and social justice: Human rights and penal practices* (pp. 65–78). Milton Park: Taylor & Francis.

Walmsley, R. (2017). *World female imprisonment list* (4th ed.). London: World Prison Brief.

Walmsley, R. (2020). *World pre-trial/remand imprisonment list.* London: Institute for Crime and Justice Policy Research.

Wattanaporn, K. A., & Holtfreter, K. (2014). The impact of feminist pathways research on gender-responsive policy and practice. *Feminist Criminology, 9*(3), 191–207.

Watterson, K. (1996). *Women in prison: Inside the concrete womb.* Boston, MA: Northeastern University Press.

West, L. (2019). The limits to judicial independence: Cambodia's political culture and the civil law. *Democratization, 26*(3), 537–553.

Whalley, E., & Hackett, C. (2017). Carceral feminisms: The abolitionist project and undoing dominant feminisms. *Contemporary Justice Review, 20*(4), 456–473.

White, R., Haines, F., Asquith, N. L. (2017). *Crime and criminology* (6th ed.). Sydney: Oxford University Press.

Whitty, M. (2021). Drug mule for love. *Journal of Financial Crime*, Vol. ahead-of-print (ahead-of-print). doi:10.1108/JFC-11-2019-0149

Willison, J. S., & O'Brien, P. (2017). A feminist call for transforming the criminal justice system. *Affilia, 32*(1), 37–44.

Wittekind, C. T. & Rhoades, E. (2018). Rethinking land and property in a 'transitioning' Myanmar: Representations of isolation, neglect, and natural decline. *Journal of Burma Studies, 22*(2), 171–213.

Woods, J. B. (2014). Queer contestations and the future of a critical "Queer" criminology. *Critical Criminology, 22*(1), 5–19.

World Prison Brief. (2021). *World Prison Brief Data*. Retrieved from https://www.prison-studies.org/world-prison-brief-data

Young, I. M. (1990). *Justice and the politics of difference*. Princeton, NJ: Princeton University Press.

Index